Lunar Voices

David Farrell Krell

Lunar
Voices

*Of Tragedy, Poetry,
Fiction, and Thought*

*The University of Chicago Press
Chicago & London*

David Farrell Krell, professor of philosophy at DePaul University, is the author of six books and the editor of Heidegger's *Basic Writings.*

The University of Chicago Press, Chicago 60637
The University of Chicago Press, Ltd., London
© 1995 by The University of Chicago
All rights reserved. Published 1995
Printed in the United States of America
04   03   02   01   00   99   98   97   96   95   1   2   3   4   5
ISBN: 0-226-45275-1 (cloth)
ISBN: 0-226-45277-8 (paper)

Library of Congress Cataloging-in-Publication Data

Krell, David Farrell.
    Lunar voices : of tragedy, poetry, fiction, and thought / David
Farrell Krell.
        p.   cm.
    Includes bibliographical references and index.
    1. Philosophy in literature.   2. Thought and thinking in
literature. I. Title.
PN49.K74   1995
809'.93384—dc20   94-46119
                                                       CIP

For Doctors Bernie Mizock and Lisa Rone
their astonished hearts
their healing hands

The Stars and the Moon

Ἄστερες μὲν ἀμφὶ κάλαν σελάνναν
ἂψ ἀπυκρύπτοισι φάεννον εἶδος,
ὄπποτα πλήθοισα μάλιστα λάμπῃ
γᾶν ἐπὶ παῖσαν.

The stars about the lovely moon
Conceal their radiant form
When she is at the full and shines
Most brightly on the earth.

—Sappho

•

To Selene

Μήνεν ἀείδειν τανυσίπτερον ἔσπετε Μοῦσαι
ἡδυεπεῖς κοῦραι Κρονίδεω Διὸς ἵστορες ᾠδῆς.

Seize the word, O Muses, well-versed in song,
And praise the Moon, daughter of Zeus, Cronos's son,
Praise her of the sweet voice.

—Homeric Hymn 32

•

I still remember how in the evenings the moon would shine on my bed, and how the golden meadow appeared before me in its silver sheen. Auntie Augusta used to recite:

Der Mond ist aufgegangen
Die goldnen Sternlein prangen, etc.

The moon has risen
The golden stars glisten, *etc.*

Oh, never will I forget these times!

—Friedrich Nietzsche, at age 13

How would it be if some day or night a daimon were to stalk you to your loneliest loneliness and say to you: ". . . and even this spider and this moonlight between the trees . . ."

—Friedrich Nietzsche, *The Gay Science,* no. 341

•

". . . and I and you in the gateway, whispering of eternal things . . ."

—Friedrich Nietzsche, *Thus Spoke Zarathustra,* "On the Vision and the Riddle"

•

The Cat and the Moon

Minnaloushe creeps through the grass
Alone, important and wise,
And lifts to the changing moon
His changing eyes.

—W. B. Yeats

Contents

Preface

What are men and women, anyway?

Thinking things, said one thinker, speaking on behalf of many thinkers before and after him, although, of course, if the bulk of human time and experience were taken into account, the answer would have to be: things that think they think. That gently ironic fold, doubling, or duplicity of thinking is literature. Literature is philosophy's duplicitous twin.

In *Griffin & Sabine: An Extraordinary Correspondence,* Nick Bantock writes of two artists who amuse and bemuse one another, that is, who serve as one another's muses.[1] From her island of Katie in the Sicmon Islands (*Sicmon?* Are they real? Check the atlas!), Sabine sees with the eyes behind her eyes the figures that Griffin Moss is drawing in London (*London?* Is it real? Check the atlas!). When Sabine finally discovers Griffin's identity and whereabouts, she writes to him and confesses her strange affinity for his work—indeed, her prescience concerning it. Baffled at first, and indignant over this invasion of his painterly privacy, Griffin replies by card and letter to the Sicmon Islands, demanding to know how Sabine is privy to the innermost secrets of his studio. His mood then shifts, and the indignation evaporates to a shimmering gratitude:

> I presume you can't see my writing as well as my pictures, or posting this letter would be superfluous. Any idea why it's only my images you see? And why can't I see yours? Tell me more about your islands, and tell me what you do. . . . I can't express to you

1. Nick Bantock, *Griffin & Sabine: An Extraordinary Correspondence* (San Francisco: Chronicle Books, 1991).

how pleased I am that you're out there. Since Verekeǿr died, I've been all alone. Now that you're there and have been all along, I feel whole again.

You don't think we're twins seperated [*sic*] at birth, do you? Or is that too simple?

Twins, separated at birth? Boy twin and girl twin? A myth and an archetype that the irritating Jungians would find flourishing in every culture and in every age, from the British Isles to the Sicmon Islands, from the eon of Empedocles to the epoch of Nietzsche. Twins? Two thinking things separated at birth, in birth, by birth? (Sabine's mother is the island's sole midwife, incidentally.) Separated from one another from the origin, and on the lookout for one another ever since?

What are women and men, anyway? Why does Zeus give birth to Athena from his head (Griffin has a picture of this, has many pictures of this), whereas he gives birth to Dionysos from his other part? The encyclopedia of myth calls this other part his "thigh," but I detect a euphemism. Should it not have been the other way around? And what is Zeus doing with a "thigh"? No, the mythmakers don't make mistakes, as the irritating Jungians never tire of pointing out. And yet nothing about these ancient stories is clear.

The third part of Robert Musil's *Der Mann ohne Eigenschaften* [*The Man without Qualities*] tells of Ulrich and Agathe, who are not twins, exactly, but brother and sister. They have been separated for many years, and come together almost as strangers. My own book, which you are holding now in hand, the book for which I am writing this preface, is not quite up to writing about Musil, not just yet, but I cannot ignore these "twins" of his.[2]

Twins: something closer than brother and sister. Siamese twins: something closer than identical twins. That is the dream elaborated by Agathe and Ulrich, by her more exuberantly than by him, when they meet as solitary adults. During one conversation late at night Agathe asks Ulrich whether he remembers Plato's old story (a story she simplifies a bit) about the bifurcation of the "originally whole human being" into two halves, man

---

2. Robert Musil, *Der Mann ohne Eigenschaften*, edited by Adolf Frisé (Reinbek bei Hamburg: Rowohlt, 1978), pp. 899–909, for the following quotations.

and woman. She is immediately embarrassed by her own question: of course he knows it, everybody knows it.

" 'And now the unhappy halves pull all sorts of silly stunts in order to get back into one another again: that story is told in all the manuals of higher education, although the story doesn't say why they fail.' "

Ulrich knows why. So many halves are in circulation that the true fit will most likely never be found. And when these wandering halves do go for their other half, they not only err but compound their silliness: a "third half" is engendered as a monument to their mistake. While Agathe has been reading *Symposium,* Ulrich has been reading Hegel, learning the lesson of our species' wicked infinity: " 'Humanity "halves itself" physiologically on and on, and the essential union stands motionless like the moon outside the bedroom window.' "

Agathe resists her brother's leap to a sadder but wiser spirit, however, and keeps her eye on the moon, even though she is on the bed and her eyes are closed.

> "You'd think that brothers and sisters must have already traveled halfway there!" observed Agathe in a voice that had gone hoarse.
>
> "Twins, maybe."
>
> "Are we not twins?"

Ulrich thinks now of Pygmalion, Hermaphrodite, Isis and Osiris. He thinks of all the figures that would delight the irritating Jungians, whom he now ventriloquizes:

" 'This craving for a double *[Doppelgänger]* of the opposite sex *[im anderen Geschlecht]* is primeval. It wants the love of a creature that is entirely the same as we are but that also has to be different from us, a magical figure that is us, but that also remains a magical figure.' " Soon Ulrich is on to the inevitable dream and delusion of "the *fluidum* of love" that the alchemist seeks in the retort. Agathe's retort is more telling: " 'That's the way it has been for thousands of years now: is it any easier to understand it in terms of two delusions?' "

Ulrich is silent. Much later in their exchange, which seems to spread over their bodies as their words become intermittent and sparse, Ulrich says:

"I'd rather have to say that a 'being-in-the-midst [*ein ‹Mitten-inne-Sein›*],' a state of undisturbed 'intensity' of life [*‹Innigkeit› des Lebens*] is probably something one cannot command when one's senses are rational."

"One would have to be a pair of Siamese Twins," Agathe rejoined.

"Well, then, Siamese Twins!" her brother repeated.

•

I cannot tell you how the story of Agathe and Ulrich ends. Neither could Musil. Nor will I tell you how *Griffin & Sabine: An Extraordinary Correspondence* ends. In a sense, they both begin rather than end. Yet let me add another word about philosophy and literature, no doubt with the same red face that Agathe shows when she tells her brother what all the world knows by now. For after Woolf, Joyce, and Beckett, the Mann brothers and Musil, the Surrealists and the Existentialists, Maurice Blanchot, and all the postmodern novelists, even the most thoroughly sterilized philosophers sense the contagion of letters at work in their own work. No one has demonstrated this contamination more relentlessly than Jacques Derrida—for example, in *Schibboleth: pour Paul Celan*. Derrida is clear about the philosopher's impatience with the merely empirical, and also with poems and stories, which are the empirical on a holiday. Philosophers want more than the spiritless empirical realm, but they do not want the pandemonium of literature. Philosophers want the bare bones of the argument, the corpse of the corpus, the stripped-down *essence* of the thing, even if all they get is a blur:

With this distinction between the empirical and the essential a limit becomes blurred, to wit, the limit of the philosophical as such, the philosophical distinction. Philosophy thus finds itself, or *rediscovers* itself, in the vicinity of the poetic, indeed in the vicinity of literature. It rediscovers itself there because our incapacity to decide about the limit is perhaps what most provokes thought. Here philosophy rediscovers itself. It does not necessarily lose itself—as those believe who in their unruffled credulity think they know precisely where this limit passes, those who hold to the limit fearfully, disingenuously, albeit without innocence, denuded of what one might call *philosophical experience*. This experience is a certain interrogative traversing of the limits, an insecurity concerning the frontiers of the philosophical field. Those who hold to the limit are, above all, denuded of the *experience of language,* which is always as poetical or as literary as it is philosophical.[3]

Admirable simplicity—from a thinker who has made everything more complicated, including tragedy, poetry, fiction, and thought, and who is rarely forgiven by the scholarly community for his gifts, his insights, and his energies.

As for my own little book, it is a triptych of triplets, its six chapters articulating nine figures over its three parts: (1) Hölderlin, Nietzsche, and Empedocles; (2) Heidegger, Derrida, and Trakl; (3) Blanchot, Kafka, and García Márquez. Presumably, a common set of obsessions unites these six inquiries, inasmuch as the triptych is dedicated to the minds, measures, menses, and manias of the moon. Allow me a few words of introduction.

•

Part One asks about tragedy and sensual love, asks it of one of the great thinkers of the "tragic age of the Greeks," Empedocles of Acragas. Because at least two moderns, Hölderlin and Nietzsche, to say nothing of Matthew Arnold, tried their hand at writing a tragedy based on Empedocles' loves, lore, life, and death, we may infer that the borderline that divides antiquity and modernity is itself put in question here. Both Hölderlin and Nietzsche believed they found in Empedocles the voice they were seeking for their own poetry and thought. The Sicilian magus, physician, rhetor, and statesman seemed to embody so much of what was utterly problematic in and about modernity: intimacy with the divine, wisdom concerning the health and illness of the human body, skill with the poetic word, and familiarity with political disaster. Moreover, Empedocles' "ironic death" or "speculative suicide," achieved by his leap into the crater of Etna, demanded of these two moderns a comprehending and comprehensive response. In both cases, the response failed.

However different the Empedocles plays of Hölderlin and Nietzsche would have been, a constellation of themes takes shape for both: a cosmos of eternal recurrence (of the same?)

3. Jacques Derrida, *Schibboleth: pour Paul Celan* (Paris: Galilée, 1986), p. 80.

that alternates between the reigns of Love and Strife, and a creature that oscillates between tender sensuality and bitter bloodletting. Hölderlin's three versions of *The Death of Empedocles* inspired all but a few of the author's "theoretical writings." Empedocles' stirring fragments and his tragic life made him the most colorful of the early Greek thinkers—also one of the most marginalized: while Parmenides and Heraclitus, Pythagoras and Zeno occupy later philosophers endlessly, Empedocles waits in the wings for the poets and thinkers who will haunt the margins, from Matthew Arnold and William Butler Yeats to Albert Camus and Luce Irigaray.

Empedocles leaps to his fiery death. Yet his downgoing is an affirmation rather than a rancorous negation or act of resignation. When Camus sought an essentially affirmative epitaph and epigraph to open his last great theoretical work, *L'homme révolté,* he found it in these lines from Hölderlin's play (here transposed into prose):

> And openly I pledged my heart to the grave and suffering land, and often in the consecrated night, I promised to love her faithfully until death, unafraid, with her heavy burden of fatality, and never to dispose a single one of her enigmas. Thus did I join myself to her with a mortal cord.[4]

For Hölderlin, however, the fire of heaven scorches the land. Everything—all the points on the line of time, every discernible epoch, every source of givenness—incinerates to ash. The fiery point is pain, felt always in searing intensity, *Innigkeit.* For even if all-living nature and humanity affect one another reciprocally and harmoniously, as Hölderlin notes in *"Das untergehende Vaterland . . ."* ["The nation in decline . . ."], so that a *new* world and a *new* life germinate Phoenix-like in the cinders of the old, and even if tragic dissolution can be felt only by the heart that senses an inchoate unification that is to come, the modality of possibility remains fixated in mournful remembrance of

---

4. Quoted by Albert Camus, *L'homme révolté* (Paris: Gallimard "Idées," 1951), p. 9; in English, *The Rebel,* trans. Anthony Bower (New York: Vintage, 1956), p. 2. These lines will be found once again in my own chap. 2, below; they are from the first version of *Der Tod des Empedokles,* ll. 372–76. In Friedrich Hölderlin, *Sämtliche Werke: Kritische Textausgabe,* ed. D. E. Sattler (Darmstadt: Luchterhand, 1986), *12,* 190; cf. 55.

what has dissolved and is lost forever to possibility. Only the rare human being who is "too intense, too singular" suffers such premonitions and such mourning. Hölderlin believed that Empedocles of Acragas was such a human being. He wanted to find in Empedocles his proper "tone," but he was not blithe about his chances. To Schiller he wrote: "I believe it is the property of rare human beings to be able to give without receiving; they can 'warm' themselves even 'on ice.' All too often I feel that I am not at all a rare human being. I freeze and petrify in the winter that surrounds me. As my sky is of iron, so I am of stone."[5]

Even though Hölderlin surrenders the three drafts of his tragedy to unending truncation, his later translations of Sophocles' *Oedipus the King* and *Antigone,* along with his "Remarks" on the plays, continue to revolve about questions concerning time, mortality, history—and intensity. His preoccupation with rhythm in the "Remarks" on the plays serves as a hinge connecting the first and second—or central—panels of my own triptych. For Martin Heidegger too remains intrigued by the rhythms of poetic speech. He denies that rhythm is preeminently a matter of versification, scansion, and metrics. Taking both Hölderlin and Trakl as his mentors, Heidegger seeks the source of the animating wave of poetic speech. In Heidegger's view, rhythm is the binding power of language, the power that both animates language and grants it its peculiar repose: rhythm is less the *flow* than the *articulation* of language. Thus the question of rhythm in Heidegger's thought and writing joins forces with much contemporary poetics and poetological poetry, which seek new ways of relating to traditional forms of versification, meter, and rhythm—new ears and new lungs for the line.

Rhythm is also a suggestive word for the alternating interplay of revealing and concealing, presence and absence, the matter that dominates Heidegger's thought early and late. Even if it seems excessive to expand the notion of rhythm to this ontological and aletheiological level, the example of Hölderlin encourages us to ask whether ἀλήθεια ("truth") as such is in some sense inherently rhythmic and periodic. Whereas, prior to Plato

5. Letter to Schiller of September 4, 1795; in Friedrich Hölderlin, *Werke und Briefe,* eds. Friedrich Beißner and Jochen Schmidt (Frankfurt am Main: Insel Verlag, 1969), p. 847.

and Aristotle, Antiphon of Athens takes being to be the *arhyth-mical* as such, the static unbudgeable immutable, Heidegger (perhaps in the company of Aristotle) is more inclined to think being and propriation in terms akin to rhythm.

If Georg Trakl is Heidegger's guide to the waves of rhythm, he is also the poet of "the lunar voice of the sister." No doubt, something in the rhythms of poetry and epiphany that concern Heidegger concern the sister as well, and perhaps her above all and in the first place. Both Heidegger and Derrida are fasci-nated by the sister's lunar voice in Trakl's poetry. That voice, an uncanny echo, rhythmic yet irregular and unpredictable, sings of sensual love and mortal fatality, of the little death and the big death, of the life—with its flood tides and ebb tides—in the bod-ies of men and women.

The hinge from the central to the third and last panel is silent. If the lunar voice of the sister dominates the central panel, the peculiar lunacies of Kafka, Blanchot, and García Már-quez prevail in the outermost panel. Yet the twin, the sister, is not forgotten. For Blanchot is above all fascinated by Kafka's am-biguous relation with "the feminine world," as though Kafka's troubled love life contained the secret of the neuter/neutral voice of the narratives. No one would or could doubt the intense intellectuality of Blanchot, his passion for the most far-reaching theoretical questions concerning literature; yet what captivates him about Kafka is not the intellect, nor even the stylistic mas-tery of this master of twentieth-century German prose, but the irremediable solitude of this forest animal. A distant cousin of the animal who haunts the rim of the woods in Trakl's poems, Kafka's forest animal cowers in the moss and mud outside the entrance to his burrow. Only when he is *writing* is the forest ani-mal "intrepid nude powerful surprising."

Whether one hundred years of solitude would suffice for Blanchot's unspeakably solitary Kafka I cannot say; but a chapter on the (eternally?) recurrent lunacy of the Buendía family seemed the proper way to end this book. Once again, at the end as in the beginning, the dominant and vexing idea is Nietzsche's thought of the eternal recurrence of the same. The puzzle is whether any of the words in Nietzsche's thought of thoughts, "eternal" "return" of the "same," can be written without scare quotes, either for Nietzsche or for Gabriel García Márquez. For each of these writers, eternity is a limited run, the return is always of nonreturn, and the same is irreducibly different. Among the differences, the sensual, sexual difference is a difference to which *One Hundred Years of Solitude* most intensely attends, especially when that difference affects brother and sister, or nephew and aunt, as they make their way to Siam.

Nine figures over three parts in six chapters. A seventh chapter was to have joined these six, and is with them in spirit, as it were: a piece on Luce Irigaray's reading of Nietzsche in *Amante marine*. However, that piece, entitled "To the Orangegrove at the Edge of the Sea," will already have appeared in print by the time these six lunar voices ask to be heard.[6]

•

One of the most remarkable fragments surrounding Robert Musil's *Man without Qualities,* a sketch dated April 16, 1933, bears the title "Lunar Rapture," *Mondrausch.* Two lovers are entrapped in the moonlight and have to cancel their social engagement for the evening. What happens to them, their "adventure," is bound up with what Musil calls "lunar nights," *Mondnächte.* On such a night, a richly sentient corporeality banishes the bustling vacuity of the day. Yet the way it does so—its particular magic—resists all codifications and all repetitions:

> Thus every inner and outer occurrence of lunar nights possesses the nature of the unrepeatable *[des Unwiederholbaren].* Every occurrence possesses an enhanced nature. It has the nature of an unselfish liberality and dispensation. Every communication is a sharing without envy. Every giving a receiving. Every reception inextricably interwoven in the excitements of the night. To *be* this way is our only way to *know* what is happening. For the "I" does not retain for itself any elixir of its past possession, scarcely a memory; the enhanced self radiates outward into a boundless selflessness, and these nights are full of the senseless feeling that something will have to come to pass that has never come to pass

---

6. See *Nietzsche and the Feminine,* edited by Peter Burgard (Charlottesville: University Press of Virginia, 1994), pp. 185–209; it offers a discussion of Luce Irigaray, *Amante marine: De Friedrich Nietzsche* (Paris: Minuit, 1980). Nietzsche's "Orange Grove" will also become the final chapter of my *Infectious Nietzsche,* forthcoming in 1995 from Indiana University Press.

before, something that the impoverished reasonableness of the day cannot even visualize. And it is not the mouth that gushes forth but all the body from head to foot, the body above the darkness of the earth and beneath the light of the sky, the body that is yoked to an excitement that oscillates between two stars. And the whispers we share with our companion are pervaded by an utterly unfamiliar sensuality, which is not some person's sensuality, but the sensuality of the earth, of all that compels our sensibility, the suddenly unveiled tenderness of the world that touches all our senses and that all our senses touch.[7]

On such a night, even the lonely and ignored nights of the past are transfigured, "like an endless bramblebush covered in silverplate, moonstains on the grass, drooping apple trees, singeing frost and gilded, opaque waters." These sheer particularities or pieces of the moonlit empirical have no rhyme or reason to come together; yet the rhythm they obey flows from a source that is itself unseen. In *Being and Time* Heidegger reminds us that even when the moon is at the full we do not see it in its entirety.

In the end, one can never be sure whether any of this is more than mere moonshine and romanticism, as the young woman in Musil's sketch comes to believe, for she sees her lover transformed into Pierrot Lunaire; the young man too quietly concedes the likelihood of lunacy, as the two go their separate ways. In the end, one can never be sure whether it is vacuous sentimentality or what—against the noise in the streets and the stillness in the heart—all the world was waiting for. In uncertainty, and in a night as alluring as it is uncertain, I invoke these lunar voices of tragedy, poetry, fiction, and thought.

•

An earlier version of my first chapter appeared in "Perspectives on Nietzsche," *Graduate Faculty Philosophy Journal,* New School for Social Research, 15, no. 2 (1991), 31–48; I am grateful to Wayne Klein for requesting the piece, and to Ernst Behler and Jim Risser, who invited me to present a version of it to the Comparative Literature Program at the University of Washington and

---

7. Musil, *Der Mann ohne Eigenschaften,* pp. 2034–35.

the Nietzsche Society, respectively. A version of the third chapter first appeared in *Heidegger and Language* (University of Warwick: Parousia Press, 1981), pp. 25–50; my thanks to David Wood for all those wonderful "Warwick Workshops" over the years. Finally, warm thanks to Anna Vaughn, Don Kelly Coble, T. David Brent, and my two (unknown but appreciated) readers for the University of Chicago Press.

Chicago   D.F.K.
Early August 1993, at the Full

Part I

Hölderlin

•

Nietzsche

•

Empedocles

1 The Sensuality of Tragedy, the Tragedy of Sensuality

> Empedocles remains forever on this *boundary,*
> and in almost all things he is a figure at the limits.
>
> —Nietzsche

> All too often I feel that I am not a rare human being.
> I freeze and petrify in the winter that surrounds me.
> As my sky is of iron, so I am of stone.
>
> —Hölderlin to Schiller

> τῶν καὶ ἐγὼ νῦν εἰμι, φυγὰς θεόθεν καὶ ἀλήτης.
> Now I too am one of them, a wanderer banished by god.
>
> —Empedocles

Given the failure of both Hölderlin and Nietzsche to complete (or, in Nietzsche's case, even to commence) a tragedy centered on the figure of Empedocles, it is perhaps a mark of success that my two initial efforts to write about these failures themselves miscarried.[1] Succeeding upon those two failures, those two or more failures, this third or nth attempt too seems bound to fail. Yet I have little choice but to carry on writing these tentative and tenuous remarks as though I were certain of what I wanted to say, which is simply that in the past several years I have become convinced that the mysterious Nietzschean and exalted Hölderlinian "Empedocles" sketches pose one of the greatest challenges to a poetics in our time. Our time? Let us agree to call it, after Hölderlin's phrase, *in müßiger Zeit,* the time of *désœuvrement.* And so, for the nth time, I am coming:

---

1. For the references to earlier versions of this chapter, see the final paragraph of the preface to the present volume.

> *Ich komme. Sterben? nur ins Dunkel ists*
> *Ein Schritt, und sehen möchtst du doch, mein Auge!*
> (B, 522; S, *12*, 170/237) [2]
>
> I'm coming. Dying? it's only into the dark,
> Only one pace; and wouldn't you love to see, O eye!

On second thought, however, what could it possibly mean to write "successfully" about the speculative suicide of Empedocles—Empedocles of Etna? Take the plunge, that's all there is to do, and if the crater spits back an old sneaker instead of the iron shoe of the master—if my reading be pedestrian and leave no traces that are worth following—*ja, ja, ich komme sowieso.*

•

I have presented Nietzsche's detailed plans and sketches for a drama concerning Empedocles of Acragas as a kind of invitation in a book entitled *Postponements.*[3] The Hölderlin texts I want to draw attention to in this chapter are the three drafts of *Der Tod des Empedokles,* along with the *Frankfurter Plan,* drawn up in the late summer of 1797, the *Grund zum Empedokles,* written two years later in Homburg, and the essay *Das Werden im Vergehen,* or *"Das untergehende Vaterland . . . ,"* which immediately preceded the 1799 sketch toward the continuation of the third draft.[4] Not only each of the three versions of Hölderlin's *Trauerspiel* but also each of these plans and theoretical writings is of staggering complexity. (I write as one who has devoted his time to simple texts, such as Heidegger's *Beiträge* and Hegel's *Phänomenologie des*

2. The first set of numbers here and throughout refers to Friedrich Hölderlin, *Werke und Briefe,* ed. Friedrich Beißner and Jochen Schmidt (Frankfurt am Main: Insel, 1982 [1st ed., 1969]), cited as "B," with page number, in the body of my text. The second set refers to Friedrich Hölderlin, *Sämtliche Werke: Kritische Textausgabe,* ed. D. E. Sattler, vols. 12–13 (Darmstadt: Luchterhand, 1986 [based on the FHA, Verlag Roter Stern, Frankfurt-am-Main, 1985]), cited as "S," with volume and page numbers. The slash in the Sattler references indicates that the quotation appears twice, first in the variorum text, then once again in Sattler's reconstructed text. While I accept Sattler's as the authoritative text today (and one must emphasize *today,* inasmuch as each year seems to bring us yet another Hölderlin edition), the Beißner-Schmidt edition remains extremely useful, especially (but not only) because of the selection of letters.

3. Krell, *Postponements: Woman, Sensuality, and Death in Nietzsche* (Bloomington: Indiana University Press, 1986).

4. See B [227], the commentary on 641; see also S, *13*, 418–19.

Geistes.) There is no way I can clarify in this brief space such recalcitrant themes as *höchste Feuer und tiefste Innigkeit* (supernal fire and the deepest intensity), *die aorgischere Natur* (the more elemental nature that resists human organization), *Zwist und Streit, Vereinigung und Versöhnung, Untergang, Übergang, Auflösung und Anfang* (quarrel and strife, unification and reconciliation, decline, transition, dissolution, and commencement), to say nothing of *das Unendlichgegenwärtige, das Endlichvergangene und das Endlichunendliche* (the infinitely present, finitely past, and finitely infinite). These complexities I am satisfied to list here as a Hölderlinian "bunch poem," to let them fall where they may, in order that they might serve as an invitation to a prolonged and intense encounter with Hölderlin.

Here I want to pursue several more modest threads that my *Postponements* introduced but then left unworked, unwoven, as though in perpetual postponement. These threads, apparently quite disparate, are:

1. The problem of the modernity of Empedocles—better, the omnipresent yet undecidable trace of Empedocles in the epochs of antiquity, modernity, and even "postmodernity," if the last-named can stand for our time-out-of-work;

2. Time and affirmation—Hölderlinian anticipations of Nietzsche's thought of the eternal recurrence of the same as an expression of *amor fati,* that is, tragic affirmation; and

3. The sensuality of tragedy and the tragedy of sensuality in all three figures (Hölderlin, Nietzsche, Empedocles), the theme of the ephemeral unification of living beings who are forever dying.

Both Hölderlin and Nietzsche spin out numberless strands in these threads—modernity, temporality, sensuality—with each strand leading back to the shadowy figure of Empedocles of Acragas. Why insist on the conjunction of Nietzsche and Hölderlin here? Because I am convinced that Curt Paul Janz and others have woefully underestimated the impact of Nietzsche's reading of Hölderlin's *Der Tod des Empedokles.*[5] Nietzsche himself testifies to the impact of that reading in one of the secondary school essays he submitted at Schulpforta, a paper dated Oc-

5. Curt Paul Janz, *Friedrich Nietzsche Biographie,* 3 vols. (München: Deutscher Taschenbuch Verlag, 1981), *1,* 78–80.

tober 19, 1861 (four days after his seventeenth birthday), entitled, "A Letter to My Friend, in Which I Recommend That He
Read My Favorite Poet."[6] This is the essay for which Nietzsche
received a mediocre mark from his teacher, Koberstein, along
with the stern counsel that in the future he should choose a
"healthier," "clearer," and "more German" poet! Although I
am not primarily interested in showing any "influence" of Hölderlin on Nietzsche, I do want to take a moment to clarify in a
provisional way one philological question concerning such possible influence.

I have been unable to discover which edition of Hölderlin's
works Nietzsche himself actually possessed, although it is certain
that he had a biography of Hölderlin in his home library by 1861.
It is also likely that either his home library or that of Schulpforta
contained the two-volume *Sämmtliche Werke* edited by Christoph
Theodor Schwab and published by Cotta in 1846.[7] I shall ignore
most of the details of this edition and merely indicate that Nietzsche would have had (via Schwab) access to the bulk of what we
today identify as the three drafts of *Der Tod des Empedokles* and to
several of the plans, notably the earliest one, the *Frankfurter Plan,*
along with the largest of the three sections of the Homburger
Grund zum Empedokles. What in fact Nietzsche did read of Hölderlin's works, how often and precisely when he did so, especially
in later years, I do not suppose we shall ever know in any detail.
However, let me set aside this philological-historical question
and proceed with my three Ariadnic threads.

6. Nietzsche's text appears in the edition of his works by Karl Schlechta,
3 vols. (München: Carl Hanser, 1956), *3,* 95–98.

7. *Der Tod des Empedokles* was first published by Aglaia in 1801; more materials
appeared in the 1826 edition of the poetry; most of the fragments and plans were
not available, however, until the 1846 edition: *Friedrich Hölderlin's Sämmtliche
Werke,* ed. Christoph Theodor Schwab, 2 vols. (Stuttgart and Tübingen: J. G.
Cotta, 1846). Volume I (pp. 124–213) contains "Der Tod des Empedokles: Fragmente eines Trauerspiels." Here the first and second versions are jumbled (e.g.,
on p. 129, act I scene 2 is actually act I scene 1 of the *second* draft: see the Beißner
edition, p. 527). Schwab presents the *third* draft (pp. 198ff.) under the title "Auf
dem Aetna." The sketch for the Chorus is missing. In volume 2, the *Grund zum
Empedokles* appears among "Prosaisches" (253–62). The first two sections, *Allgemeiner Grund* and "*Die tragische Ode . . . ,*" do not appear in the Schwab edition.
The detailed plan of the *third* draft does not appear there either, even though
Schwab cites several phrases from it on pp. 304–5. Finally, the *Frankfurter Plan* for
the *first* version appears in Schwab's essay, "Hölderlin's Leben," *2,* 300–303.

Antiquity and Modernity:
The Epochal Suspension of Empedocles

For both Hölderlin and Nietzsche Empedocles was a trace of the past so painfully present that nothing could have been more futural. In the figure of the ancient magus as they descried him—and in this they are joined by Matthew Arnold, whose suppressed *Empedocles on Etna* contains much magnificent poetry—antiquity and modernity strangely elide. Nietzsche underscores several times the name *Empedokles* when in a note of 1875 (KSA, *8*, 104–5)[8] he declares that his own "general task" is "to show how life, philosophy, and art can be related to one another in a more profound affinity, without the philosophy becoming banal or the philosopher's life dishonest." In the same way, Hölderlin's *Grund Zum Empedokles* betrays the extent to which Nietzsche's forebear felt compelled to struggle with this elemental poet, physician, and statesman, born to be a singer in an age that demanded a sacrificial victim, in order to find his own poetic voice and establish his own "character" (B, 917; cf. 576–77). There are many moments in both Nietzsche's and Hölderlin's Empedocles plans when it is impossible to distinguish the respective authors' voices from what in a more innocent age one might have called their historical "object" or "subject matter." The third and final fragment of the first cluster of Nietzsche's Empedocles plans (1870–71) reads as follows:

5 [118]

Empedocles, compelled through all the stages, religion, art, science; bringing science to dissolution, he turns against himself.

Departure from religion, through the insight that it is deception.

Now, joy in artistic semblance, driven from it by the recognized sufferings of the world. Woman as nature.

Now he observes the sufferings of the world like an anatomist, becomes *tyrannos*, uses religion and art, becomes steadily harder. He resolves to annihilate his people, because he has seen that they cannot be healed. The people are gathered about the

8.   I cite Nietzsche's works (with the exception of some not yet contained in the historical-critical edition) throughout by volume (in italics) and page of the *Kritische Studienausgabe* [KSA], ed. Giorgio Colli and Mazzino Montinari, 15 vols. (München: Deutscher Taschenbuch Verlag, 1980).

crater: he goes mad, and before he vanishes, he proclaims the truth of rebirth. A friend dies with him. (KSA, 7, 126)

It is as though Empedocles, the pre-Socratic thinker, presides over the final turns of what Nietzsche's *Birth of Tragedy* calls the Socratic "supplement" (KSA, *1*, 96). Here the age of science, which is Nietzsche's own age, the epoch of modernity, finds itself in the throes of a transformation to an age of art. That Empedocles himself, as rhetor and poet, cannot sustain the joyous affirmation of artistic semblance, that he becomes steadily harder, that he legislates in order to annihilate, and that the communication of rebirth precipitates his own madness and death—these things strike home for the figures of both antiquity and modernity, these things recoil uncannily across all epochal demarcations and suspend all epochal suspensions. Similarly, the second fragment of the central cluster (dated 1871–72) also touches something at the heart of both epochs:

8 [31]

An Apollonian god turns into a human being who craves death.

The strength of his pessimistic knowledge enrages him.

In an irruptive excess of pity, he can no longer bear existence.

He cannot heal the city, because it has degenerated too far below the Greek standard.

He wants to heal it radically, namely, by destroying it; but here it salvages its Greek standard.

In his godlike nature, he wants to help.

As a man, full of pity, he wants to annihilate.

As a daimon, he annihilates himself.

Ever more passionate waxes Empedocles. (KSA, 7, 234)

These Nietzschean fragments accord with Hölderlin's description of Empedocles as a sacrificial victim of his times, *ein Opfer seiner Zeit* (B, 578; S, *13*, 344/364), of times long gone but also of times imminent and about to expire, as perhaps also of time "itself," if such a thing may be said, time "as such." [9] Em-

9. This is the thesis of one of the most remarkable philosophical books on Hölderlin's Empedocles: Françoise Dastur, *Hölderlin: Tragédie et modernité* (La Versanne: Encre marine, 1992), esp. pp. 38 (" . . . the subject of tragedy is time"),

pedocles is the victim "in whom the extremes appear to be united actually and visibly in One, yet precisely for that reason are united too intensely *[zu innig]*, so that the individual goes down, must go down, in an ideal deed." As we shall see, it is the character of that *idealische Tat* of speculative suicide that haunts Hölderlin throughout all three versions of *Der Tod des Empedokles,* and ĭt will trouble Nietzsche as well.

> *Daß du des Überwinders Freuden all*
> *In Einer vollen Tat am Ende fändest?* (B, 522) [10]

> That you would find the conqueror's joys all
> In one full deed at the end?

Hölderlin's *Allgemeiner Grund* (a text, incidentally, to which Nietzsche could not have had access) shows him wrestling with the very possibility of the tragic poet's identification with an "image" or alter ego in a bygone time and foreign place. That identification becomes all the more discomfiting and even treacherous in the measure that tragic *Innigkeit* ("fervor" or "intensity") approaches *nefas,* nefarious hubris. Hölderlin allows this Latin name to stand, as though it were a taboo object (*nefas* meaning "blasphemy" or "sacrilege"). The identification of the

---

59 (" . . . tragedy's theme is nothing other than time itself"), 63(" . . . that god [i.e., Zeus] is nothing other than time itself"), 76, and passim. See in particular her discussion of what she calls, not "temporality," but *temporarité,* which is "nothing other than the tragedy of time itself, which grants no final repose but continues its infinite process relentlessly in ever-new dissolutions and reconfigurations" (61). The importance of Dastur's book for my own argument will become clearer in the second part of the present chapter and throughout chap. 2, below. Finally, one should also note Friedrich von Hardenberg's (Novalis's) emphasis on the essentially tragic character of *past* time. In the *Poëticismen* of 1798 he writes, "Every representation *[Darstellung]* of the past is a mourning-play *[Trauerspiel]* in the genuine sense." See Novalis, *Werke, Tagebücher und Briefe,* 3 vols., *Das philosophisch-theoretische Werk* (vol. 2), ed. Hans-Joachim Mähl (München: Carl Hanser, 1978), p. 326; cf. p. 541; cited hereinafter simply by volume and page, e.g., *2, 326.* I shall have to leave for another time the question of the nexus of time, tragedy, and *Trauerspiel*—along with the notion of the *Messianic*—in the thought of Walter Benjamin, although I shall mention now my thanks to Peter Fenves for his insights into this theme.

10. Sattler's analytical text construction exhibits the many rewritings of these lines, even though these particular lines do not appear in his final reconstruction (S, *12,* 237); but see pp. 168–69. The phrase "*in einer idealischen Tat*" appears in the *Grund zum Empedokles* (B, 577; S, *13,* 343/363).

poet with a figure of the past is most treacherous, and even nefarious, in the case of Empedocles on Etna (B, 571; S, *13,* 332/ 359).[11] These various forms of imbrication, elision, or overlap in identification, especially such *nefarious* identification, make it impossible to posit from the outside, as it were, the "epochs" of antiquity and modernity. No temporary suspension of the struggle between celestial fire and imperturbable calm supervenes in order to allow the story of history to unfold in such neatly circumscribed epochs. No ultimate suspension shatters the suspense that holds all identifications of subjects and objects in a kind of hermetic *neutral* zone (B, 789).

A further indication of the interlacing and ringdance of roles across the boundaries of epochs: Nietzsche's school essay on Hölderlin draws particular attention to *Der Tod des Empedokles,* "this remarkably significant dramatic fragment in whose melancholy tones resounds the future of the hapless poet, the living grave of years spent insane; resounding not as you believe in turgid chatter but in the purest Sophoclean language and in an infinite richness of thought." Whether "the future of the hapless poet" is fully consummated in Empedocles' antiquity, or

11. Hölderlin continues to employ the notion of *nefas* in his *Anmerkungen zum Oedipus* (see B, 731). My question to Philippe Lacoue-Labarthe, who sees the notion of *faute* gaining force in the *second* version of *Der Tod des Empedokles,* would be how to bring the issue of sacrilege (i.e., *nefas*) to bear on Hölderlin's notion of *Zäsur,* which Lacoue-Labarthe places at the center of his own reflections. See Philippe Lacoue-Labarthe, *L'imitation des modernes: Typographies II* (Paris: Galilée, 1986), esp. "La césure du spéculatif," p. 61. The question is too difficult and too far-reaching for me to reduce it to a note. Perhaps the only thing we can be certain about is the fact that the accusation of impiety laid against Empedocles gains force as Hölderlin's versions succeed upon one another. Klaus Düsing argues that the growing emphasis on *nefas* is evidence of the failure of "aesthetic Platonism" in Hölderlin, who is no longer confident that man and divinity are balanced in the absolute accord of beauty and love: when Empedocles identifies himself with divinity as such, argues Düsing, he succumbs to "religious guilt" and must "purify himself." Thus the gods are no longer mere Schillerian *Gebilde der Kunst,* but have "independent existence." Yet is it a matter of the gods coming to have "independent existence"? Or is it rather the case that a presentiment of the failure of all *Kunstgebilde* arises precisely in the *infidelity* and the *flight* of the gods, who now attain something like independent *inexistence?* See Klaus Düsing, "Ästhetischer Platonismus bei Hölderlin und Hegel," in *Homburg vor der Höhe in der deutschen Geistesgeschichte: Studien zum Freundeskreis um Hegel und Hölderlin,* ed. Christoph Jamme and Otto Pöggeler (Stuttgart: Klett-Cotta, 1981), pp. 101–17.

whether it waits upon Hölderlin's problematic modernity or
even the indefinitely postponed epoch of Nietzschean postmodernity (and in the Great Year of 30,000 seasons Empedocles of
Acragas can afford to wait); whether the poet is given the name
Empedokles, and whether he be Hölderlin's or Nietzsche's Empedocles; whether the "living grave" will entomb Nietzsche's
Hölderlin or will encrypt, as it were, Hölderlin's Nietzsche; and
whether the "purest Sophoclean language" to which Nietzsche
refers points toward the caesurae and the hard rhythmic jointures of tragedy, lyric poetry (especially in the late hymns), *and*
speculative philosophy—these questions defy hasty response. If
the juxtaposition of names in the title of Part I of the present
book seems to produce a brusque parataxis and an epochal
anachronism, it is perhaps because here the epoch of syntax and
of reliable chronology fails.[12]

Finally, the modernity and postmodernity of antiquity resounds in certain fragments attributed to Empedocles, such as
Diels-Kranz fragment 124,[13] which Nietzsche cites in his lecture
course, "The Pre-Platonic Philosophers," taught at Basel in 1872,
1873, and 1876:

> *O du elendes, ganz unseliges Geschlecht der Sterblichen, aus welcher
> Zwietracht, aus welchem Wehklagen seid ihr entstanden!*

> Oh, you wretched, miserable race of mortals! What discord and
> lamentation have spawned you?

Is this the voice of Empedocles, resounding ages prior to Hölderlin? Or that of Georg Trakl, lamenting long after him? (Compare Trakl's *"O des verfluchten Geschlechts,"* from *Traum und Um-
nachtung,* or well-nigh *any* poem of Trakl's—including all those
discussed in chapter 4, below.) Nietzsche calls Empedocles a figure "at the limits," *eine Grenzfigur,* as radically undefinable as he

---

12. See Theodor W. Adorno, "Parataxis: Zur späten Lyrik Hölderlins," in
Noten zur Literatur III (Frankfurt am Main: Suhrkamp, 1965), pp. 156–209; see the
French translation of this text in Philippe Lacoue-Labarthe, ed., Hölderlin, *Hym-
nes, élégies et autres poèmes, suivi de Parataxe etc.* (Paris: Garnier Flammarion, 1983),
pp. 131–80, esp. p. 167. See also the introductory essay by Lacoue-Labarthe,
pp. 7–20.

13. Hermann Diels and Walther Kranz, eds., *Die Fragmente der Vorsokratiker,*
3 vols., 6th ed. (Zürich: Weidmann, 1951), *I,* 361.

is ubiquitous. And it seems that Empedocles will always have invited others from every age—among them Arnold, Camus, Blanchot, Bataille, Derrida, and Irigaray—to join him at the edge.

Time, Tragic Downgoing, Affirmation

Commentators have recently stressed the radical shift in Hölderlin's portrayal of Empedocles' struggle—in search of the fitting deed, the fitting end—from the first to the second, or from the second to the third (and final) draft of Hölderlin's *Trauerspiel*. They are no doubt right.[14] Yet I risk suggesting that a certain continuous theme runs through all three versions, a continuous yet increasingly radicalized theme; it is admittedly a theme so broad in scope that it perhaps defies designation *as* a theme. I mean *time*, time as tragic downgoing, and *affirmation*.

As Hölderlin endeavors to hone the "accidental" elements of his drama down to an "essential" core, he poses in ever more

14. Walter Müller Seidel, "Hölderlin im Homburg: Sein Spätwerk im Kontext seiner Krankheit" (in Jamme/Pöggeler, pp. 161–88), argues that the *first* version centers about an individual conflict (Empedocles' hubris and blasphemy [i.e., *nefas*] against the gods), whereas the later versions, especially the *third*, depict Empedocles' death as a sacrifice that transforms tragic occurrence itself into a world-historical process, a national, *vaterländische* reversal into what Nietzsche would have called "grand politics." Christoph Jamme radicalizes this view by asserting that the conflict of the first two versions can be reduced to what Hegel criticized as the bootless sufferings of "the beautiful soul," the soul that cannot mediate between nature and life, the soul that refuses to commit itself fully to life. Jamme, who contrasts Hölderlin's Empedocles to Hegel's Jesus, particularly in terms of the text *Der Geist des Christentums*, sees the legitimation of Empedocles' suicide changing radically between the *Frankfurter Plan* and the *Grund zum Empedokles*. He describes it as a process in which the emphasis on *nefas* dwindles and Empedocles' suicide is brought into accord with an economy of sacrifice. Empedocles plunges to his death, not as a man of despair or as a penitent, but as the prophet of a fundamental historical turn or a turning of the tide (*Zeitenwende*), a turn in which the downgoing of the prior epoch embodies the upsurgence of the new. Thus by the *third* version of his *Trauerspiel* Hölderlin has learned how to mediate between his hero and the *Zeitgeist* in such a way that Empedocles' death attains "historically transformative power." See Jamme, "Liebe, Schicksal und Tragik: Hegels 'Geist des Christentums' und Hölderlins 'Empedokles,'" in Christoph Jamme and Otto Pöggeler, eds., *Frankfurt ist der Nabel dieser Erde": Das Schicksal einer Generation der Goethezeit* (Stuttgart: Klett-Cotta, 1983), pp. 300–324, esp. pp. 312–15. See also Christoph Jamme, *Ein ungelehrtes Buch": Die philosophische Gemeinschaft zwischen Hölderlin und Hegel in Frankfurt 1797–1800*. Hegel-Studien Beiheft no. 23 (Bonn: Bouvier, 1983), esp. pp. 296–316.

radical fashion the question of time and affirmation. Can Empedocles go down with joy? Can he bless his life and his now
vanished gods? Or will he plunge with a snarl and a curse on his
lips? It is as though a daimon has stalked Empedocles to the moment of his loneliest loneliness in order to pose this question.
In the very first sketch, the *Frankfurter Plan*, dated August–
September, 1797 (B, 567–70; S, *12*, 19–28), Hölderlin's initial
statement about his hero culminates in a remark about time,
"Kantian time," we might say—the regime of the *Nacheinander*,
or pure succession. This notable passage, which anticipates
Nietzsche's Empedocles plans in several ways, also broaches the
first and third of my own themes, namely, epochality and
sensuality:

> Empedocles, by temperament and through his philosophy long
> since destined to despise his culture, to scorn all neatly circum-
> scribed affairs and every interest directed to this or that object; an
> enemy to the death of all one-sided existence, and therefore also
> in truly beautiful relations unsatisfied, restive, troubled, simply
> because they are special kinds of relations, relations that are felt
> solely in that magnificent accord with all living things which sates
> him utterly; simply because he cannot live in them and love them
> fervently with omnipresent heart, like a god, freely and expan-
> sively, like a god; simply because as soon as his heart and his
> thought embrace anything at hand he finds himself bound to the
> law of succession. (B, 567; S, *12*, 20/26)

Empedocles' "full deed at the end," his idealized suicide,
must somehow either transgress or consummate, either breach
or confirm, the rule of succession. Consummation, confirma-
tion, and transgression are all involved in this matter of rebirth
and recurrence *(Wiedergeburt, Wiederkehr)*. It is not simply the
repetition of the word *Wiederkehr* in all three versions of Hölderlin's play that interests me here, but the intensification of the
theme of *downgoing* and recurrence—the theme of time, *Untergang*, and tragic affirmation—as though Hölderlin too were pre-
occupied with the question that lies coiled at the heart of Nietzsche's *Thus Spoke Zarathustra*, or Gabriel García Márquez's *One
Hundred Years of Solitude*.

Nor is it simply a question of the decline and transition of
the fatherland, the transmutation of a particular region of space

and regime of time, the possibility of a "new world" rising from the ashes of the old, even though the essay so closely associated with Hölderlin's sketch of the third version, *Das Werden im Vergehen* (B, 641–46; *"Das untergehende Vaterland* . . . *,"* S, *14,* 81–100), does emphasize this historico-political dimension. It is also and perhaps preeminently a question of the passing of the son of Ouranos, the passing of Cronos himself—Pausanias addresses Empedocles as *Uranussohn* ("son of Ouranos")—who is or once was so intimate with nature that it seemed he would recur eternally like the morning sun; it is, both in the first version and in the final sketches toward the third draft, a question of the festival of Saturn, *die Saturnustage* and *das Saturnusfest* (B, 513 and 587; S, 144/229 and 419/438); it is, as the later "Remarks on *Antigone"* so enticingly suggest, also and perhaps preeminently a question of the passing of Zeus himself, Zeus as "the father of time" or "the father of the earth," "the more appropriate Zeus" who precisely as a figure of death *(Gestalt des Todes)* " *compels us more decisively toward the earth"* (B, 786–88); it is, in short, a question of the fitting celebration of, and sacrifice to, the divinity of *time.* In all three versions of *The Death of Empedocles* there seems to be a waxing tension, one that becomes ever more intense as the versions succeed one another, a tension between recurrence and absolute passing, between *Wiederkehren* and *Nimmerwiederkehren,* between *Bleiben* and *Vergehen, Wiedersehen* and *Es ist vorbei!* Held in suspense by that waxing tension, we experience the concomitant oscillation between bitter resentment and joyous affirmation in the face of downgoing and death.

In act 2, scene 3 of the first draft, we find Empedocles transfigured. Hölderlin indicates in a note jotted onto his manuscript page at this point: "From here on he has to appear as a superior being *[ein höhers Wesen],* altogether in his earlier love and power" (S, *12,* 112/216). Thus transfigured, an affirmative and affirming Empedocles raises the gourd to his lips:

> *Ich trink es euch!*
> *Ihr alten Freundlichen! ihr meine Götter!*
> *Und meiner Wiederkehr, Natur. Schon ist*
> *Es anders. O ihr Gütigen!* . . .
> (B, 500; S, *12,* 112/216)

I drink to you!
You, my friends of old, you my gods!
And to my recurrence, Nature. Already
It is otherwise. O you propitious ones!

Confronted by Pausanias' bewilderment in the face of his exultation—"But you should be in mourning!" the young disciple cries—the transfigured Empedocles offers him the following encouragement:

Siehest du denn nicht? Es kehrt
Die schöne Zeit von meinem Leben heute
Noch einmal wieder und das Größre steht
Bevor; hinauf, o Sohn, zum Gipfel
Des alten heilgen Aetna wollen wir.
Denn gegenwärtger sind die Götter auf den Höhn.
(B, *501; S, 12,* 114–16; 217).

Do you not see? Today recurs
The lovely time of my life
Once again and something grander yet
Is still to come; upward, my son, to the peak
Of ancient holy Etna. That is where we shall go.
For the gods are more present on the heights.

However, scarcely a moment later the joyous transfiguration of an affirmed, affirmative eternal return collapses back into rancor, resentment, and gall. Or, at least, so it seems when one examines Hölderlin's manuscript, which especially here reveals a struggle between transfigurative, affirmative passages like the one we have only now read and starkly negative passages such as the following one, which was apparently excised from the final copy:

—Natterbisse sinds
Und nicht der erste bin ich, dem die Götter
Solch giftge Rächer auf das Herz gesandt.
(B, 501; S, *12,* 218/118) [15]

15. These lines, and those cited immediately above, are extremely difficult to reconstruct from the manuscript, which shows a vast number of revisions. The lines cited here, on the adder's bite, so reminiscent of the stricken shepherd (in "The Vision and the Riddle" and "The Convalescent") of *Thus Spoke Zarathustra*, disappear from Sattler's reconstruction, although they are present in Beißner's.

> —They are adders' bites
> And I am not the first to whose heart the gods
> Have sent such venomous avengers.

These same tensions inform the final scene of the third and final draft, in which Manes and Empedocles debate Empedocles' intended "ideal deed," his epochal sacrifice, his speculative suicide. (I am uncertain as to whether the figure of Manes is Oriental, Egyptian, or utterly Junonian Greek, but am tempted to hear his name in Latin as "You shall remain," inasmuch as this would make him the alter ego of Empedocles, if indeed the hero's name has something to do with ἔμπεδος, "steadfast," "continuous in time.") Although Empedocles calls Manes his *böser Geist* (B, 562; S, *13*, 409/433), as though in anticipation of Nietzsche's *Geist der Schwere,* and although Hölderlin at least implies that Manes is Empedocles' opponent (B, 582: *Sein Gegner* . . .), it is not so easy to distinguish this "poor mortal" from the "idol" that Empedocles himself has become. Manes' questions are by now quite impossible for Empedocles (and for all his retinue, across all the epochs) to answer:

> *Bist du der Mann? derselbe? bist du dies?*
> *[. . .]*
> *O sage, wer du bist! und wer bin ich?*
> *[. . .]*
> *Wie ists mit uns? siehst du es so gewiß?*
> (B, 562–65; S, *13*, 409–17/433–35)

> Are you the man? the very one? are you this?
> [. . .]
> O tell who you are! and who am I?
> [. . .]
> How is it with us? are you so sure of what you see?

Empedocles will not wax confident where even Hyperion was so unsure. On the one hand, to the extent that he claims the right of "free death" as an end to "the long tallying of suffer-

---

Sattler explains that they are rejected lines written in the left-hand margin of the manuscript: it is as though Hölderlin were trying to purge his text of ressentiment precisely as his hero tries to purge his affirmation of all negativity. The (impossible) reconstruction of the text would be worth studying in great detail at this very point, where the tension between affirmation and negation seems most intense.

ings" he has endured, Empedocles' "full deed at the end" certainly does seem to be full of poison, and to imply an infidelity to the earth. On the other hand, Empedocles himself postpones his plunge into Etna because—and these are the last words we hear from him in the play—he dare not go "without joy." Whether Empedocles' downgoing will be what Nietzsche in his own most detailed Empedocles plan calls "a rebirth of penitential death" *(eine Wiedergeburt des Sühnetodes),*[16] or whether it will be—whether it *can* be—a "creative act" of "ideal dissolution" and "tragic unification" (B, 644–46), that is, an *epochal* and essentially *affirmative* sacrifice, is a capital question for all three figures, a question for the parataxis "Hölderlin • Nietzsche • Empedocles." Penitential death, haunting the very possibility of affirmative downgoing, leads us to our third and last theme.

Sensual Tragedy, Tragic Sensuality

Does the tragic unification *(tragische Vereinigung)* of which Hölderlin speaks have anything to do with the apparently more ephemeral unions of sensual, sexual love? In Hölderlin the connection seems to be tenuous, to say the least. The two earlier drafts of *Der Tod des Empedokles* break off in the middle of scenes involving Pausanias, Panthea, and Delia, as though something in those scenes will not resolve, as though Empedocles' lovers and devotees have nothing essential to say about his grand suicidal deed "at the end." Thus the role of the two women in particular is radically reduced as the versions proceed: these personages are presumably among those "accidents" that will be cut as the play approaches what Hölderlin believes to be what is "essential" in it.[17]

16. See *Postponements,* pp. 49 and 92.

17. Extremely significant in this regard are Hölderlin's remarks on *Emilie vor ihrem Brauttag,* which interrupted (forever) his work on the *second* draft of *Der Tod des Empedokles,* remarks contained in a letter to Neuffer dated July 3, 1799 (B, 904–5). He indicates that the most difficult formal challenge for him, as far as the integration of the "modern" and the "ancient" is concerned, is to prevent his "love story" from aping the diction and the manner of high tragedy. Retain the elevated diction, and the lovers sound as though they are always wrangling; sacrifice the diction and one inevitably loses the exalted form of the *Trauerspiel.* Thus the poet of tragedy must opt for a "proud denial of everything accidental," and this seems to be the strategy Hölderlin follows when he marginalizes the

Always an "Antigonal" figure, Hölderlin's Panthea is either
patronized or fraternized—in the third draft she becomes Empedocles' naive and idealistic sister, *Schwester naiv. idealisch* (B,
585; S, 355/370). At the same time, it has to be admitted that
Empedocles himself is characterized by the very same words,
naiv. idealisch, so that the "sister" is perhaps to be understood as
an alter ego, a kind of twin, though perhaps not of the Siamese
variety. But then, why not a brother? A question not only for
Hölderlin but also for Robert Musil's Ulrich and Agathe, a question for Georg and Grete Trakl, a question for Franz and Ottla
Kafka, a question to which we will have to return in later chapters of the book.[18]

Be that as it may, such marginalization of the female characters is disturbing in the light of what Hölderlin had earlier
seen as the essential trajectory of Empedocles' life and death.
For Empedocles' gods are daimons of the earth, of "omnipresent Nature." From Hölderlin's late "Remarks" on Sophocles'
Oedipus the King and *Antigone,* one learns that Zeus himself, as
the father of time, is also the father of earth, so that one must be
less inclined than ever to identify Hölderlinian divinities as
ageless, deathless, and sexless. Indeed, in the "Remarks on *Oedipus,*" Hölderlin avers that the god is "nothing but time *[der Gott,
weil er nichts als Zeit ist]*" (B, 736). In the ode entitled "Empedocles," a first version of which Hölderlin composed in 1797, the
period of the first draft of his *Trauerspiel,* he designates the cause
of Empedocles' plunge into Etna as *schauderndes Verlangen,*
"shuddering desire," words he also employs in the first draft of
his play (see B, 67; 522–23; S, *12,* 170/237). He apostrophizes Empedocles as a fellow poet who has squandered his riches. Giving
a bizarre twist to the ancient Empedocles' invocation of Queen

---

characters of Delia and Panthea in the *third* version of his tragedy. To such
"proud denial" Hölderlin contrasts the "*tender timidity that characterizes the accidental* [mit dieser zarten Scheue des Akzidentellen]," which would characterize
the drama of sentiment. His "only question" is what form such a "beautiful spirit
of love" would take, and he seems by no means to be confident of an answer.
One might speculate that he would be even less confident about the possibility
that the tragic and sentimental forms might be successfully integrated—for example, in his own twice-interrupted Panthea/Delia scenes. Here once again a
careful reading of the letter's text, which is long and difficult, would be necessary—perhaps elsewhere, at a later time, in another context.

18. See esp. note 4 in chap. 6, below.

Kypris-Aphrodite and her reign of Love (Diels-Kranz, fr. 128), Hölderlin evokes the scene of the Egyptian queen Cleopatra melting pearls in a chalice of wine. The final stanza of the ode reads as follows:

> *Doch heilig bist du mir, wie der Erde Macht,*
> *Die dich hinwegnahm, kühner Getöteter!*
> *Und folgen möcht ich in die Tiefe,*
> *Hielte die Liebe mich nicht, dem Helden.*

> Yet you are holy to me, like the power of earth
> That took you away, O bold one! O murdered one!
> And I would follow into the depths,
> If love did not hold me, this hero.

Indeed, it is in despair over the death of his beloved Diotima, that is to say, in despair over the ephemeral character of mortal love, especially the sensual love of man and woman, that Hyperion suddenly introduces the figure of Empedocles into Hölderlin's work:

> And now tell me, is there any refuge left?—Yesterday I was up on Etna. I recalled the great Sicilian of old who, when he'd had enough of ticking off the hours, having become intimate with the soul of the world, in his bold lust for life plunged into the terrific flames. It was because—a mocker afterwards said of him—the frigid poet had to warm himself at the fire.
>
> O how gladly I would precipitate such mockery over me! but one must think more highly of oneself than I do to fly unbidden to nature's heart—put it any way you like, for, truly, as I am now, I have no name for these things, and all is uncertain *[es ist mir alles ungewiß]*. (B, 431–32)

If Hölderlin's first plans for a *Trauerspiel* involved the death of *Socrates* rather than Empedocles, as his letter to Neuffer dated October 10, 1794 testifies (B, 829), and if those plans found their lyrical consummation in the ode "Sokrates und Alcibiades," then one only need recall the tenderness of that ode—Socrates' loving what is most alive—in order to become convinced that sensual love and tragedy cannot be altogether strangers to one another in Hölderlin's vision. For Hölderlin too loves what is most alive, a Diotima of his own who, inaccessible in life, soon passes into the perfect inaccessibility of death.

Nevertheless, no matter how Empedocles is first invoked in Hölderlin's work, the Greek magus's love for Panthea and Pausanias appears to play less and less active a role as the project of the *Trauerspiel* proceeds, so that *Nietzsche's* insistence on the centrality of sensual love in and for tragedy emerges as the single greatest difference between the Empedocles plans of Hölderlin and Nietzsche. Nietzsche makes the connection between sensuality and tragic death seem so indissoluble that we are at first oblivious to it, and it is only in retrospect that one demands more of *Hölderlin's* play than it perhaps can give. Yet Nietzsche's demands for a sensual tragedy can be made on purely Hölderlinian grounds: in his Basel lectures on the pre-Platonic philosophers, Nietzsche borrows a number of essential words from Hölderlin's vocabulary in order to show that every tragic philosophy, every philosophy of unification and discord, of becoming and passing away, must be a philosophy of Aphrodite.[19] Empedocles' encounter with Pantheia, a woman he had rescued from the plague (she is renamed Corinna in Nietzsche's early Empedocles plans, and later on, in the sketches surrounding *Thus Spoke Zarathustra,* she is called Pana), is at the very center of the Nietzschean conception. Empedocles' "ironic"[20] plunge into Etna will also be the plunge of this woman, his beloved, and the irony will turn out to be the inextricable *fatality* of sensual love—the love that is most alive precipitating a most fiery death.

Woman, sensual love, and tragic death is the disconcerting, asymmetrical constellation that *Postponements* is all about—and so I will curtail discussion of it here. Suffice it to say that Nietzsche's "thought of thoughts," the eternal recurrence of the same, to which we too will return in the final chapter of this book, will be brought into the selfsame constellation ten years after his abortive Empedocles drama. What Hölderlin shuns, Nietzsche indeed proposes, but then postpones. Upon that proposing and postponing hangs the fate of the Dionysian philosophy as a whole, as of every philosophy of ephemeral unification and inevitable dissolution. Whether the festive celebration of life within time, the time of tragic downgoing, can counteract

19. Note the words *Vereinigung, Zwietracht, Werden und Vergehen* in Nietzsche's lectures, reprinted in the Großoktav edition (Leipzig: A. Kröner, 1913), *19,* 196.

20. Not "Ionian," as I mistakenly wrote in *Postponements* (p. 44), following the Großoktav text, which has *ionisch* instead of *ironisch.*

the plague of pity and penitence, or whether Dionysos will flee from the tragic stage, shun Ariadne and skirt Aphrodite—these questions are as yet unanswered. Or perhaps they have always already been answered—to the god's embarrassment. It is as though for aeons now we have been waiting upon the word that will be spoken by the lunar voice of the goddess herself.

•

Both Nietzsche and Hölderlin would grant the last word to Empedocles, the philosopher of agony and insight. I am painfully aware that these few remarks of mine do not much clarify either Hölderlin's or Nietzsche's Empedocles. As convinced as I am about Empedocles' ubiquity as the thinker of religion, science, art, and sensual love, who transgresses the epochal boundaries and thus suspends the very suspension in which our historical knowledges are held (for ἐποχή is suspension), I am at a loss to think in a lucid and confident fashion about the themes of tragic downgoing, affirmation, and sensual love. For the moment, I am reluctant to attach my own inchoate questions to the far more ambitious schema developed by Philippe Lacoue-Labarthe, for which the collapse of tragedy in Hölderlin marks a gap or caesura in philosophical speculation as such.[21]

21.   Lacoue-Labarthe perceives in Hölderlin's "imitation" of Greek tragedy the modern and contemporary "limitation" of speculative philosophy. In such (l)imitation he sees the evanescence of catharsis in tragedy, the demise of the absolute standpoint in speculative philosophy, and the collapse of "mimetology"—the ruin of the imitable—in both tragedy and philosophy. I would very much like to respond some day to his call for a patient and precise exposition of the three *Empedokles* drafts from the point of view of the "caesura," especially inasmuch as his own point of departure is the later *Anmerkungen* to the translations of Sophocles. Françoise Dastur notes one of the difficulties concerning Lacoue-Labarthe's thesis on the caesura, suspension, and catharsis of speculative philosophy, although whether or not it is her Empedoclean point of departure that reveals the difficulty I cannot be certain. At all events, Dastur objects to Lacoue-Labarthe: " . . . the caesura is not a 'caesura of the speculative' in the sense that it would interrupt the speculative process of *Selbstbespiegelung* [self-mirroring] or auto-reflection; it is rather the very condition of speculation, of spiritual repetition itself, which can take place only if the movement of reality is interrupted, if there is a suspension, a cessation *[arrêt]*, which authorizes its gaze back upon *itself*. Thus the caesura permits the apparition of time itself, permits a view upon the entirety of time. . . . The caesura is this point of indifference on the basis of which the whole process can be perceived and in which the opposi-

For the moment, I am satisfied with the thought that Hölderlin himself seems to have found his voice precisely in being at a loss. Even the "heroic life of a hermit," the life of one who translates Sophocles and who seems assured of "the most appropriate viewpoint" (B, 786), continues to be a life that is troubled by all these "awkward" points (B, 790). For his part, Nietzsche never manages to grant Ariadne, Corinna, and Pana the time and space they need to speak or act out their parts. Yet all these failures have to do with what Empedocles of Acragas identifies as the alternating reigns of Love and Strife, the striving of these two periods of rule, or their loving interplay and clasp. If my remarks here are disappointingly thin, tenuous, precarious, it is perhaps because the words of Empedocles and of Φιλία herself remain to be heard—as Hölderlin and Nietzsche undoubtedly once heard them, and as, after them, Yeats heard them.[22]

In the first of Empedocles' two poems, the one we call "Of Nature," which Heidegger would insist we translate, "Of Upsurgence," Empedocles celebrates the reign of Φιλία, which surely must be coming. Fragment 17 (lines 18–26) of that poem issues a pledge or a promise whose allure neither Hölderlin nor Nietzsche can resist:

Fire and water and earth and vast height of air . . .
And in their midst, Love . . .

---

tions can find their equilibrium." However, Dastur herself, I believe, would experience some discomfiture over the words *authorize, entirety, whole process, equilibrium,* etc. For like Lacoue-Labarthe, Dastur emphasizes the caesura as a mark of radical *separation,* radical *finitude.* The caesura as a product of *fire* and a figure of *rhythm* will return to haunt us in chaps. 2 and 3, below. On this entire question, see Lacoue-Labarthe, *L'imitation des modernes,* esp. pp. 40, 56–57, 60–61, and 77; and Françoise Dastur, *Hölderlin: Tragédie et modernité,* pp. 79–80 and 119. In this same context I would want to read quite closely Christopher Fynsk, *Heidegger: Thought and Historicity* (Ithaca, NY: Cornell University Press, 1986), chap. 5, and Andrzej Warminski, *Readings in Interpretation: Hölderlin, Hegel, Heidegger* (Minneapolis: Minnesota University Press, 1987), esp. chaps. 1 and 2. Finally, I would want to read the materials collected in Christoph Jamme and Otto Pöggeler, eds., *Jenseits des Idealismus: Hölderlins letzte Homburger Jahre (1804–1806)* (Bonn: Bouvier, 1988), in particular the articles by Klaus Düsing, Gerhard Kurz, and Uvo Hölscher (esp. pp. 331–34). Another time, perhaps.

22. See William Butler Yeats, *A Vision* (New York: Collier, 1966 [1st ed., 1926; 2d ed., 1937]), p. 20.

Gaze on her with the mind's eye, do not be astonished.
You know her, she surges in the limbs of mortals.
Through her they dwell on loving thoughts and do the unifying deed,
Calling her by name: Delight! and Aphrodite!
As she whirls with the other elements there
No mortal man can make her out. But do trace
These footsteps of my logos: it will not disappoint you.

2 Stuff • Thread • Point • Fire
Hölderlin's Dissolution

> What are we? personified *almighty points.*
>
> —Novalis, *Vorarbeiten* 1798 (*2*, 329)

> To climb down a mountain, to embrace the region with one's eyes, and all the while to feel an unsated craving. Passionate lovers who do not know how to achieve *unification* (in Lucretius) [.] The knower *demands* unification with the things and sees himself *apart from* them—that is his *passio.* Either everything should dissolve in knowledge or he himself will dissolve in the things—that is his tragedy. (The latter is his death and its *pathos.* The former is his striving to *make* everything into spirit: *enjoyment* in conquering, vaporizing, and violating *matter.* Enjoyment of the atomism of mathematical points. *Cupidity!*
>
> —Nietzsche, notebook M III 1 (Spring–Fall, 1881), 11 [69]

The point of all dialectical, internalizing remembrance (Hegelian *Erinnerung*), as of all commemorative thinking (Heideggerian *Andenken*), is to hold in memory and to preserve from obliteration the contents (Hegelian and Heideggerian *Inhalt*) of thought and experience. For both Hegel and Heidegger, to remember is to heed, hold, and keep.[1] Sometimes the same seems to be true of Hölderlin. Yet at virtually every moment in his theoretical writings from the Jena through the Homburg and even into the final periods   he only mourns   all dialectical punc-

---

1. See Krell, *Of Memory, Reminiscence, and Writing: On the Verge* (Bloomington: Indiana University Press, 1990), chaps. 5 and 6, where I have discussed the cases of Hegel and Heidegger, respectively. I am grateful to my students and (present as well as former) colleagues at DePaul University, especially Anna Vaughn and Paul Davies, and to colleagues at the Collège International de Philosophie, especially Françoise Dastur, for their willingness during the fall of 1990 to listen to some of the strange thoughts contained in this chapter and to help them along.

tuation catches fire; the ostensible inwardness (*Innigkeit* as it is usually rendered) and internalizing remembrance *(Erinnerung)* that Hölderlin emphasizes without cease, as well as the punctuated line of time as such, are consumed utterly. This accounts for the ambiguous fate of Empedocles, who is Hölderlin's obsession during the years in which most of the theoretical sketches were composed: Empedocles feels himself to be fettered by time as succession, and yet is unable to find liberation in a death that would be freely chosen at a certain point in time; he remains on the verge of the crater, so to speak, consumed in the very delay that wards off his "one full deed at the end." However, if *Der Tod des Empedokles* remains but a fragment, or three fragments, forever disrupted and disruptive, returning always only as a tragedy, then the ardor or intensity (*Innigkeit* as I shall render it throughout these remarks translation is wholesome gymnastics for language) of its very fragmentation incinerates the time of succession, consumes the time of identity, purges the time of imitation. In Hölderlin's punctilious yet hardly punctual time of tragic dissolution, a time bereft of punctuation, all points, as we shall see, become fireballs.

All points. Points of view, points of commencement and culmination, starting, middle, and end points; points of rest, unification, dissolution, and scission *(Gesicht[s]-, Anfangs-, Mittel-, End-, Ruhe-, Vereinigungs-, Auflösungs-, Scheidepunkte).* Even what Hölderlin calls the elongated or distended point, *der verlängerte Punkt,* is less a productive line or a usable, weavable thread than a burning fuse. *All* points in Hölderlin's theoretical writings are consumed by the fire of heaven, which is not so much an ethereal, crystalline memory of a bygone life as an ecstatic, intense reliving of the same life in ineluctable downgoing. As Nietzsche too will have known.

In this chapter I shall restrict myself to commenting on several passages from *Wenn der Dichter einmal des Geistes mächtig . . .* (which earlier editors of Hölderlin's works called "On the Poetic Spirit's Manner of Proceeding"), *Das untergehende Vaterland . . .* ("Becoming and Passing Away"), and the *Grund zum Empedokles.*[2]

2. The intrusions in my text are from either Hölderlin's letters or the three drafts of *Der Tod des Empedokles.* The translations are my own. Note that for the

The Reproductive Act

"If the poet should ever attain power over the spirit," begins Hölderlin, such spiritual power would enable her or him to reproduce himself or herself in the same or in an other. Such power would guide all inclination and appropriation *(Zueignung)*, would allow the poet to capture and secure *(festhalten, versichern)* both self and poetic work through "the reproductive act." Such spiritual power would reproduce itself *(sich reproduzieren)* in the very stuff of poetry as it does in an individual's memory—through the harmonious alternation and interplay of spiritual import and form. Yet alternation and interplay of content and form in and of themselves are insufficient. The reproductive stuff of life and of dramatic action remains to be *found.* And even when it is found, appropriation of it commands a certain temporal order of differentiation and deferral, distribution and delay:

> Thus the stuff must be distributed, the total impression must be delayed, and the identity must become a striving forward from one point to another, whereupon the total impression naturally finds itself, so that the point of commencement and the midpoint and the point of culmination are most intensely drawn to one another, in such a way that closure occurs, with the point of culmination turning back to the point of inception, and the point of inception to the midpoint. (S, *14,* 143)

---

most part I am limiting myself here to the theoretical writings of the Jena, Frankfurt, and Homburg periods, having very little to say about Hölderlin's later "Remarks" on his Sophocles translations—on which so much of the contemporary discussion has focused. My reading of Hölderlin's *Der Tod des Empedokles* will at times intersect that of Warminski, *Readings in Interpretation,* chaps. 1–2, esp. pp. 11–22. Like Warminski, I am interested in reading the final scene of the (truncated) third draft, the Manes scene, reading it "a little longer," reading it "*as* a scene of reading" (13). Like Warminski, I take it to be disconcerting and yet undeniable that "the transition from one world and time to another"—the transition that is *history*—hinges and unhinges "simultaneously" on "radical forgetting and radical remembering" (16). The themes of *fire* and *intensity,* themselves burning through the distinctions between the Hesperian (Christian-Germanic), Greek, Egyptian, and Oriental realms, I take to be themes particularly appropriate to such radicality of reading.

The point of poetic creation articulates a thread of circular unity, a unity of linear unification and linear opposition or juxtaposition—as in the central junction or intersection in the sign for infinity: ∞. For the poetic process is alive, seasonal, and cyclical, drawn at one and the same time or in rhythmic alternation toward its midpoint and its extremes. Life alternates endlessly, precisely because it is the only alternative. Life itself is the elongated or distended point, *der verlängerte Punkt,* which strives simultaneously for intensity *(Innigkeit)* and distinction or difference *(Unterscheidung).*   That I am still in the cloister is a result of my mother's request. For her sake I can certainly afford to let a couple of years go sour.   The identity of the extenuated point cannot come to rest absolutely, for that would be its death. Nor can that identity depend on a sequence of infinitely isolated moments ("as it were, a row of atoms"). It must be constituted by "*a thoroughgoing and characteristic drawing into relation*" (Beziehung). Such identity, which is always something more than mere serial unity, confronts as its "ultimate task"

> having a thread, a remembrance, in harmonic alter(n)ation *[Wechsel];* so that the spirit never is in a single moment and then again in another single moment, but is perdurance in one as in another, remaining present to itself in its various attunements precisely as it is altogether present to itself *in infinite* unity, which on the one hand is the point of disjunction of the singular as singular, while on the other is the unifying point of the singular as juxtaposed, and finally both at the same time, so that in it the harmoniously juxtaposed is neither juxtaposed as singular nor unified as juxtaposed, but felt   for the past few days my work has stumbled to a halt, at which point I always employ reason concerning it   as both in *one,* as singularly and inseparably juxtaposed, and is invented as so felt. (S, *14,* 150)

Thus the artist who seeks an inspired voice and vision in foreign climes and distant times struggles to achieve self-identity and a measure of autonomy, but also to distinguish himself or herself in the world, all the while yearning to preserve a harmonious relationship between self and world. The poet usually either collapses back into childlike complacency or prods the self with merciless commands and bootless contradictions.

Yet this wretched alternative is all but unavoidable. . . . The boy has to deal with men.   Only one maxim, applied to the poet's life, can rescue her or him from what at one point Hölderlin calls "this sad alternative," namely, the alternate regression into a childhood of intense personal feeling and sallying forth into a world of distinctions and differences. The only maxim that will help the poet survive such alter(n)ation is the following: "Posit yourself *with free choice* in harmonious juxtaposition to an external sphere, precisely in the way you are in *harmonious* juxtaposition within yourself, by nature, and yet unrecognizably so, as long as you remain within yourself" (S, *14*, 153–54). Presumably, the only obstacle to a successful application of the maxim   You have become clearer about who you are than I have   is how one can *avoid* remaining within oneself, how one can sally forth at least long enough to recognize (on the outside) the harmony of oneself (within). Hölderlin's fascination with Empedocles may be explained by the circumstance that the ancient Greek magus develops a unique approach to this struggle between inner self and outer world, although in the three drafts of Hölderlin's play the poet is unable to bring Empedocles to the point of radical (dis)solution, to the idealized deed of suicide.

Hölderlin's essay "The fatherland in decline . . ." indicates that the poet is never alone, whether in harmonious or cacophonous juxtaposition. Born to be a singer, he may find that his age requires him to be a sacrifice. To be sure, the essay generally takes the larger, more distant view, according to which the new world and new life   I am in a new world   come to be from the passing away of the prior ones. For a point of time, or in between two points of time, the new age seems to hover tremulously between being and nonbeing; nevertheless, Hölderlin attributes to the new age all three modalities—possibility, actuality, and necessity. Looking fore as well as aft, in anticipation of what Nietzsche will describe as the Apollonian dream-state, Hölderlin calls the process of becoming and passing away (insofar as it is captured in the unconstrained and therefore scarcely mimetic art of tragic-dramatic poetry) "a terrifying yet divine dream" (S, *14*, 97). Terrifying inasmuch as the divine dream is invariably haunted by disruption and dissolution; divine inasmuch as the thread of remembrance can nonetheless be woven into the "stuff" of the drama.

Thus the dissolution, as necessary, from the viewpoint of ideal remembrance becomes as such the ideal object of newly developed
life, a backward glance to the path that had to be traversed from
the beginning of the dissolution to the point at which the new life
[produced] a remembrance of the dissolved; and from that, as an
explanation and unification of the gap and of the contrast that
takes place between the new and the bygone, remembrance of
the dissolution can proceed. Ideal dissolution does not terrify.
The point[s] of commencement and culmination are already established, found, secured; hence this dissolution is always more
secure, more relentless, bolder; and it presents itself as it properly
is, as a reproductive act, whereby life runs through all its points
and, in order to attain the entire sum, tarries on none of them,
dissolving itself in each in order to produce itself in the next; except that the dissolution is more ideal to the degree to which it
distances itself from its point of commencement, whereas the restoration is more real to the same degree, until finally from the
sum of these sensations of passing away and originating, infinitely
run through in a moment, a whole feeling of life comes to the
fore; and from this [arises] the sole excluded element, what was
primally dissolved in remembrance (by the necessity of an object
in its most accomplished state). And after the remembrance of
the dissolved, the individual, unites with the infinite feeling of life
through remembrance of dissolution, and after the gap between
them is filled, there proceeds from this unification and comparison of the past singularity and the infinitely present the new situation proper, the next step that is to succeed upon the past. (S,
14, 97)

   Early on in the long and tortuous passage I have reproduced
here, Hölderlin interrupts the phrase "a backward glance to the
path that had to be traversed." He introduces into his manuscript three quick sketches—drawings, graphics, or doodles.
The ink drawings, evidently in a hasty hand, look something
like this:

The first of the three sketches (counting from the left) is partly
gathered up by a swooping, scooping, sweeping line that appears

to have been meant to encompass the figure as a whole, but inadvertently sunders it:

The drawings are as difficult to "read" as the text is. Do they depict the problem of the contiguity of points, or of the communication between points, in Hölderlin's historical continuum or "thread," two points juxtaposed and conjoined by some unknown *x* of "ideal" or "tragic" dissolution? Does the middle sketch depict a single point of the dissolved past, trebled and infinitized within itself? (Does it not look like an open eye, the eye of Franz Baader's and F. W. J. Schelling's sun, heart, and theocosmic eye?[3] Whatever the case, this middle figure will reappear in the final chapter on Nietzsche and Gabriel García Márquez as the wheel of recurrence.) Does the final graphic represent the periodic wave of a halved infinity, replacing the usual straight line of succession? Are the straight lines in the final figure introduced in order to graph or measure the waves of the period, to calculate the rhythmic intensities of peak and valley? The problems of such a retrospective "window" (the window itself seems an Egyptian eye, the eye of Manes, accustomed to the longer historical view) on the past point of dissolution, a window that would itself be an opening of ongoing life, *futural* life, are, as Hölderlin well knows, immense.

Hölderlin's "explanation and unification of the gap and of the contrast that takes place between the new and the bygone" remains mysterious indeed. Ideal dissolution may not terrify, but it certainly baffles. And even if the points of inception and termination in the process are "already established, found, secured," the reproductive act that runs through them and provides the thread seems hardly as straightforward, relentless, and bold as, say, Descartes' *enumeratio* does.[4] In the following paragraph of Hölderlin's text, which consists of a single sentence, the

---

3. See F. W. J. Schelling, *Über das Wesen der menschlichen Freiheit,* in volume 7 of the *Sämmtliche Werke* (Stuttgart, 1830), p. 367n.

4. See *regulae* 3 and 7 in Descartes' *Rules for the Direction of the Human Mind,* in Descartes, *Œuvres et lettres,* ed. André Bridoux (Paris: Pléiade, 1953), pp. 44–45 and 57–61.

optimism of the reproductive act (odd equivocation, as though reproduction alternated somewhere between memory and life, or between memory, life, love, and the poetic work) reaches its apogee: "Thus, in remembrance of dissolution, the latter, because both of its ends stand firm, becomes altogether the secure, relentless, and bold act that it properly is." The ubiquitous, vigorous, and yet altogether ambiguous reproductive act   It's peculiar—I'll probably never fall in love except in dreams   appears to disseminate its power and surrender its act to dissolution as such. Dissolution envisaged and remembered therefore seems to involve much more than merely filling a gap. Could it be the daring leap of Empedocles into Etna? And yet is not that vaunted leap   I know that everything godlike / Must go down postponed endlessly? As though given infinite pause   I shall not go yet, old man!   by Hölderlin's sudden recollection of Empedocles stranded on the brink of his reproductive act of dissolution, the next paragraph of the text begins with an *Aber*, "But." An *Aber* that takes us from foreign *stuff* to the temporal and significative *thread* and on to a *point* that is ablaze with *fire*—an *Aber* that would have served as the midpoint of these remarks of mine, had they been so bold:

> But this ideal dissolution is distinguished from the actual also by the fact that it goes from the infinitely present to the finitely past, such that (1) at every point of the same dissolution and restoration, (2) at one point in its dissolution and restoration with every other, (3) at every point in its dissolution and restoration, it is infinitely more interlaced with the total feeling of dissolution and restoration, and everything is more infinitely permeated, touched, and confronted by pain and joy, strife and peace, movement and rest, form and formlessness, so that a heavenly fire rather than an earthly one works its effects. (S, *14*, 98)

One should never underestimate the devastation wrought by idealized heavenly fire in the ideal dissolution of ideal points. Does it not seem as though every point of dissolution in Hölderlin's historical vision, taken in itself and also in its relation with every other, whether of the beginning, middle, or end, whether of unification or disjunction, is incinerated? Would not cinder and ash alone be left as the barest signs or traces—always something less than punctual points—of the bold reproductive act? Where stuff, thread, and point meet fire, all inwardness melts in ardor and intensity, all economies of punctuality and containment shrivel in what Bataille will have called the general economy of solar expenditure without reserves.   O you well-known to me, you magic, / Frightful flame! how quietly you dwell / Here, then there, how you shy from yourself / And flee yourself, you soul of the living! The next paragraph of *Das untergehende Vaterland . . .* , the last I shall cite, begins with the word *Endlich*, "finally," but also "finitely," "endlike." To be sure, the passage commences with the optimism of an infinitely present present, the pure presence of perfect (re)production and restoration *(Herstellung),* and an ideal envisagement of a dissolution that is always safely past:

> Endlike, once again, because on the other hand the ideal dissolution goes from the infinitely present to the finitely past; ideal dissolution differs from the actual in that it can be more thoroughly determined, it does not have to conflate in anxious disquiet several essential points of dissolution and restoration into one, does not have to wander anxiously in the direction of things inessential, toward the feared dissolution, nor toward things that would hinder the restoration, things quite properly dead; it also does not have to limit itself, one-sidedly, anxiously, and to the bitter end, to one point of dissolution and restoration, so that it is made to go toward its proper demise. Rather, it goes its precise, straight, open way, at each point of dissolution and restoration being entirely what it can be at that point, and only at it, hence truly individual; naturally, nothing foreign or distracting, nothing itself insignificant forces itself onto this point; but it traverses the individual point freely and completely in all its relations with the remaining points of dissolution and restoration that lie between the first two points that are *capable of* dissolution and restoration, namely, the juxtaposed infinitely new and finitely old, the real whole and the ideal particulars. (S, *14,* 98)

Hölderlin himself concedes and even emphasizes the advantage of proceeding from the infinitely present to the finitely (or finally) past, from the ideally "real" totality to the really "ideal" yet truncated particulars of history. To proceed the other way would require that one go to encounter disquiet, anxiety, contingency, and death. Unfortunately, this "other way" is the only way available to those who act or think *in* time and history, without the idealized and idealizing window on the "real," which is to say "finite," past.   You know me and you and death and life not.   If heavenly fire consumes the points of dissolution and restoration in the ideal, the infinitely present, then the gaps between these incinerated points themselves become infinite—in the sense of the unbounded and indeterminate. If the theoretical fragment in question begins with the phrase "The fatherland in decline," and if it peters out in a Fichtean lucubration *(Ich/ Nichtich)* and a fragmentary recollection of tragic unification, nothing in Hölderlin's meditation can halt or even slow the irremediable decline, the downgoing and decrease, behind all the brave reproductive racing back and forth between points of ideal dissolution and restoration.

The Bypassed Terminus

There is in Hölderlin's text   I am on the way to becoming a really good boy   what one might call "the missed terminal" or "bypassed terminus," *der verpaßte Endpunkt.* (The locution is not Hölderlin's.) Not the elongated point that produces a narrative thread and the dramatic stuff of historical life, but a repeated point of repetitious culmination, which the text itself repeatedly reaches but then bypasses into redundancy. Such a missed opportunity for closure occurs in *"Wenn der Dichter einmal des Geistes mächtig . . . ,"* and I will therefore return to it for an instant, to the very point at which I stopped citing earlier. After naming the thread of remembrance that binds beginning and end and midpoint, thus transforming a series of atomic and discrete units into one continuous invention or narrative cycle,   Thus it had to be. / Thus the spirit wills it / And the ripening time. / For sometimes we / The blind need a miracle   Hölderlin indicates the "properly poetic character" of that thread. Remembrance in the poet lies beyond the powers of both art and genius, and its thread is spun and twisted in the direction or sense or meaning *(Sinn)* that the poet will fatefully come to have. Such direction or sense or meaning, *der Sinn,* constitutes poetic individuality. "To such individuality alone is given the identity of inspiration, the accomplishment of genius and art, the presentification of the infinite, the divine moment *[die Vergegenwärtigung des Unendlichen, der göttliche Moment gegeben]*" (S, *14,* 150). Full stop.

Phenomenology itself, whether Hegelian, Husserlian, or Heideggerian, would doubtless be more than satisfied with such givenness and presentification. Philosophical speculation of every kind would certainly allow and even insist on a full stop or a period or (as the French say) a *point* to terminate the sentence and the paragraph. For what more could be given or written after this divine moment of infinite presentification? Unfortunately, Hölderlin never knows when to stop fully. Never fully knows when to stop. Never knows fully when to let the period fall. It is as though he were drawn, spun, and twisted in the direction of disquiet, death, and dissolution—as though he were born to play with heavenly fire.   Daily I must call upon the vanished godhead. When I think of great men in great times, and how they spread holy fire on all sides and transformed everything that was defunct, everything wooden, all the straw of the world into flames, so that it soared heavenward with them; and when I think of me, of how often I drift about like a flickering little lamp begging for a drop of oil so that I can shine a bit longer through the night—behold! a wondrous shudder passes through all my limbs, and softly I say to myself a terrifying word: the living dead!

The bypassed terminus. Never knowing when to stop. Always either hyperbolic or elliptical. The (in)famous first sentence of *"Wenn der Dichter einmal des Geistes mächtig . . ."* contains 109 lines and over a thousand words; a semicolon appears in line 50 in order to slow the sentence down for a brief interval, for it is all about control and points of rest *(Ruhepunkte),* although also about strife, alter(n)ation, and the receptivity of poetic stuff, which is almost always recalcitrant. The poetic process can therefore never be purely   Do you know what the cause of it is? Human beings are afraid of one another, afraid that the genius of the one will consume that of the other; that's why they gladly provide one another with food and drink, but nothing that nourishes the soul, and they can't bear it when something they say or do starts up like a flame of spirit in the other. The fools! As though anything human beings might say to one another were more than kindling, which burns only when it is ignited by spiritual fire, inasmuch as it came to be out of life and fire. And if only they were to grant one another nourishment, both parties would live and illumine, and neither would consume the other   about purity. Pure presentification of the infinite in the infinitely present, the divine moment, does not avail. More is needed, more of something else must be found, if such a thing dare be said. "In its operations, the poetic spirit's manner of proceeding can never end with this. If it is true, something else must be found in it *[aufzufinden sein]*, and it must show itself to be the case that the procedure that gives the poem its significance is merely the transition from what is pure to this to-be-found *[der Übergang vom Reinen zu diesem Aufzufindenden]*, as also backward from this to what is pure. (Mediation between spirit and sign)" (S, *14*, 148). As long as the to-be-found remains to-be-found, ensconced in the gerundive of necessity, the regression to purity   Do you recall our unruffled hours, when we and we alone were rapt to one another? How triumphant! The two of us, so free and proud and alert, blossoming, gleaming in heart and soul and eye and face, and each alongside the other in such heavenly bliss! Even then I sensed it and said it: one could travel the world over and still not find anything like that again. Daily I can feel it, and ever more gravely   remains problematic. The Ariadnic thread that ought to guide us back point-by-point smolders, burns as a fuse, untwists, ravels to ash. Mediation between spirit and sign loses itself among signs of intensity *(Innigkeit)*. No stop can be a full stop, no point a point to which the poet might return and from which he or she might set out boldly, relentlessly, straightforwardly, on the way (back) to spirit. The very possibility of mediation loses itself in the interminable hiatus of the caesura, as Hölderlin long ago observed and as Walter Benjamin, Maurice Blanchot, and Philippe Lacoue-Labarthe have recently reminded us.[5]

The only possible punctuality or punctuation for a discourse

5. Hölderlin, B, 729–36; 783–90; Walter Benjamin, Part III of "Goethes *Wahlverwandtschaften*," in *Illuminationen* (Frankfurt am Main: Suhrkamp, 1977), esp. pp. 116–19; Maurice Blanchot, *L'espace littéraire* (Paris: Gallimard, 1955), pp. 374–75; and Philippe Lacoue-Labarthe, *L'imitation des modernes*, esp. pp. 59–69. Lacoue-Labarthe calls *hyperbologic* what one would perhaps also have to call *ellipsis*. That is to say, Hölderlin's "regression" from a classic Aristotelian (i.e., mimetological and cathartic) to a more Sophoclean reading (and writing, and directing) of tragedy, insofar as it speaks regressively as a *speculative* discourse, always both falls too short and goes too far with regard to the Aristotelian model for tragedy. Hence the (apparent) confusions of Lacoue-Labarthe's own account—of Hölderlin's paralysis, dislocation, immobility, interdiction, distention, suspension, split, spiral hollow, foundering, and "spasm." While I cannot follow Lacoue-Labarthe's reading of the three drafts of *Der Tod des Empedokles* as precise stages of such a regression (60–62), and while I regret his acceptance of the traditional reading of *Innigkeit* as *l'intériorité* (62–64), I celebrate his search in Hölderlin for a logic of excess, a logic of alternance, a logic of what I will here call *hyperbollipsis*.

that perdures in the white heat of caesura and hiatus   Many people excel in this or that. But a nature like yours, where all is gathered in an intense indestructible living union, is the pearl of our times. Whoever has known her, and whoever knows that her own happiness, born of heaven, is also her profound unhappiness, he too is eternally blessed and eternally wretched   consists of comma, semicolon, and . . . *verpaßter Endpunkt.*[6]

After Hölderlin invokes the presentification of the infinitely present, the divine moment of perfect givenness, his paragraph ends . . . but his text goes on, beyond the pure word, in search of what remains *aufzufinden,* locating only a dead and deadening unity *(eine tote und tötende Einheit).* Defunct unity appears in the form of "a positive nothing" *(eines positiven Nichts),* "an infinite cessation" *(eines unendlichen Stillstands),* and matchless "hyperbole" *(es ist die Hyperbel aller Hyperbeln der kühnste und letzte Versuch des poetischen Geistes)* (S, *14,* 150–51). This boldest and most reckless leap beyond perfect givenness would take us to the question of freedom, and to what we earlier invoked as "this sad alternative": the poet happy in his or her childhood, like Empedocles in his garden, but wretched in the world of distinguished men—distinguished, but always vying, always envious.   Ah! I'd rather you knew nothing / Of me and all my mourning. No!   A hyperbolic or elliptical leap would never grant the poet a sign that might guarantee the safe return to purity; it would be a leap into endless complications, where there would always remain something to be found, something beyond the repeatedly bypassed termination . . .

6. On the caesura, see both Lacoue-Labarthe, cited above, and the following from Andrzej Warminski, which in a way synthesizes the findings of Lacoue-Labarthe and Françoise Dastur, discussed in chap. 1, note 21, above: "What Hölderlin means by 'caesura' is a very peculiar 'cutting off,' for it is an interruption that, in brief, allows the tragedy to continue. . . . It is what Hölderlin calls 'the pure word'. . . . Like the Manes scene, the caesura is the place where the tragedy explicitly turns upon itself, where, in short, representation represents itself *as* representation. That this turning is not the reflection of a Subject (absolute or otherwise) but rather of a text is clear from Hölderlin's using explicitly linguistic terms to name it: that is, caesura, the pure word. Indeed, rather than allowing the human subject to recognize himself in his own other, the caesura rips him out of his own sphere of life, out of the center of his own inner life, and carries him off into an other world and tears him into the eccentric sphere of the dead" (Warminski, *Readings in Interpretation,* p. 17). For further discussion, see the remarks on *rhythm* and *counterrhythm* in the final section of chap. 3, below.

At the Burning Point

Can we learn a little more about the point of combustion? When and where and how in Hölderlin's text does the *point* of every *thread* of all narrative *stuff* catch *fire* and burn itself out? From the outset Hölderlin was fascinated by the necessity of separation *(Trennung)*. Every point, including the midpoint, was for him the point that opens upon a sheath of separation *(Scheidepunkt)*.   I live a very lonely life, and I believe it is good for me.

Even in the early essay, "Judgment and Being," composed early in 1795, "original separation" was the primal division and allotment that others were calling *Urteil,* "judgment." For Hölderlin it was more like an ordeal, an *Ur-Teilung,* more like crisis and divorce than confident critique. From the outset the ordeal was as much of life as of thought.   I am happy and unhappy as a result of your kindness. . . . Dear Mother! What is wanted is a human being who is good for something. But am I that, if I am to be honest about it?

In one of the "Seven Maxims" from the Spring of 1799 (S, *14,* 48), he appealed to "the profound feeling of mortality, of change, of life's temporal limits." A mournful sense of separation and loss always accompanied and perhaps even encompassed Hölderlin's meditation on unification, serving as its horizon, its harrowing season. "For he has attained much who can understand life without mourning." Yet the point is not to try to attain too much, not to blast away at the horizon or season of mourning with hopes for too much.   I was always tempted to see you, and when I saw you it was only to feel that I could be nothing for you. . . . Because I wanted to be so much for you, I had to tell myself that I would be nothing for you.

Every bit as early in his life as a thinker, Hölderlin tried to meet the necessity of separation and loss with the force of remembrance. Human beings would elevate themselves above mere need and necessity only if they remembered with gratitude their destiny or proper "skill," "calling," or "sending" *(Geschick).* The "Fragment of Philosophical Letters" (1795–96; S, *14,* 36) invoked   In philosophical letters I want to find the principle that will explain to me the separations *[die Trennungen]* in which we think and exist   a memory of life that is thankful *(dankbar),* a "thinking that dares to enter into the more intense nexus of life *[den innigeren Zusammenhang des Lebens zu denken wagt]*" (S, *14,* 37). Every

bit as early in his life as a poet, and certainly by 1797, the necessity of separation and the destiny of remembrance joined in a
thinking of *tragedy*. In *"Das lyrische dem Schein nach idealische
Gedicht . . ."* ("On the Differences among the Kinds of Poetry";
S, *14*, 184; B, 598–602), Hölderlin invoked his own version of the
famous Fichtean-Schellingian "intellectual intuition," according to which tragic thinking depends upon insight   I almost
believe that I am pedantic out of sheer love   into the unity of all life,
life being the scene of love, separation, and loss.

Tragedy rises as a flame from what seems to be a "primally
unified life," an Edenic state or an Empedoclean sphere in
which everything encounters everything else and each thing receives its "rights," its "entire measure of life." At a certain point
in primally unified life, at a certain *uncertain* point, which is to
say, at each indeterminate and unbounded point of the infinitely present, separation invariably supervenes and disrupts
the unity. Diremption occurs with, in, and through a feeling of
excess. The parts that constitute the whole of life come to "feel
too unified *[zu einig]*." The hyperbolic, ironic, excessive "too"
(zu)   He must die, for he lived too well, / The gods all loved him over-
much. / . . . What can the son of god do? / Boundlessly the boundless one is
struck   marks the moment of scission and separation at the
very point of most intense unity. In the *Grund zum Empedokles*
Hölderlin will say: ". . . too intensely, too singularly *[zu innig, zu
einzig]*."

When, where, and how does the excess transpire, disrupting
unity at the point of life's supreme intensity? The parts of the
unified whole of life separate not only when they wander from
the center but also when they are "closer to the midpoint *[Mit-
telpunkt]* of the whole" (S, *14*, 185). At the fulcrum too, where the
radius of every circle begins, and where beginning and end
should be balanced for all eternity, disruption invariably occurs.
The reign of the sky god, the celestial monarch, is periodically
overthrown.   The Lord of Time, troubled in his enthroned rule, /
Scowls gloomily over all raging. / His day is done, his lightning flashes, / Yet
what kindles above merely burns, / While the striving below is savage discord.   Hölderlin cites as the cause of such disruption and discord the necessitous free will or contingent arbitrariness—for
Willkür means both—of Zeus, son of Cronos, lord of heaven,
father of earth, and wielder of the lightning bolt: ". . . *in dieser*

notwendigen Willkür des Zevs *liegt eigentlich der ideale Anfang der wirklichen Trennung."* The moment or point of excess is the central point, the midpoint, of all life, where extremes meet; the point of excess and separation is none other than the central or middle point of unification. A smaller point burning at the center of every middle point, like the smoking axle of a wheel, and a still smaller point burning at its center, in turn, and so on into abyssal infinity. It is god. It is strife. It is the very life of life. It is death. It is miracle. It is mirage.   O mirage! It is gone forever! It is truth. It is the lie. It is, as Hölderlin obsessively says, "both together."

Yet whatever else it is, the fiery point is *pain*, felt always in searing intensity. For even if nature and humanity affect one another reciprocally and harmoniously, as Hölderlin notes in *Das untergehende Vaterland . . . ,"* so that a new world and a new life germinate in the ashes of the old, and even if tragic dissolution can be felt only on the grounds of a nascent and as yet undiscovered unification, it remains the case, as every hermit knows, that the modality of possibility remains fixed in mournful remembrance of what has dissolved and is lost forever to possibility. The access and the excess of *pain*   the best simply have to perish one way or the other   rise in the course of dissolution, blotting out any possible apprehension of the new life, up to the point at which a genuinely tragic language transforms amorphous pain into a tremor of terror. For the language of tragedy   O Greece, with your genius and your piety, where have you gone?   does not manage to communicate "the first pain of dissolution." (That modest phrase, "the first pain of dissolution," from "Becoming in Passing Away," a phrase that hides well its excess, Hölderlin later reworks to read: "not the first, raw pain, *still too* unknown in its depths to those who suffer and those who observe *[nicht der erste rohe in seiner Tiefe dem Leidenden und Betrachtenden n o c h z u unbekannte Schmerz der Auflösung]"*; Beißner and Schmidt read: ". . . *dem Leidenden und Betrachtenden* noch ZU *unbekannte . . ."* [S, *14,* 84, 94, and 97; B, 642].) All of which suggests that *pain* is the celestial element of fiery excess that remains to be found, *das Aufzufindende,* which transcends all pure spiritual import and artistic form in the direction of the sign. Pain, a sign? No doubt, a sign that is not read, a sign undeciphered, a sign too isolated to be twisted into a thread of narrative. *Zu einzig.* A sign too intense for any gleaning of meaning in and through the stuff of drama. *Zu innig.* A sign seared of its sense, a sign graved in fire.

> Passing away? And yet
> To remain is like a stream chained
> By frost. Foolish boy! Does the holy
> Spirit of life sleep and keep itself anywhere
> So that you might tie him down, the pure one?
> The ever joyous one will never shudder anxiously
> In prisons for you, or hesitate hopelessly on one spot.

Digression on Heidegger and *Innigkeit*

Heidegger's avowed purpose in his lecture course of 1934–35 on "Hölderlin's Hymns, *Germanien* and *Der Rhein*," is to prevent the word *Innigkeit* from collapsing into anything his students (and now his readers) might recognize.[7] Heidegger's avowal is both a gesture of fidelity to Hölderlin's exceptional legacy and a betrayal of Hölderlin's text. For as recalcitrant and as resistant to interpretation as Hölderlin's own "fundamental attunement" may be (*Grundstimmung* is also Hölderlin's word for *Innigkeit*, it

---

7. Martin Heidegger, *Hölderlins Hymnen 'Germanien' und 'Der Rhein',* Martin Heidegger Gesamtausgabe vol. 39 (Frankfurt am Main: V. Klostermann, 1980), cited in the body of my text by volume and page. My thanks to Will McNeill of DePaul University for the reference and for his own work on Heidegger's Hölderlin. Warminski's brief treatment of Heidegger's course reduces its reading of "holy mourning" as Hölderlin's "grounding mood" *[Grundstimmung]* to a mere "ontologizing" gesture on Heidegger's part (*Readings in Interpretation*, pp. 64–71). Yet it is a mistake to see in Heidegger's reading of the "Not" of *Germanien* a mere retreat to the mood of dread or anxiety in the fundamental ontology of *Being and Time* or "What Is Metaphysics?" One would have to discuss Heidegger's extensive development of the theme of *Grundstimmung* after the period of *Being and Time*, for example, the fundamental mood of the 1929–30 lecture course, which is somewhere between "profound boredom" and "melancholy" *(die tiefe Lange-weile; Schwermut).* One would then have to take up Heidegger's explicit reference in the *Germanien* lecture course to the founding mood of Hölderlin's *Empedokles,* namely, *Innigkeit.* Quite surprisingly, Warminski neglects these pages of Heidegger's *Germanien* course, the very pages that would have been most important for his own project. For the 1929–30 course, see Martin Heidegger, *Die Grundbegriffe der Metaphysik: Welt—Endlichkeit—Einsamkeit,* Martin Heidegger Gesamtausgabe vol. 29/30 (Frankfurt am Main: V. Klostermann, 1983), esp. 270–71, on melancholy, and the entire first part of the course, on profound boredom. Will McNeill and Nicholas Walker have translated the volume into English, forthcoming in 1995 from Indiana University Press.

is not merely Heidegger's, so that Heidegger is doubtless correct to associate the two words), Heidegger's own desire to prevent his students from "understanding" that attunement is both rigorously faithful and insidious. His reading, in terms of "the historical existence of a people and the decision touching them" (*39*, 116), may well be the most terrifying betrayal, precisely because of the proximity of Hölderlin and Heidegger in the matter for "decision," to wit, "the sending of a people and their relation to the gods" (*39*, 116–17). It is a proximity felt too intensely by Heidegger for him to ignore it, no matter how much farther down the raveling threads of time, history, national destiny, social order, and generation he may have been. It is also a proximity, incidentally (and obviously), never felt by Hölderlin toward Heidegger. No window opens onto the unbounded *future*. The same limitation applies to Heidegger and to ourselves, of course, even if we should feel, perhaps too intensely, a certain proximity to Heidegger. But who, we? Among other things, we who, like Hölderlin and Heidegger, have no window on the future, even and especially when we feel too intensely.

Nevertheless, let me at least try to cite a moment of difference in Heidegger's lectures that allows us to separate Hölderlin from Heidegger, without, however, dreaming of originals and innocents. The moment of difference might emerge at the core of Heidegger's *double rejection* of the "usual" ways of reading *Innigkeit*. He begins: "The originally unified nexus of the most extensive conflict is what Hölderlin, especially in his later years, called by a single word of his own: *Innigkeit*" (*39*, 117). Heidegger then refers us to a later moment in his lecture course, in which *Innigkeit* is identified as "the original unity of powers in the *Reinentsprungenen* [the purely engendered], and as the mystery of such being" (248 ff.); indeed, for Heidegger the word *Innigkeit* recurs as his essential clue concerning the "endowment and assignment" of the German people and their own unbounded, or too terribly bounded, future (291 ff.). But to continue:

> This word *[Innigkeit]* confronts us again and again in the most varied domains, in sundry transformations and configurations. It is one of Hölderlin's principal words. Naturally, a schoolbook definition cannot capture its import. However, let us immediately guard against a misunderstanding: *Innigkeit* does not mean

simply the "interiority" *['Innerlichkeit']* of sensibility in the sense of the closing-off-in-itself of a "lived experience" *['Erlebnisses'].* Nor does it mean an especially high degree of "warmth of feeling" *['Gefühlswärme'].*

In effect, these "two misunderstandings" are but one: in the final era of metaphysical subjectivity, as portrayed in many of Heidegger's texts, including the *Beiträge zur Philosophie,*[8] all interiority is reduced to the tepid sentimentality of "lived experience." If metaphysics begins with the yoking of ἀλήθεια ("truth") under "correctness," and continues in modernity with "certitude of representation," it ends when thinkers expose the mushy interiority of a psychologizing life-philosophy. Heidegger wants to rescue the poet's word from the swamp of inwardness, whether in Descartes' cogito or in life-philosophy's "lived experience."

Yet why do we sense that Heidegger is more troubled by the latter than by the former, that he is more resistant to feeling than to cogitation? *Gefühl* is by no means a word Hölderlin forbids himself to write. Does Heidegger's trouble have to do with an allergic reaction not only against life-philosophy but also against the disquieted relationship of his own thought to all "other" forms of life, for example, animal and vegetable life, in this my life as a plant "just-plain-life," and even "divine life," all-in-all, what one might have to call δαίμων life?[9] But to continue: "Nor is *Innigkeit* a byword of the 'beautiful soul' and of the sort of attitude it takes toward the world. With Hölderlin, the word has nothing of the aftertaste of a dreamy and deedless sensitivity *[einer verträumten tatenlosen Empfindsamkeit].*"

To be sure, Hölderlin's Empedocles pursues nothing other than an ideal deed, a full deed at the end—his speculative sui-

8. Martin Heidegger, *Beiträge zur Philosophie (Vom Ereignis),* Martin Heidegger Gesamtausgabe vol. 65 (Frankfurt am Main: V. Klostermann, 1989), passim.

9. See Krell, *Daimon Life: Heidegger and Life-Philosophy* (Bloomington: Indiana University Press, 1992), passim. In addition, one would only have to examine Novalis's uses of *Innigkeit*—for that is an essential word for him as well—in order to ascertain the *intensity of feeling* that the word radiates. While "interiority" is at most only a peripheral sense of *Innigkeit* for both Novalis and Hölderlin, as Heidegger insists, the white heat of intensity should not be denigrated as mere "feeling." See Novalis, *Werke, 2,* 557, 607, 614, 669, 789; cf. 669, on *Dichtigkeit* and *Intensität.*

cide—even if that deed is frustrated throughout the three versions of *Der Tod des Empedokles*. What sorts of deeds is Heidegger thinking of? Why does he oppose them to dream-states, to which Hölderlin (and indeed Heidegger himself, who consistently favors the Apollonian over the Dionysian) is certainly not foreign? Why does Heidegger reenact with little or no refinement Hegel's scornful reproach of *die schöne Seele*? Is Heidegger's Hölderlin more Hegelian than we believed? Finally, why does Heidegger resist sensitivity and sensibility, which Hölderlin himself never spurned? Whatever we may reply, Heidegger wants all these things reversed:

> Altogether to the contrary. It *[Innigkeit]* means first of all the supreme force *[höchste Kraft]* of Dasein. Secondly, this force proves itself in successful confrontation with the extreme conflict in beyng from the ground up *[diese Kraft bewährt sich im Bestehen der äußersten Widerstreite des Seyns von Grund aus]*. In short, it *[Innigkeit]* means the attuned, cognizant inherence in *[Innestehen]* and carrying out of *[Austragen]* the essential conflict of that which in the juxtaposition has an original unity, the "harmoniously juxtaposed." (*39*, 117)

Heidegger prefers to persist within and to carry out from within, to confront, engage, withstand, settle, and survive the conflict surrounding what is essential. He prefers the original unity of the harmoniously juxtaposed. He prefers to be cognizant *(wissend)*. He prefers supreme force, the point, and unity, over pain, fire, and dissolution. One might rejoin that Hölderlin prefers these as well, so that it is merely the tonality of the preference—and of its inevitable frustration—that constitutes the difference. At all events, with regard to the matter of *Innigkeit*, Heidegger   Also one of the wretched / Of this race, a mortal, like you   prefers what metaphysics always and everywhere prefers, and in the most traditional of tones. "Openness for beings, letting ourselves into them *[das Sicheinlassen]* and persisting through their discordance, does not exclude *Innigkeit;* rather, it alone grants proper possibility to beings' power, a power that unifies on the basis of the ground *[zu ihrer aus dem Grunde einigenden Macht]*" (*39*, 118).

Heidegger acknowledges that *Innigkeit* plays a decisive role in Hölderlin's *Grund zum Empedokles*, to which we shall soon turn, where the theme (in Heidegger's words) is "tragic beyng" as such. He cites Hölderlin's "most profound *Innigkeit,* expressed in the tragic-dramatic poem," and notes the poet's references to a variously "modest," "bold," and "excessive" *Innigkeit.* He then quotes the following cryptic lines from the *Grund:* ". . . for the *innigste* sensation is exposed to transiency precisely to the degree in which it does not repudiate the truly actual [or truly *temporal*] [10] and sensuous relations (and therefore it is also a law of lyric poetry, if the *Innige* in itself is less dead [or less *profound*] [11] there, thus easier to keep, to repudiate the physical and intellectual nexus)." Even though it is impossible for me here to recover the context of the quotation—inasmuch as the *Allgemeiner Grund,* from which it is taken, discusses the difficult and delicate negotiation of the poet's own experience with a foreign, analogous "stuff"—Heidegger's interpretation is bold, to say the least:

> Here it is said clearly that the nexus of beings, whose being is to be founded in poetry—in this case, the fundamental relation of an historical people to their gods—, that is to say, the fundamental attunement in the original unity of its conflict, must be repudiated precisely in order to preserve the *"innigste Empfindung,"* the fundamental attunement, in the face of transiency, of overhasty utilization and leveling. Thus the fundamental attunement is nothing that dare be made immediately "popular."
> (*39,* 119)

No negotiation, nothing foreign, and thoroughgoing contempt for the *populär,* in a fatherlandish thinking that craves to heed, hold, and keep. How vastly different Hölderlin's own national pedagogy is from all this! While veiling and repudiation *(Verhüllung, Verleugnung)* are indeed essential to the tragic dramatist's search for the foreign analogue, these words sound remarkably different in Heidegger's mouth ("—concealing preservation of being proper—," "its concealing power," "Poetic saying of the mystery is *repudiation* [*die* Verleugnung]"), even before the word *Vaterland* comes to occupy him excessively.

10. Beißner-Schmidt and Sattler alike read *wahren zeitlichen* rather than Hellingrath's *wahren wirklichen.* See B, 572; S, *13,* 359.

11. Beißner-Schmidt and Sattler read *weniger tief* rather than Hellingrath's *weniger tot.* Ibid.

To be sure, *Vaterland* is a crucial word for Hölderlin as well, and not only in *"Das untergehende Vaterland . . ."* A reading of the Heidegger/Hölderlin confrontation dare not stop with *Innigkeit*. It would have to double back on itself   and pray for the French   in order both to examine Hölderlin's national pedagogy more critically and to grant Heidegger's text its own irreducible strangeness and resistance to all narrative reductions—including the political reduction. Another time, perhaps.

Hyperbollipsis

In *pure* life, nature and art are merely juxtaposed harmoniously, with the divine as the midpoint between the two. How nature and art confront or affront one another in an *impure* life, a life that is never transparently clear, never pristine, a life that always collapses back into the old confusions   uralte Verwirrung after bypassing the illusory end point: this is the principal question posed in Hölderlin's *Grund zum Empedokles,* with which these points of mine will close.

Even in *pure* life the divine midpoint   Now I can say that Apollo has struck me   would have to be the point of excessive intensity *(Übermaß der Innigkeit)*, the point-of-change for all things in unstable juxtaposition. The undulating wave of periodic alter(n)ation intersects the midpoint at each crest or peak of its apogee and at each valley of its nadir. The ruling divinity of every midpoint is πόλεμος, as Heraclitus would have said, or, in Empedocles' own vision, a vision that remains vital in Freud, Yeats, and countless others, Νεῖκος, "Strife." Indeed, the broad, flattened *X* of Hölderlin's first sketch may depict the interpenetrating cones or vortices of Empedoclean Love and Strife. To dwell *in* the chiasmic midpoint is to be twisted aorgically *out* of it, and thus to dwell undecidably in the very midst of the to-be-found. Such is the case with Schelling's Archäus, who in spite of all that he can do is dislodged from the center of the circle, catapulted to its circumference, and then thrust back again, without respite. "In the middle," says Hölderlin's *Grund,* "lies struggle and the death of the individual" (S, *13,* 361). Thus the fulcrum, the central point and unifying moment of tragic drama *(der vereinende Moment)*, appears as an illusion or mirage on the point of irretrievable evanescence *(wie ein Trugbild, [das] sich immer mehr auflöst).* In the final scene of the third draft of *Der Tod des Empedokles,* Manes taunts Empedocles himself as such a specter. *Trugbild!* he cries. If Manes, who is perhaps the old Egyptian priest of Neith, is the *Di Manes* or δαίμων, that is, the tutelary genius of Empedocles, who is himself the tutor of young Pausanias, then the colorful philosopher-physician is indeed, as Hölderlin says he is, no more than a "momentary unification" of extremes. Manes is therefore neither one nor the other extreme exclusively: neither Pausanias returned and wizened from his (impossible) regressive-progressive voyage to Imperial Rome, Sophoclean Athens, and antediluvian Egypt, nor Empedocles redoubled as his own opponent *(Gegner),* nor Solon's Egyptian priest fresh from the pages of *Timaeus.* Manes is nonetheless manifold: the very figure of figurative reading, Manes is these three, plus many more figures of di-manic reading.

For his part, Empedocles of Acragas is utterly duplicitous. His text on "nature" (fr. 17) contains the words διπλ' ἐρέω, "I shall tell a double tale," "I shall redouble my tale," "I, being double, shall tell . . ." In his well-rounded sphere of truth he unites the extremes of Φιλία and Νεῖκος "too intensely" *(zu innig).* Thus the "felicitous betrayal" *(der glückliche Betrug)* of unification—as though the knot of destiny *could* be either tied or cut once and for all—"is dissolved precisely to the degree that it was too intense and singular *[zu innig und einzig]"* (S, *14,* 361). As an individual, Empedocles must go down. As an individual uniting the extremes of his age, he must go down in the performance of an ideal deed, which the first draft calls "one full deed," accomplished "at the end." Such would be Empedocles' consummation, his speculative suicide, his historic and epochal sacrifice, inasmuch as   I am now full of parting   he is the avatar of his city's destiny and the destiny of all mortals.[12]

12. "Hölderlin's Empedocles, reaching by voluntary steps the very edge of Etna, is the death of the last mediator between mortals and Olympus, the end of the infinite on earth, the flame returning to its native fire, leaving as its sole remaining trace that which had to be abolished precisely by his death: the beautiful, enclosed form of individuality. After Empedocles, the world is placed under the sign of finitude, in that irreconcilable, intermediate state in which reigns the Law, the harsh law of limit. The destiny of individuality will be to appear always in the objectivity that both manifests and conceals it, both denies it and forms its

Yet a visible, sensuous avatar of destiny, as the law of limit, can never resolve the *universal* problem of destiny, can never solve it visibly, sensuously, and individually—otherwise the life of an entire world would perish with a mortal who is but one of its particulars, however exceptional he or she may be. An odd situation results. Empedocles *must* be a sacrifice, he *must* go down, and yet he *cannot* do so. His suicide represents the double bind of an imputed ὕβρις and *nefas* that pertain undecidably to both mortals and gods, both of whom, as the later "Remarks" suggest, practice betrayal and infidelity; for only a godlike child of godlike parents   Now, I fear, I must see to it that I do not end as Tantalos did, who became more of the gods than he could digest   could tantalize the gods. Thus no fateful resolution is possible, except as illusory *(scheinbar),* that is to say, tragic. Solution and resolution dissolve in perpetual postponement and perplexity. The very excess of intensity and singularity in Empedocles makes every solution *(Lösung)* sheer dissolution *(Auflösung).* The dramatic narrative of the death of Empedocles can be played out only as a thread that consists of points of fire, only as an ellipsis, only in between the gutted points that reproduce themselves to infinity   I've seen the sad and lonely Earth   within and without. A fire burns out of control in the heart and hearth of each point and blanc of hyperbollipsis . . .

Late in the *Grund zum Empedokles* Hölderlin indicates two traits of the tragic hero, the hero whose very excesses frustrate the excessive death in which the drama would otherwise culminate. The first trait seems at first to be a mere *epistemological* excess, the second an excess of *music* and *charm.*

In his fury to know, says Hölderlin, Empedocles had to tear himself from his own midpoint, penetrating his object so excessively *(so übermäßig penetrieren)* that he "lost himself in it, as in an abyss" (S, *13,* 365). In his ardor to penetrate all the points of cognition, Empedocles found himself swallowed up in them. Whether hyperbolic or elliptical, whether lunging too far or falling short, Empedocles was excessive. As the result of a

basis: 'Here too the subjective and the objective exchange faces'." Michel Foucault, *The Birth of the Clinic: An Archaeology of Medical Perception,* trans. A. M. Sheridan (London: Tavistock, 1973), p. 198.

bizarre reversal, he felt himself penetrated by the objects. He became "more infinitely receptive" *(unendlicher empfänglich)*, more boundlessly gravid with things. He found in retrospect that he had always surrendered himself to people and things in erotic devotion *(hingegeben hatte)*.[13] Hölderlin's words here suggest the reproductive act—an equivocal phrase, as we noted earlier, suggesting a remembrance and a coupling of life and work, a remembrance that in some eminent sense, a sense very difficult to determine, is *of woman*. Perhaps Hölderlin's Empedocles plays out the untold fate of the woman-man Teiresias, whose words in Sophocles' plays serve as the caesura of the dramatic action, that is, as the secret of the tragedies' dramatic *rhythm*?

The second excess, no doubt related to the first, has to do with the esteem in which the hero's people hold him. The citizens of Acragas, the jealous priest (Hermokrates), the archon-father of Panthea (Kritias-Mekades), the hero's brother (Strato), the women Panthea and Delia, the beloved Pausanias, and even the oriental alter ego of Empedocles, Manes—all are ardently drawn to him, as though torn from their own distinct mid-points and dragged into the outermost orbit of his life. Hölderlin explains: "Nature . . . appeared with all its melodies in the spirit and in the mouth *[im Geiste und Munde]* of this man, and so intensely and ardently and personally." One is reminded of Hölderlin himself, in the circle of his own friends: a secondary-school teacher of Hölderlin's describes him in an official report as *venusta*, *"liebreizend,"* that is to say, as stimulating or inspiring love. It must be difficult sometimes to be a secondary-school teacher. Heidegger says that teaching is more difficult than learning because the teacher must let the pupils learn. Hölderlin tells us of Empedocles' *Anmut*, usually rendered as "grace," although a reading of one of Hölderlin's most important

---

13. On *Hingebung* in Friedrich Schlegel's *Lucinde*, and in Hegel's polemic against that novel, see Krell, "Lucinde's Shame: Hegel, Sensuous Woman, and the Law," *Cardozo Law Review* 10: 5–6 (March–April 1989), 1673–86; reprinted in *Hegel and Legal Theory*, ed. Drucilla Cornell, Michel Rosenfeld, and David Gray Carlson (New York and London: Routledge, 1991), pp. 287–300; also revised and reprinted in *Re-reading the Canon: Feminist Interpretations of Hegel*, ed. Patricia Jagentowicz Mills (University Park, PA: Pennsylvania State University Press), forthcoming in 1994.

sources, Schiller's *Über Anmut und Würde,* would teach us to render the word   I only wish I could show you her picture, then I wouldn't need to say a word   as "charm" or "attractiveness" or "stirring beauty," meaning the stunning beauty of a sexed creature.

They worshiped him, they all accepted him, says Hölderlin of the "foreign" yet analogous personage of Empedocles, who is to be the stuff of Hölderlin's own tragedy. Among those people he lived for a time, supremely independent, yet always in supreme intensity, always teaching his doctrine of excess.   Oh, give yourself to nature, before she takes you!   He drew them all toward himself, and they gathered about his fire. Yet because he appeared among them too conspicuously, too outrageously, and ultimately too sensuously, too threateningly *(zu sichtbar und sinnlich erschien),*   the most familiar virtues and faults of the Germans can be reduced to a rather dull-witted domesticity   he had to go down. Or, rather, he had to *remain* in downgoing, to *persist* on the brink, precisely because his teaching was all about *not* persisting, *not* remaining. He had to express himself in "some one most determinate point." Which point? "In a point where they were most in doubt concerning the unification of the extremes in which they lived" (S, *13,* 367). In the end, he had to express himself out of the open point of his beautiful mouth, singing its flow of excessive words.

Like Schelling's God, "whose every path culminates in embodiment," [14] Hölderlinian and Empedoclean divinity must undergo perpetual alter(n)ation of sexes and sexualities.   How is it with us? are you so certain of what you see?   The first words of the earliest manuscript of *Der Tod des Empedokles* (S, *13,* 30; 179) are *Panthea. Rhea.* Panthea we recognize: she is the woman cured by the physician Empedocles, the woman whose midpoint never went cold. [15] But who is Rhea?

Rhea is Hölderlin's original name for the woman he eventually called Delia, associated with the Antigone of Sophocles' Athens. Panthea Rhea. Their conjoined names reverberate with

14. F. W. J. Schelling, *Stuttgarter Privatvorlesungen,* quoted in Krell, "The Crisis of Reason in the Nineteenth Century: Schelling's Treatise on Human Freedom (1809)," in *The Collegium Phaenomenologicum: The First Ten Years,* ed. John Sallis, Giuseppina Moneta, and Jacques Taminiaux (Dordrecht: Kluwer Academic Publishers, 1988), p. 25.

15. See Krell, *Postponements,* pp. 45–46 and 111.

the saying of one of Empedocles' forebears, for in it we can hear Heraclitus' πάντα ῥεῖ.[16] All divinity flows. As if the points of fire in Hölderlin's Empedocles meant to take us in the direction of fluid mechanics, the molten mechanics of divinity and woman.[17]

Rhea, the consort of C(h)ronos, or Time, is the mother of all the primary Olympians—of the brothers, Zeus, Poseidon, and Hades, as well as of Hera, the sister and queen of Zeus. Rhea is the great titaness of the earth, Magna Mater, Kybele. If she disappears from the manuscript of *Der Tod des Empedokles,* it is not because she is one of the "accidents" to be eliminated from the play as a result of Hölderlin's "repudiation of everything accidental" (903–6). Rhea recurs. In the flow of every fiery point.

Panthea Rhea. All divinity flows. The great titaness returns as the fiery magma of Etna. She stretches out her arms to Empedocles, the son of Aither, supernal fire, in order to reclaim him.   You too must go down. / You beautiful star! and it won't be long now.   Fire will ultimately join fire, in an act of ultimate fidelity to the earth. As Françoise Dastur says in a striking phrase, "The fire of spirit rises toward the heights, but love and pain, which are the mortals' lot, bend the flame back *[courbent la flamme]* to earth."[18]

> To me too life became a poem.
> For your soul was in me, and openly, like you,
> My heart gave itself to the earnest Earth,
> The long-suffering, and often in the sacred night
> I swore it to   her, unto death,
> Without fear; faithfully to love her who is fateful.

To be sure, Hölderlin's Empedocles never takes the plunge. His full deed at the end remains a deed on the verge. Suspended among the points of hyperbollipsis . . . threading points of fire . . . through the needle's eye of dissolution.

Fidelity to the earth is not a deed done at one go, not a leap of faith. It could take one hundred years. The tapestry or *stuff* of

16. I am grateful to Dr. Andrea Rehberg of the University of Warwick for this suggestion.

17. See chap. 6, "The 'Mechanics' of Fluids," in Luce Irigaray, *This Sex Which Is not One,* trans. C. Porter with C. Burke (Ithaca, NY: Cornell University Press, 1985), esp. pp. 108–9, and 117–18.

18. Françoise Dastur, *Hölderlin: Tragédie et modernité,* p. 52.

tragedy ravels to the *thread* of finitely finite historical time, frays at the precise point of excessive intensity, consumed forever in that beautiful mouth   *venusta Panthea Rhea venusta*   where the ardor of unification bursts into the *fire* of an utterly precise dissolution.

Forgive me, dearest Mother! if I cannot make myself altogether clear to *you*. I repeat to you courteously what I was able to have the honor to say. I beg our good Lord, inasmuch as I speak as a learned person, that he help you in every way, and me. Take care of me. Time is precise, down to the letter, and all-merciful.

For the nonce,

your

most obedient son,

Friedrich Hölderlin.

Part II

Heidegger

•

Derrida

•

Trakl

3 The Source of the Wave

Rhythm in the Languages of Poetry and Thinking

> All method is *rhythm*. Remove rhythm from the world and you remove—the world. . . . In the temporal world, beyng is a rhythmic relation.
>
> —Novalis, *Fichte-Studien* IV (Spring, 1796; 2, 146, 157)

> I sensed the rhythm coming over me. The dance began in me, a powerful temptation—now that nothing more could help me—to give myself up to it and to step outside of time. My feet went more willingly, as the rhythm commanded, and I was about to surrender myself to it utterly. Let the wilderness close over us all again. Let the primal ground swallow us all, showing no fissure, knowing no shape. Dance, Cassandra, bestir yourself! Yes, I am coming. Everything in me compelled me to join them.
>
> —Christa Wolf, *Kassandra*

It is not surprising that little has been said or written about rhythm in Heidegger's work: in his essay "Language," in which he considers Georg Trakl's poem "A Winter Eve" as an illustration of speech in its purest and most essential unfolding, Heidegger eschews all formal poetic analysis. No amount of scansion or versification can tell us what is poetic in or about the poem, says Heidegger.[1] Fixing the rhyme scheme, identifying figures of speech, turning up tropes, subsuming fragments of the poem under given categories of poetics and metrics—none of these things truly aids us in our efforts to hear the language in and of the poem. In short, Heidegger rejects the collective

---

1. Martin Heidegger, *Unterwegs zur Sprache* (Pfullingen: G. Neske, 1959), p. 18, hereinafter cited as US, with page number, in the body of my text.

apparatus of poetics and announces his search for "another kind of measure" (US, 20).

In his earlier essays on Hölderlin and Rilke as well, references to rhythm or to other formal or structural aspects of poetry are exceedingly rare. Heidegger pursues instead what one might call *Seinsmetaphorik,* a metaphorics of being and propriation. He conducts a thematic inquiry into various topics such as wandering, homecoming, nearness to the origin, the holy, and withdrawal, always with a view to his own consuming interest in the questions of *Sein* and *Ereignis.* There are, it is true, several references to rhythm in the preliminary remarks to the last lecture on Hölderlin, "Hölderlin's Earth and Sky" (1959).[2] One reference takes up a remark by Paul Valéry, who celebrates the poem as a "protracted hesitation between sound and sense."[3] However, Heidegger's own efforts, at least at first glance, are devoted more to sense than to sound. His passion for *Dichten* seems to be constrained by the guidelines, strictures, and habits of *Denken.* Thought has little to say about blank verse, and even less about what some contemporary poets celebrate as the demise of "iambic five."

In Heidegger's view, however, meter and rhythm are not at all identical. Heidegger's lack of interest in the former reflects a fascination with rhythm more broadly conceived. Two important sources for Heidegger's conception of rhythm are his 1953 essay on Trakl, "Language in the Poem: A Discussion [or Placing] of Georg Trakl's Poem" (US, 35–82), and his remarks during the Heraclitus seminar conducted jointly by Heidegger and

2. Printed in the fourth, expanded edition of Martin Heidegger, *Erläuterungen zu Hölderlins Dichtung* (Frankfurt am Main: V. Klostermann, 1971), pp. 152–81, hereinafter cited as EHD, with page number. In the present instance, see EHD, 153–54: in these preliminary remarks Heidegger cites Bettina von Arnim, who calls the poet an arrow that leaps from God's bow, embodying the "rhythm" of that bow; von Arnim also refers to the "primal rhythm" that lies at the very roots of the "tree of language."

3. EHD, 153. It would be intriguing to compare Heidegger's reference, and the entire metaphorics of font, source, and wave, to Jacques Derrida, "Qual Quelle: Valéry's Sources," in *Margins of Philosophy,* trans. Alan Bass (Chicago: University of Chicago Press, 1982), pp. 273–306, a task I cannot undertake here. See also Michael Naas, "Rien ne m'est plus étranger qu'un lac," in *Le passage des fontières: Autour du travail de Jacques Derrida* (Paris: Galilée, 1994), pp. 467–75.

Eugen Fink in 1966–67.[4] After examining these and other passages on rhythm, I shall turn to Heidegger's discussion of "metrics" in an expanded sense, the sense suggested by Hölderlin's "measure" or *Maß*, the μέτρον by which the poet of the late hymns surveys the mortal dimension between earth and sky.

Antiphon

An early allusion to rhythm occurs in Heidegger's 1939 treatise "On the Essence and Concept of *Physis:* Aristotle's *Physics* B, 1."[5] Aristotle uses the word with reference to Antiphon, a sophist trained in the Eleatic tradition, who seeks the "being" and "nature" of things in what is permanent and immutable. Antiphon proves to be one of the earliest philosophers (or sophists) to take for granted what we normally attribute to Aristotle, if not Plato, as their greatest discovery—the matter-form distinction, which itself rests on the distinction between (material) transiency and (formal) immutability. Antiphon, and neither Aristotle nor Plato, is in Heidegger's view the first metaphysician.

What is truly in being, as far as Antiphon is concerned, is τὸ πρῶτον ἀρρύθμιστον καθ' αὐτό, "the primordially arhythmical in itself," which is to say, the constant, the steadily and uninterruptedly· present. The word ῥυθμός may therefore be understood as meaning everything in beings that does not last, the transient and transitory. Antiphon's own example—which is an example that could have worked as much *against* metaphysics as *for* it—is that of an old wooden bedframe that is cast onto the junkheap, one post of which begins to take root and sprout leaves. The post does not sprout another bedframe, but only a tree. What lasts, in other words, is the wood, literally, ὕλη, which after Aristotle we call *matter*. The bedframe itself is a particular fleeting structure, a temporary, transient jointure or articulation of the wood, a ῥυθμός. Heidegger translates the Greek word ῥυθμός as "articulation," "coinage," "imprint," "jointure," "constitution," or "structure." Aristotle complains (and

4. Martin Heidegger and Eugen Fink, *Heraklit* (Frankfurt am Main: V. Klostermann, 1970), pp. 91–92, cited throughout the book as Hk, with page number.

5. Martin Heidegger, *Wegmarken* (Frankfurt am Main: V. Klostermann, 1967), pp. 309–71; cited hereinafter as W, with page number.

Heidegger is sympathetic to the complaint) that Antiphon un-
derestimates the significance of movement and change in beings: movement and change constitute the very nature and being of beings. By bypassing κίνησις and μεταβολή, and insisting
on stasis, Antiphon becomes the prototypical metaphysician,
against whom Aristotle struggles in order to rescue the early
Greek understanding of being as presencing in unconcealment
and withdrawal into concealment.

However, Antiphon is not only the prototypical metaphysician: to the extent that the matter-form distinction pervades
Western conceptions of language, speech, and writing, Antiphon is also the first aesthetician and literary critic. Yet the An-
tiphonal inception of metaphysics and aesthetics is bizarre, to
say the least, inasmuch as it reverses the hierarchy—the superi-
ority of pure and immutable form over composite and corrupt-
ible matter—that will prevail for two millennia in metaphysics,
aesthetics, and criticism. If metaphysics begins with Antiphon, it
will end when Nietzsche reinstates Antiphon by once again ele-
vating matter over form. Or, to be more accurate, when Nietzsche finally twists free of the Platonistic hierarchy altogether, he
will not merely invert the relative positions of matter and form
but urge the question of primal *rhythm* as the very *power* of both
language and world. Heidegger inherits from Nietzsche the
questions of *both* the reversal of matter and form *and* the dis-
placement of the metaphysical hierarchy as such, a displace-
ment in which the mysteries of rhythm loom large.[6]

After this "Antiphon," as it were, let me now proceed to Heidegger's major offering as regards rhythm—his extended essay
on Georg Trakl.

The Animating Wave

The opening paragraphs of Heidegger's Trakl essay include an
intriguing passage on rhythm. That passage (US, 38) finds itself
echoed at two later points in the essay (US, 65 and 73), although
neither echo clarifies the initial cryptic remark. Heidegger's en-

6. On the matter-form distinction, see Martin Heidegger, *Ursprung des
Kunstwerkes* (Stuttgart: P. Reclam, 1960), pp. 19–22; English translation in *Basic
Writings,* revised and expanded edition (San Francisco: HarperCollins, 1993),
pp. 152–53. (*Basic Writings* will be cited henceforth as BW, with page reference.)

tire discussion or "placement" of Trakl attempts to locate the
site of Trakl's poetry, the place where Trakl is "gathered" in poetic utterance. The site of Trakl's poetry is that *single unsung poem*
which gathers all of Trakl's lyric poetry and grants it its inimi-
table style, a world all its own—what Joseph Leitgeb calls *die
Trakl-Welt.*[7]

Previewing the site of Trakl's encompassing yet always un-
uttered poem, Heidegger writes:

> From the site of the poem wells forth *[entquillt]* the wave that in
> any given poem animates [Trakl's] speech as creatively poetic. Yet
> the wave so little abandons the site of the poem that its rippling
> flow lets all animation of speech flow back into the ever more
> veiled wellspring. The site of the poem, as the source of the ani-

---

7. Leitgeb is quoted in Otto Basil, *Trakl* (Reinbek bei Hamburg: Rowohlt,
1965), p. 165. Walther Killy too has stressed the unity or gathered center within
Trakl's poetry: "Such poesy wends its way as *one* infinite poem." See Killy, "Bestand und Bewegung in den Gedichten Georg Trakls," in *Zur Lyrik-Diskussion,*
ed. Reinhold Grimm, "Wege der Forschung," vol. 111 (Darmstadt: Wissenschaft-
liche Buchgesellschaft, 1966), p. 445. See also Killy's monograph, *Über Georg Trakl*
(Göttingen: Vandenhoeck und Ruprecht, 1960), p. 52. Concerning the "Trakl-
world," I believe that Heidegger would insist—against Karsten Harries—that
Trakl does inaugurate a "world," that he is not unalloyed "earth." True, Trakl's
poetry is, as Killy writes, a "response to the dissolution of the world," a response
that is therefore always reminiscent of Hölderlin. Trakl's poetry derives its elements from the fragments of the world that is passing and constructs a novel
world with them. His images—the seasons, times of day, brother and sister, lovers, forest and town, bread and wine—are, again in Killy's words, "the first gifts
of creation." Yet even though they constitute the traditional stuff of lyric poetry,
in Trakl these images are not threadbare, trite, or hackneyed. Trakl presents
these beings as they are for *our* world, which is to say, as remote and estranged,
fremd. Precisely in their "enigmatic foreignness," both "things and world are
returned to us." (Killy, "Bestand und Bewegung," p. 449.) Cf. Karsten Harries,
"Language and Silence: Heidegger's Dialogue with Georg Trakl," in *Martin Heidegger and the Question of Literature,* ed. William V. Spanos (Bloominton: Indiana
University Press, 1979), esp. pp. 167–68. On the intimate relation of the poetry of
Trakl and Hölderlin, especially after 1912, see Bernhard Böschenstein, "Hölderlin und Rimbaud, Simultane Rezeption als Quelle poetischer Innovation im
Werk Georg Trakls," *Salzburger Trakl-Symposion,* ed. Walter Weiß and Hans Weich-
selbaum (Salzburg: Otto Müller Verlag, 1978), pp. 9–27. Böschenstein argues that
Trakl's "mosaic procedure," that is, his Rimbaudian alignment of apparently un-
related images, is gradually replaced by a rhythm and a syntax that are distinctly
Hölderlinian. Böschenstein also concurs that in the later poems one can hardly
speak of the absence of "world," no matter how *strange* that world may be.

mating wave *[als die Quelle der bewegenden Woge]*, shelters the veiled
essence of what—to metaphysical-aesthetic representation—at
best can appear as rhythm. (US, 38)

Here Heidegger distances himself not only from metrics but also
from all notions of rhythm in traditional aesthetics, poetics, and
rhetoric. He insists on that distance inasmuch as aesthetics—
long after Antiphon—is itself ensconced in the metaphysical
gap between the mutable sensuous and immutable supersen-
suous as "content" and "form," respectively. The opening remarks of Heidegger's essay "On the Origin of the Work of
Art" (1935) apply here as well: rhythm cannot be an extrinsic
formal-structural element that rescues the stuff of language
from chaos, disorder, and cacophony. Rhythm has essentially
nothing to do with the conformity of spoken or written language
to inherited standards of measure and versification. It does have
to do with the intrinsic motion and animation of language as
such. It is the marvelous motion of a ripple or wave that swells
and sinks and thus both moves and stays in place. In his commentary on Stefan George's poem "The Word" (US, 230), Heidegger notes that rhythm can bestow a kind of calm, repose, and
tranquillity, *Ruhe*, on the poem: "Rhythm, ῥυσμός [the Ionian
form] . . . is what enjoins the getting under way *[Be-wegung]* of
dance and song, thus letting these rest in themselves. Rhythm
lends repose." Finally, the wave allows all motion in speech to
flow back to its source, as Hölderlin says of *Der Ister;* the wave
thus points toward the wellspring of language, which nonetheless remains ever more concealed and protected.

At this point, one might interject a suspicion developed by
Jacques Derrida over the past two decades in many essays and
books. When Heidegger spurns the "sciences" of literary criticism, rhetoric, and poetics, is it in order to preserve a certain
nostalgia concerning an "essence" of language that would be
untouched by the vulgarities of a technologized science, an "essence" of language that would be reserved for divine poesy and
privileged thought? When Heidegger denies that the essence of
technology is anything technological, he appeals to a pristine
realm that fatally resembles the metaphysical realm of pure essences. Does rhythm lend repose precisely in the way that *all*
metaphysical ideas "beyond" the sensuous world offer solace

and rest? The suspicion cannot be readily quelled. We will have to allow it to haunt our own inquiry into the source of the wave, returning to it periodically in these remarks of ours—especially in the following chapter, which takes up Derrida's reading of Heidegger's Trakl essay more explicitly.

Heidegger's Trakl essay proceeds for many pages without further reference to the wave and its source. Various themes, some of them familiar to readers of Heidegger's earlier essays on poetry, others totally unfamiliar, emerge: wandering in search of the earth, descent into silence and death, the undetermined animality of human beings, the decomposition of human being, the location or site of mortality as one of perpetual departure and apartness, *Abgeschiedenheit,* and the trajectory of humanity through the spiriting years, *die geistlichen Jahre,* which are years that seem to propel humankind forward and backward at the same time. All this is of course hopelessly cryptic, especially when it is accompanied by no extended commentary on these motifs—on their relationship to one another and to particular poems by Trakl. The curious thing is that no amount of commentary here could render Heidegger's own essay comprehensible. Like the advance of a Trakl poem, where stark images muster in rows, often as dissociated, noncontextualized individuals, forming an intense *Nebeneinander* of ghostly appearances in spectral space [8]—a radical parataxis of colors (bleeding reds and purples, frigid blues and silvers), shapes, shades, and motions (almost all of them descensional)—Heidegger's own discussion of Trakl's poetry remains startling, bewildering, so that it is no exaggeration to say that the extended essay on Trakl is of an order of difficulty that is unmatched by any of Heidegger's other essays. Compared to it, "Time and Being" (1962) and the *Beiträge* (1936–38) are child's play.

If I now abandon the Trakl essay—until its return in the lunar voices of later chapters—it is with no illusion of having greatly clarified the source of the wave, the site of the singular poem of Trakl. Perhaps all that can be said at this point is that the way toward the source of Trakl's poetry requires something more than a metaphorics of being, something more than the

8. See Friedrich Georg Jünger, "Trakls Gedichte," in *Text und Kritik,* no. 4, *Über Georg Trakl* (April 1964), p. 7.

recapitulation of themes that are bound up with those of either fundamental ontology or the "other" thinking of propriation. It requires the cultivation of a new (or perhaps old, even ancient) sensibility, a sensibility for something akin to what the tradition, according to Heidegger, has called *rhythm.*

Fetters

The question of rhythm arises once again during the Heraclitus seminar of 1966–67. In the course of a discussion of a "speculative approach" to the Heraclitean fragments, Eugen Fink concedes the necessity and the difficulty of heeding Heraclitus's "multidimensional speech." [9] At that point Heidegger draws the seminar participants' attention to a lecture and a monograph by Thrasybulos Georgiades, historian of music at the University of Munich.[10] Heidegger praises Georgiades' work, especially his insight that the word ῥυθμός does not derive from ῥέω, to flow, as has long been supposed; the Greek *rhythmos* is to be understood either as coinage, imprint, distinguishing characteristic (in a word, as *Gepräge*), or as chains and fetters *(Fesseln),* such as those that bind Prometheus to his rock. (Heidegger does not mention that his own translation of ῥυθμός in the 1939 Aristotle essay on φύσις anticipates the translation by Georgiades.) "Rhythm," understood as imprint, bond, and linkage, suggests *measure* and *order* rather than the uninterrupted and unpunctuated flux of the Heraclitean πάντα ῥεῖ. It is, as we shall see, more "just" than "unjust," more δίκη than ἀδικία. The wave of rhythm does not simply flow by; it entwines, links, forges, and inscribes.[11]

9. See chap. 5 of the published protocol of the Heraclitus seminar, Hk, cited in note 4, above.

10. Thrasybulos Georgiades, "Sprache als Rhythmus," in *Die Sprache,* "Gestalt und Gedanke, Nr. 5," ed. Bayrische Akademie der schönen Künste (München: Oldenbourg, 1959), pp. 109–35. The lecture appears also in Georgiades, *Kleine Schriften* (Tutzing: Hans Schneider Verlag, 1977), pp. 81–96. The monograph is entitled, *Der griechische Rhythmus: Musik, Reigen, Vers und Sprache,* 2d ed. (Tutzing: H. Schneider, 1977), originally published in 1949.

11. I find no specific reference to ῥυθμός at those places where fetters or chains are discussed in Aeschylus's *Prometheus Bound.* Yet the Liddell-Scott entries for ῥυθμόω and ῥυθμός, which do cite ῥέω as the etymon, do not not entirely disconfirm the Heideggerian-Georgiadian reading. The first means to shape, and, in the passive, to be molded; the second means "any regularly recurring

Nietzsche too appears to have anticipated these senses of rhythm. In a now famous passage of *The Gay Science* (no. 84; KSA 3, 439–42) he describes rhythm as the most useful and even "utilitarian" aspect of language. When language orders the atomic units of a sentence anew, seeking to fix the right word in the right place, when it tints the thoughts a new shade, making them "darker, more foreign and remote," it is rhythm more than anything else that preserves the thought in the memory of man and telegraphs that thought to the gods. Indeed, rhythm seeks to overpower the gods by granting them so much unalloyed pleasure that they can only capitulate and accede to the poet-shaman's wish. "Without verse man was nothing; by means of it he became well-nigh a god." Philosophers, otherwise so self-certain and secure in their office, appeal to the asseverations of poets precisely in order to lend their own thoughts "force and credibility"; in spite of the ancient quarrel between poetry and philosophy, and the hegemony of philosophy, there are times when the philosopher readily forgets Homer's admission that "singers lie a lot," and negotiates an alliance.

Precisely in this Nietzschean and Heideggerian context, we ought to recall the theme of "the measure and the order of dissemination," developed by Derrida in "La double séance."[12] There $\rho\upsilon\theta\mu\acute{o}\varsigma$ is taken to mean "the law of espacement," "the cadence and character of writing," and "the regular period of the blank in the text." Mallarmé himself does not doubt that poetry is in full crisis, a crisis concerning the very meaning of rhythm, a crisis that extends to all literature, whether prose or poetry. For his part, Derrida would insist that the crisis of *poetic* language—the irruptions and caesurae of *rhythm*—is precisely

---

motion," such as: 1. measured motion, time; 2. measure, proportion or symmetry of parts, at rest as well as in motion; 3. proportion, arrangement, order; 4. state or condition of anything, temper, disposition (citing Theognis and Archilochus); 5. form or shape of a thing; 6. manner, fashion of a thing, kind or type. The figure of *Prometheus Bound,* so important to Nietzsche—one thinks of Prometheus alongside Oedipus in section 9 of *The Birth of Tragedy* (KSA, *1,* 64–71)—will no doubt return to haunt us as a figure of fettering and excess, of rhythm and counterrhythm, linkage and breakage—in a word, *caesura.*

12.   Jacques Derrida, *Dissémination* (Paris: Seuil, 1972), pp. 204 and 312; English translation by Barbara Johnson (Chicago: University of Chicago Press, 1981), pp. 178–79 and 279–80.

what invariably contaminates *thought,* no matter how desperately the philosophers flee those rhythmic entanglements. In short, the preoccupation with rhythm would unite many obsessions of our "postmodern" epoch, our Blanchotian time out-of-work, with those of Heidegger and, via Heidegger, those of the Western metaphysical tradition as a whole. But let us return now to Heidegger and Georgiades.

Heidegger appears to have been influenced by Georgiades' thesis that the ancient Greek language, in contrast to later European tongues, is ordered by a quantitative measure of long and short syllables that leaves little room for subjective or "psychological" variations of intonation and inflection. Even the *speaker* of ancient Greek, argues Georgiades, is compelled to adopt the stance of a *listener.* For the ancient Greek rhetor and poet, Hegel somewhere remarks, speech is "active listening." The speaker's own utterance comes from afar, as it were, bearing audible traces of its divine origin. Its rhythm is not left to the caprice of emphasis but belongs to the very "substrate" of the language itself. Archaic language does not make "statements" or elaborate "propositions" that possess "meaning." "In the sentences of archaic language," insists Heidegger during the Heraclitus seminar, "the matter speaks, and not the meaning *[spricht die Sache und nicht die Bedeutung]*" (Hk, 91). Ancient Greek is therefore a prime case of Heidegger's dictum that in a certain sense language—and not the mortal—speaks.[13]

Although even poetic language in our time and on our tongues has lost its divine resonance, so that a development of the sensibility in question can never be a matter for some sort of religious "Greek revival," poetry does possess the trait (here expressed negatively, by way of defense, and therefore inadequately) that its words and phrases do not yield propositions in the formal sense. Any poem in fact subverts the reign of logic, syntax, and semantics in language. MacLeish's famous conclusion to "Ars Poetica"—

> A poem should not mean
> But be—

13. See Georgiades, "Sprache als Rhythmus," p. 128. Heidegger makes the phrase *die Sprache spricht* the central refrain of his essay "Die Sprache" (US, 11–33).

proposes what in fact we have always suspected. Indeed, the preceding couplets of MacLeish's lunar poem, which *enact* the being of the poem, are altogether more thought-provoking than the assertory conclusion:

> A poem should be palpable and mute
> As a globed fruit,
>
> Dumb
> As old medallions to the thumb. . . .
>
> A poem should be motionless in time
> As the moon climbs,
>
> Leaving, as the moon releases
> Twig by twig the night-entangled trees,
>
> Leaving, as the moon behind the winter leaves,
> Memory by memory the mind—
>
> A poem should be motionless in time
> As the moon climbs.[14]

What is perhaps essential to the poem is neither its "meaning" nor its exhibition of inherited "metrical patterns," its iambs, but its being linked to, or coined by, language in a special way. The question of the wave's source would then be that of the peculiar binding power of language beyond the mere linkage of syllables, or even of words and things, a binding power beyond both "naming" and "predicating."

It is precisely the question of the binding power of poetic language that Heidegger raises in the essay ". . . Poetically Man Dwells . . ."[15] In the poem or posthumous fragment of Hölderlin's that gives Heidegger the title for his essay—and a rubric that is essential for his later thought—the following lines appear:

> *Gibt es auf Erden ein Maß? Es gibt*
> *Keines.*[16]

14. *The Collected Poems of Archibald MacLeish* (Boston: Houghton Mifflin Company, 1962), pp. 50–51.

15. Martin Heidegger, *Vorträge und Aufsätze* (Pfullingen: G. Neske, 1954), pp. 187–204; cited henceforth in the body of my text as VA, with page number.

16. See the discussion of these lines by Fynsk, *Heidegger,* chap. 5, esp. pp. 220–29. It must also be noted here that the lines just quoted are conjectural, including the break at "gibt / Keines." The poem "In Lovely Azure" is recorded

> Is there a measure on earth? There is
> None.

These lines appear immediately after the poet has identified "the measure of man" as God, a god who is "as open as the sky," albeit the night sky, "with stars," and presumably with the moon as well, the sky of "lovely azure." The tension produced in these lines that are lost somewhere between night and day is unbearable: human beings must be measured upon the standard of God, who is not so much "unknown" as open and manifest, *offenbar*, as open as the infinite depth of the heavens; and yet on this earth, where humans dwell, "full of merit, yet poetically," *there is no measure.* Heidegger understands this to mean that human beings dwell between earth and sky, which constitute their essential space, their "dimension"; they dwell by taking the measure of that dimension. "Such measuring has its own $\mu\acute{\epsilon}\tau\rho\text{o}\nu$ and therefore its own metrics" (VA, 196). Such measuring is in fact poetic creativity, *Dichten,* as such. To poetize is to take the measure of humanity as mortality.

> Human beings are essentially as mortals. They are called mortals because they can die. To be able to die means to make death as death possible. Only human beings die—indeed, they do so continuously, as long as they linger on this earth, as long as they dwell. Yet their dwelling rests on the poetic. Hölderlin discerns the essence of the "poetic" in the taking-measure by which the essence of human being is surveyed. (VA, 196)

The problem is not the infinite depth of the standard. For the god who is manifest as the one who remains unknown, the god whose depth is unplumbed by mortals, is in its own way the most familiar of themes. The difficulty is the relationship between "measure" in the sense only now noted and the more technical sense of the word in poetics. Heidegger stresses the importance of hearing and listening for poetic dwelling, a letting-come of whatever is to be measured; he urges an insinuation, as it were, into the rhythms of the dimension that encom-

---

solely in Wilhelm Waiblinger's novel, *Phaëton* (Stuttgart: F. Franckh, 1823), pp. 153–56, where it is transcribed into prose, without line breaks, without jointures, although the "original" is said to have been composed in Pindaric verse.

passes sky and earth, immortals and mortals. Yet Heidegger says nothing about Hölderlin's own poetic measures. Why the *line* such as we have it, the brittle, broken line, as it appears here—if only as a conjecture?

> *Gibt es auf Erden ein Maß? Es gibt*
> *Keines.*

Why "the hard rhythmic jointures" of Hölderlin's late hymns, as Beda Allemann calls them?[17] Why, later and elsewhere, does Walt Whitman insist on "the free growth of metrical laws," and why do poets after him, like William Carlos Williams and Charles Olson, search desperately for a new measure, seeking it in acquisitions of the ear and the pressures of the breath, the measure that will set poetry on its variable feet again?[18] The need to take the measure of the poetic line in unheard-of ways announces from Hölderlin on (and in the English-language tradition perhaps from Wordsworth on) the absence of all fixed measures on the earth. Such taking-measure never presumes to think of itself as anything other than a *response* to natural, cultural, communal, or perhaps even ontological rhythms, rhythms over which it has no control, certainly not the control or the options exercised in traditional poetics.

For example, Charles Olson's "projective verse," which defines itself as composition by *field* and as radically *open,* is ultimately a response to the rhythms of sound and breath:

> It would do no harm, as an act of correction to both prose and verse as now written, if both rime and meter, and, in the quantity words, both sense and sound, were less in the forefront of the mind than the syllable, if the syllable, that fine creature, were more allowed to lead the harmony on. With this warning, to those who would try: to step back here to this place of the elements and minims of language, is to engage speech where it is least careless—and least logical. . . . But the syllable is only the first child of the incest of verse (always, that Egyptian thing, it produces

17. See Beda Allemann, *Hölderlin und Heidegger,* 2d ed. (Zürich and Freiburg: Atlantis Verlag, 1956), p. 180.

18. For Whitman's phrase, see the Preface to the first edition of *Leaves of Grass* (1855), in *Leaves of Grass,* ed. Sculley Bradley and Harold W. Blodgett (New York: W. W. Norton, 1973), pp. 711–31. Charles Olson's poetics will be considered below.

twins!). The other child is the LINE. And together, these two, the syllable *and* the line, they make a poem, they make that thing, the—what shall we call it, the Boss of all, the "Single Intelligence." And the line comes (I swear it) from the breath, from the breathing of the man who writes, at the moment that he writes, and thus is, it is here that, the daily work, the WORK gets in, for only he, the man who writes, can declare, at every moment, the line its metric and its ending—where its breathing, shall come to, termination.[19]

From here it is but a half-step (perhaps the half-step of the lunar *woman* who writes) to Olson's "Proprioception," to the "working 'out' of 'projection' " in terms of "sensibility within the organism by movement of its own tissues." [20]

The question of the binding power of language thus continues to point toward the source of the wave that the tradition calls "rhythm." At the same time, the question routs all traditional notions concerning language—the syllabic or phonemic "body" of the word, its referential "soul," its signified "spirit." We cannot even be certain that Heidegger's interrogation of the "source" remains true to the wave itself, whether that interrogation follows the wave in spite of all the distractions and aberrations of metaphysics and metaphorics to which it is heir. We can be sure of this alone: the fetters of the traditional measures and modes of taking-measure are broken forever; perhaps not even the ancient linkages of $\rho\nu\theta\mu\delta\varsigma$ can hold; perhaps the coinage of rhythm is marred or worn away, its exergue scarcely recognizable, as legal tender altogether useless. Poetic language itself in our time, a time out-of-work, withdraws, secrets itself, ironizes itself, as though confronting an impossible dying. William Empson wryly reviews the conceptions of death held up as amulets by Christians, Buddhists, aesthetes, communists, psychoanalysts, and liberals. "We are happy to equate it [death] with any conceived calm," he writes, as though in rec-

19. Charles Olson, *Selected Writings,* ed. Robert Creeley (New York: New Directions, 1966), pp. 18–19. Olson would have been pleased by Nietzsche's concurrence: "A period, as the ancients understood it, is above all a physiological whole, inasmuch as it can be contained within a single breath." See *Beyond Good and Evil,* 247; KSA 5, 190.

20. Charles Olson, *Additional Prose,* ed. George F. Butterick (Bolinas, CA: Four Seasons, 1974), p. 17.

ollection of Heidegger's equation of $\dot{\rho}\upsilon\theta\mu\acute{o}\varsigma$ and repose, *Ruhe*. Empson concludes his droll series of triplets with a bemused confession, the rhythm of which lopes and limps along, blank and uncomprehending:

Heaven me, when a man is ready to die about something
Other than himself, and is in fact ready because of that,
Not because of himself, that is something clear about himself.

Otherwise I feel very blank upon this topic,
And think that though important, and proper for anyone to bring up,
It is one that most people should be prepared to be blank upon.[21]

Do such self-concealing, self-ironizing, and self-withdrawing measures reveal themselves as the (hidden) source of the wave? We will return to this at the conclusion of the chapter.

Saxifrage

The following remarks concerning rhythm in Heidegger's *own* writing may be taken as an addendum to the work of Johannes Lohmann and Erasmus Schöfer on Heidegger's language and style.[22] Schöfer's thesis is that the central demand of Heidegger's thinking, namely, the demand that we put into question the *is* that constitutes the very basis of our predicative language, compels him to shatter the constraints of normal *syntax* and to search for the telling *word* of being. The first part of Schöfer's study, on Heidegger's neologisms and novel interpretations of particular words, presupposes the second part, on syntax and style. However, in these remarks I merely want to adjoin a word about what Schöfer calls Heidegger's "metalogical thought-forms."

Schöfer identifies Heidegger's extensive use of (1) paradox and oxymoron *(aprosdoketon)*, as in the following examples: *das schweigende Reden des Gewissens* [the silent speech of conscience],

21. William Empson, "Ignorance of Death," in *Collected Poems* (New York: Harcourt, Brace, 1956), pp. 58–59.

22. See esp. Erasmus Schöfer, *Die Sprache Heideggers* (Pfullingen: G. Neske, 1962), the essential text for this aspect of Heidegger's writing. See also Johannes Lohmann, "Martin Heideggers 'ontologische Differenz' und die Sprache," *Lexis*, vol. 1 (1948); and "SEIN und ZEIT, SEIN und WAHRHEIT in der Form der Sprache," *Lexis*, vol. 2 (1949).

die helle Nacht des Nichts [die bright night of the nothing]; (2) circular reasoning, exemplified in the familiar phrase *das Wesen der Wahrheit ist die Wahrheit des Wesens* [the essence of truth is the truth of essence]; (3) deliberate tautology, in the form of *figura etymologica,* in such phrases as *die Welt weltet, das Ding dingt, das Nichts nichtet* [the world worlds, the thing things, the nothing nihilates]. These tropes or figures of speech, plus the use of image and metaphor to say what is essential to thought— the devotion to the particular word, the passion for etymologies and word constructions, the appeal to irony, negation, and the interrogative form—all are devices by which Heidegger avoids normal predication, assertion, and definition without lapsing into total silence. Schöfer is surely correct in arguing that in spite of all the talk about the ostensible "turning" *(Kehre)* in Heidegger's career, his language remains remarkably homogeneous. Yet the essays and lectures from at least 1935 onward (Schöfer cites 1945 as the pivotal time, but the publication of materials in the *Gesamtausgabe* keeps pushing the date farther and farther back) do show a greater willingness on Heidegger's part to indulge in language play, or, better, his willingness to submit his line of thought to the always obtrusive and occasionally violent play of language.[23]

One aspect of that submission is visible in the enhanced rhythmical character of Heidegger's essays from the 1930s on, particularly in crucial passages where the themes and lines of argument developed in a given essay are about to converge. I cannot pretend to have canvassed Heidegger's corpus in order to tally the places where this happens; nor will I pursue here the perhaps more fruitful matter of the general "economy of means" in any given piece—the macro-rhythm of its rhetorical structure, its rhythmic chains and caesurae. Here I want to examine only one passage where rhythm and other poetic and rhe-

23. In *What Calls for Thinking?* Heidegger writes: "If we may talk here of playing games at all, it is not we who play with words; rather, the essence of language plays with us, not only in this case, not only now, but long since and always. For language plays with our speech—it likes to let our speech drift away into the more obvious meaning of words. It is as though human beings had to make an effort to live properly with language. It is as though such a dwelling were especially prone to succumb to the danger of commonness. . . . This floundering commonness is part of the high and dangerous game and gamble in which, by the essence of language, we are the stakes" (BW, 388–89).

torical features dominate the text. I have selected a brief passage from the penultimate page of "What Are Poets For?" (*Wozu Dichter?* 1946), an essay cited by Beda Allemann as marking the "apotheosis" of Heidegger's absorption in poetic speech.[24] Similar passages can be found, however, in many of Heidegger's nonpoetological texts, especially in the peroration or *chute* of the text.

The context of the argument in "What Are Poets For?" (in which Rainer Maria Rilke figures prominently), is the relation of historical evil to the flight of the gods, and the remote possibility of the gods' return—in a word, the Empedoclean context. Heidegger concludes his discussion with the following four sentences:

> *Unheil als Unheil spurt uns das Heile. Heiles erwinkt rufend das Heilige. Heiliges bindet das Göttliche. Göttliches nähert den Gott.*

> Unhale as unhale traces the hale. The hale, calling, signals the holy. The holy binds the divine. Divinity nears the god.

Perhaps the first trait that strikes us here is the approximation to *rime enchaînée*. The last word of each sentence, altered syntactically from accusative object to nominative subject and morphologically from the definite to the indefinite neuter noun, becomes the first word of the next. We hear too the alliteration and assonance, resulting principally from word and syllable repetitions; we note prosopopoeia throughout, but especially in the present participle *rufend*, "calling." Viewed as a whole, the passage reproduces a kind of metonymic play of parts and wholes, from *Unheil* to *Heile, Heiles* to *Heilige, Heiliges* to *Göttliche, Göttliches* to *Gott,* thus suggesting that the initial and final terms, the unhale and the god, are themselves related as parts to a whole, and that the linkage of the two is performed by ῥυθμός as such. The declining number of syllables in the third and fourth sentences (nine and seven, respectively, instead of ten as in the first two sentences) suggests a compression and convergence that conform to the meaning of the final verb in the chain, "nears" or "approaches," *nähert.* Finally, the move-

24. Allemann, *Hölderlin und Heidegger,* p. 192. The essay "Wozu Dichter?" appears in *Holzwege* (Frankfurt am Main: V. Klostermann, 1950), pp. 248–95; the quotation cited below appears on p. 294.

ment from parts to wholes, the advance to the ultimate term (ultimate, that is, at least for Rilke's poetry), is sustained by the
strongly rhythmical line, which can be scanned as dactylic te-
trameter and trimeter:

> Ünheĭl äls / Ünhēil / spūrt ŭns dăs / Hēĭlĕ.
> Hēĭlĕs ĕr / wĭnkt / rūfĕnd dăs / Hēĭlĭgĕ.
> Hēĭlĭgĕs / bĭndĕt dăs / Gŏttlĭchĕ.
> Gŏttlĭchĕs / nāhĕrt dĕn / Gŏtt.

Why these approximations to poetic speech, why these Malachi Mulliganish dactyls, as unmistakable as they are enigmatic?
Beda Allemann observes that Heidegger's own language, "in
ways that are difficult to define, becomes ever more intimately
bound up with the language of Hölderlin," especially the language of those "hard rhythmic jointures" of the late hymns.[25]
Such intimacy is of course—as we shall see in a moment—easy
prey for parody and ridicule. José Ortega y Gasset calls Heidegger "one of Hölderlin's ventriloquists," although he surely
means the reverse, namely, that the poet is Heidegger's ventrilo-
quist.[26] Indeed, the jab seems witty until one tries to decide
which of the two, Hölderlin or Heidegger, is the dummy: in the
Hölderlin/Heidegger encounter there are no dummies.

Is it then merely a case of what Merleau-Ponty somewhere
describes as a gradual absorption or seduction into the style of
the author with whom one happens to be occupied? Or, if it is
more than that, can we perhaps relate such rhythmic language
to the notions of coinage, imprint, and linkage (Gepräge, Fesseln)
discussed above? It seems as though Heidegger is in search of
that binding power of language, of the telling measure that will
calculate the distance between the unhale mortal and the sky
god, when he lets his language become bound by rhythm. Does
he then use language, as Nietzsche says, as a "magic sling" to
toss at the flying feet of the fleeting gods? Or is the effort both
more modest and more desperate than that?

Heidegger wants to leave to its own devices the tradition for
which language is a system of ciphers and propositions, or at best
a vehicle of meanings, a tradition for which the cocksure ma-

25. Allemann, *Hölderlin und Heidegger*, pp. 180 and 182.
26. José Ortega y Gasset, "Martin Heidegger und die Sprache der Philosophie," in *Universitas* (Stuttgart, 1952), vol. 7, p. 903.

nipulation of predicates suffices. He responds and corresponds to *(ent-spricht)* the language of rapture, of the *mystes*, which tries to perform or enact what it says. Heidegger is rarely willing to allow the constative to pretend that it can speak without the performative. Indeed, Heidegger's is the responsive rapture of something that he would like to call *thinking:* the initiate is expected to remain sober at the feast of thought, even though the language will begin to dance.

If a word of suspicion is in place here, a suspicion related to Derrida's concerning Heidegger's nostalgia for essences, mine would be that Heidegger's approximations to the rhythmic jointures of poetic speech are often *insufficiently* hard. Heidegger's language of thinking is not poetic enough. The lines scanned above have a lilting quality about them, as though they were an ontotheological jingle—Malachi Mulligan's scampering "Ballad of Joking Jesus." They sound like a ditty played on a barrel organ, as Zarathustra complains to his animals.[27] To say the least, the lilting or singsong quality is altogether absent from Hölderlin's late hymns and fragments, the meter and measure of which are excessive, or even recessive, constantly cut by caesurae:

> Is there a measure on Earth? There is
> None.

Es gibt / Keines. Hölderlin's lines are scored in meteoric rock, they are *saxifrage* in William Carlos Williams's sense. The mea-

---

27.   Lest readers think that I have been unfair in my selection of Heidegger's lines from "Wozu Dichter?" I offer these still more bizarre lines from that essay, lines that are more lilting than anything Zarathustra's animals ever produced: "*Das wagendere Wagen, wollender als jedes Sichdurchsetzen, weil es willig ist. . . . Das wagendere Wagen des willigen Wollens. . . .*" (H, 275); "*Die Wagenderen wagen das Sagen*" (H, 287); "*Das sagendere Sagen der Wagenderen ist der Gesang*" (H, 292); and, finally, "*Das Wollen der Wagenderen ist das Willige der Sagenderen*" (H, 294). Such "more daring" and "more telling" lines were caricatured cruelly by a recent German satirist of whom I do not approve, and whom I will therefore not properly cite, but whose singsong nonsense has "Wozu Dichter?" as its obvious source, just as Günter Grass's *Die Hundejahre* had Heidegger's "Was ist Metaphysik?" as its source. This satirist writes: "I can still hear his highpitched raspy voice, slow and deliberate—Professor Wolkenweber reading from his treatise 'On Essence and Ducks': *'Es ist es ist es ist . . . die wagende Sage des ereignenden Seins, das vage Sagen des erregenden Weins, die reissende Rage der segenden Sage, der aufgeregte Reigen des sengenden Soundsos, das Zeichen des Siechtums des wagenden Wegners, oder aber auch des wëgenden Wagners des sägenden Seins'.*"

sure of the lines from Heidegger's "What Are Poets For?" is, in contrast to it, pudding. In short, Heidegger's later thinking is not "too poetic," which is the complaint we always hear; often it is not poetic enough, if Hölderlin, Rilke, and Trakl are any measure. Indeed, Heidegger's closest approximations to the language of poetry may—in spite of what I may have implied in these pages—occur in his hardest, sparest prose, as in the passages on *das Man*, anxiety, and mood in *Being and Time*, or in the discourse on the mortals, as in the passage cited earlier in this chapter, "Human beings are essentially as mortals. . . ." The German of that passage, which I reproduce here in part, resounds as follows:

> *Der Mensch west als der Sterbliche. So heißt er, weil er sterben kann. Sterbenkönnen heißt: den Tod als Tod vermögen. Nur der Mensch stirbt—und zwar fortwährend, solange er auf dieser Erde weilt, solange er wohnt. . . .*

Is there a measure that can readily scan these lines? *Es gibt / Keines.* "Pure prose is never 'prosaic'; it is as poetic—and as rare—as poetry" (US, 31).

Rhythms of Presencing and Absencing

If there is a guiding thought behind both the theory and practice of rhythm in Heidegger's work, it is the sobering thought of the enigmatic periodic presencing and absencing of beings in time. Heidegger's adventure with poetic language is not a tourist flight on the viewless wings of poesy. It is a way of experiencing the meaning of being and time as presencing, that is, as presence bound by a twofold absence—the not-yet and the no-longer that articulate a being's giving-itself as it is, or the not-as-such, which articulates its giving-itself-out-to-be what it is not. Heidegger's adventure with the language of poetry is intimate with the self-concealing manifestation that marks both being and language. In the years following *Being and Time* that adventure becomes all-absorbing for Heidegger.

Here it will not be possible to discuss the transformations undergone by the notion of ecstatic temporality in Heidegger's thought after the publication of his magnum opus, although any discussion of rhythm in connection with Heidegger can scarcely avoid the question of temporality.[28] Neither the definitive emergence of history (as the history and sending of being) in his thought nor the indefinite expansion of his destructuring of the history of ontology illuminates the path to be taken here, the path that Heidegger himself trod in the direction of the work of art, the work of language and of poetry, the poetry of the deaths of God and Man and the thought of dwelling on the earth—where Nietzsche and Hölderlin accompany.

During the 1950s in Germany, literary criticism in the form of *Stilkritik* sought to illuminate that path by concentrating on Heidegger's suggestive but enigmatic remarks on rhythm. However, *Stilkritik*, the German equivalent of text-immanent criticism, doubtless reminiscent of New Criticism in America and England, soon foundered in the tidal wave of neo-Marxian social-critical thought during the 1960s and then drowned in the successive waves of semiotics, structuralism, and poststructuralism in the 1970s and 1980s. The problem of rhythm (in this ontological context) has not advanced since the days when Emil Staiger, Ernst and Friedrich Georg Jünger, and Beda Allemann began to concentrate their energies on it. Further, there are many indications in the work of Jacques Derrida that rhythm remains the great unresolved theme of text-immanent criticism and perhaps of deconstruction as well. Finally, as the references to Williams and Olson in this chapter suggest, poets in the "postmodern" United States have been relentlessly reworking the question.[29]

At the conclusion of his *Hölderlin und Heidegger,* Beda Allemann broaches the question of "the historicity of the poetic."[30] "Historicity" here does not have the sense of "history of

28. See chaps. 2–3 of Krell, *Intimations of Mortality* (University Park, PA: Pennsylvania State University Press, 1991), and chap. 6 of Krell, *Of Memory, Reminiscence, and Writing.*

29. A number of American poets and critics might be cited here, but I will mention only the now disbanded Yale group and the circle associated with the journal *boundary 2* at the State University of New York at Binghamton, under the leadership of William V. Spanos. See the latter's excellent introduction to the problem, "The Destruction of Form in Postmodern American Poetry: The Examples of Charles Olson and Robert Creeley," in *American Studies (Amerikastudien)* (Stuttgart: J. B. Metzler Verlag, 25, no. 4: 375–404.

30. Beda Allemann, *Hölderlin und Heidegger,* pp. 211–18, for this and the following.

ideas," "historicism," or indeed any sort of developmentalist approach. It designates "the more profound and authentic historicity" of the literary work. It seeks what Goethe called the "life-
force," *Lebenskraft,* of a work of art. Citing Emil Staiger's *Die
Kunst der Interpretation* (1955), Allemann argues that criticism
comes closest to the "inner historicity" of the literary work
when it takes the "most fundamental" and "primary" element
of the work to be its *rhythm.*[31] Allemann tries to grasp such
rhythm in terms of Heidegger's "unsurpassed temporal analysis
of Dasein": the unity of a work of art derives from its "historizing
suspension in the ecstases of original time." He concedes that
a thorough temporal analysis of the poetic work remains un-
achieved, and confesses that "every attempt at a temporal analysis" automatically leads him, as it led Heidegger, to the problem
of the *origin* of the work of art—the hidden source of the wave,
as it were. By virtue of the "purity of rhythm" in the work, that
is to say, the "gathering of the ecstases of time" in it, the artwork
transports us to the "more original dimension of time," the
dimension Allemann regrettably calls "perfect presence," *voll-
kommene Gegenwart.* However, such perfection has little to do
with the Husserlian and Hegelian dreams of a living present, full
presence, absolute presence to self. For "perfect presence," as
source or origin, is in Allemann's view an irreducible dyad, *Zwie-
falt.* It is perhaps the fold Derrida calls the *hymen.* In any case,
presence is always presence/absence. Presence designates a perpetual to-and-fro, *Hind-und-Her,* that arises from "the strife of
clearing and concealing."[32] The source or origin itself, the *Ur-*

31. Friedrich Georg Jünger agrees with Staiger and Allemann; indeed, he
even extends the scope of rhythm to include all language. In the same lecture
series in which Heidegger presented "Die Sprache," and Georgiades his theory
of Greek rhythm, Jünger calls rhythm—in contrast to the semantic realm—the
"more powerful experience of language." He continues: "The rhythm of speech
is the uninterrupted movement itself in which language is embraced in its unity,
in which it is cradled. . . . We can hear how language is pre-formed, shaped in
terms of its rhythm. It yearns for that rhythm; in its very articulation it anticipates
its rhythm." Later he adds: "To the question of whence rhythm, and why its regularly recurring movement is festive and joyous, the Greeks responded that it
stems from the gods. They saw in rhythm a basic relation of motion that could
not be derived from anything else and that they simply accepted." See Jünger's
lecture in *Die Sprache,* cited in note 10, above, pp. 106 and 108.
32. Allemann, *Hölderlin und Heidegger,* pp. 216–17. Cf. the following from
Heidegger's "Language" (US, 21): "The beckoning [of the poem] calls into a

sprung and *Quelle* whence the wave of rhythm emanates and whither it returns, is both clearing and concealing at once. It is a source that in its untraceable flow reveals the nonorigin of origins in the work of art.

Beda Allemann is unable to show why and how the historicity of the poetic, as uncovered by an ecstatic-temporal analysis, inevitably leads to the problem of the source or origin, much less to what I have called (after Derrida) the nonorigin of origins in the work of art. The work of art "by itself," under its own power, seems to lead to the problem of (non)origin. I suspect that it may be possible to show how the ecstatic movement from absence to presence and back again to absence occurs in a given work, by considering the way in which all the ecstases of time converge on the impossible horizon of *Präsenz*—that is, how all the tenses remain in tension to the undecidable horizon of presence/absence and the disseminative action of revealing/concealing. Consider the following selected lines from Whitman's "Crossing Brooklyn Ferry," in which the italicized verbs suggest something like a rhythm of revealing/concealing:

—I *see* you face to face!
—Others *will watch* the run of the flood-tide.
—I *am* with you.
—Just as you *feel* . . . so I *felt*.
—I too *had been struck* from the float *forever held* in solution, I too *had received* identity by my body.
—We *understand* then do we not? [33]

If we do not "understand," it is because the rhythmic interplay of future, past, and past perfect tenses makes the horizon-of-the-present in this and every "Crossing" radically undecidable.

Perhaps the more subtle tense-shifts in the Trakl poem with which—after two brief detours—I shall conclude this chapter will shed some unsteady light on the advance *within* Heidegger's ecstatic analysis of temporality to the invocation of the duplici-

---

nearness. All the same, the call does not tear what is called away from its remoteness; a calling holds what is called in remoteness. The calling calls in itself, and therefore calls always here and away: here into presencing; away into absencing."

33.   Walt Whitman, "Crossing Brooklyn Ferry," in *Leaves of Grass*, pp. 159–65. Of course, I have wrenched these lines out of their place in Whitman's poem.

tous origin of revealing/concealing, to the source of the poem as of the "things" of poems, to the (non)origin of world and earth.

However, before closing I want to refer explicitly to Heidegger's "The Anaximander Fragment" (1946), which defines the nature of δίκη, the enjoining or binding order—that is to say, the *rhythm*—of what emerges and passes away, and in passing away surmounts disorder, ἀδικία.[34] Δίκη expresses, as Heidegger insists, the *tragic order*. It is the hard rhythmic play of what is present with the not-yet-present and the no-longer-present, the play in which beings confront their own processual presenc*ing* / absenc*ing*. That very play pervades Georg Trakl's poetry. Its sequences of tableaus conjure "things" that arrive, linger awhile in presence, and then evaporate and are gone. Trakl is rapt to the rhythm of presencing and absencing. The "stress" of his line, his measure, doubtless falls on absence and withdrawal: Friedrich Georg Jünger characterizes Trakl's poetry as the incantation of "transient appearance," *vergängliche Erscheinung*. Yet it is not Platonic "transiency" that Jünger has in mind. Behind or above or beyond this coming-to-appear there stands nothing. The source of the wave remains inscrutable. The rhythmic wave of Trakl's poetry is, as one of his last poems affirms, "the icy wave / Of eternity." The wellspring of the sacred grove, as we shall soon hear in *De Profundis*, murmurs "the silence of God," pulsing with the irregular rhythm of the coming and going of things. The source of the wave is the usage, order, and reck of δίκη.

Yet is there not something overly expansive, even excessive, about taking the question of rhythm to the realm of revealing and concealing, presencing and absencing? Can rhythm—whether as coinage, fetter, recurrence, or periodicity—be thought in terms of self-showing and self-concealing, coming to presence and withdrawal into absence? Can the ontology of Dasein or the poetics of ἀλήθεια employ the word *rhythm* without flattening it out, crippling it, bringing it to a standstill?

To expand the usage of *rhythm* in this way is doubtless dangerous. Yet there is a kind of precedent. When Hölderlin inter-

34. In *Holzwege,* pp. 328–30; see the English translation in *Early Greek Thinking,* 2d ed., by D. F. Krell and Frank A. Capuzzi (New York: Harper & Row, 1984), pp. 42–44, for the following.

prets the dramatic structure of Sophocles' great plays *Oedipus the King* and *Antigone*, he uses the word *rhythm* in an unaccustomed way, so that one might be tempted to think that his "Remarks" serve Heidegger as the proper "school" of rhythm. At the risk of reverting to matters already discussed in chapters 1 and 2 of this book, let me return to Hölderlin's *Anmerkungen* with the question of rhythm in mind.

The "lawful calculus" of the ancient dramas might well serve the modern poet as a school. No doubt the "living meaning" of the particular content of a play cannot be *reduced to* a "general calculus"; yet the stuff of a play must be brought into relation with such a rule. To be sure, the words *law* and *calculus* cannot be understood here as meaning a standard meter or verse-form. For the tragic play involves a proper balance (rather than a mere sequence) of representations, sensations, and thoughts: "The law, the calculus, [is] the way in which a system of sensibility *[ein Empfindungssystem],* the whole human being, develops under the influence of the element . . . " (B, 730). It is not clear what that influential element is, but it is apparent that the succession involved in tragedy involves more than scansion and versification: " . . . and presentation and sensibility and ratiocinations, in sundry successions, always come one after the other according to a secure rule *[nach einer sichern Regel]*." Tragic transport, the ecstasy, rapture, or seizure produced by the play (perhaps what Aristotle took to be purgation), depends upon this rule, precisely because tragic transport is so indeterminate, "properly empty, and utterly unconstrained." Hölderlin now introduces the word *rhythm* and explains its expanded sense, that is, the sense in which rhythm can only be understood as *counterrhythm.*

> Therefore, in the rhythmic sequence of presentations in which the *transport* portrays itself, what is needed is *that which in versification is called caesura,* the pure word, the counterrhythmic interruption, in order to encounter the surging alternation of presentations at its summit, in such a way that what comes to the fore is not the alternation of presentations but presentation itself. (B, 730)

The rhythm of tragedy involves less the line of verse than the depiction of the incidents. The tragedy of rhythm is that its element, which is what is played out on the stage, is precisely what must truncate the flow. Only such interruption can "protect" the parts of a play from the "eccentric rapidity" by which the play tears along. The calculus that Hölderlin applies to the tragedies estimates whether the later parts of a play run away with its beginning, or whether they are somehow prodded and compelled by that very beginning. The first is the case with *Oedipus the King*, the second with *Antigone*. Accordingly, the caesura in *Oedipus* must come early in the play (_____), whereas in *Antigone* it must perform its counterrhythmic work late in the play (___/___) (B, 731; 783).

What serves as the counterrhythmic interruption in both cases, whether early or late, are the speeches of Teiresias, the blind seer, the man-woman. "He steps into the course of destiny as the one who oversees the power of nature, the power that tragically snatches a human being out of his or her sphere of life, and tears the midpoint of their inner life away to another world and into the eccentric sphere of the dead" (B, 731).

It is striking that Hölderlin's word for the seizing or snatching away of a human being is the very word that Heidegger chose in *Being and Time* to designate the operation of ecstatic temporality, namely, *Entrückung*. It is as though Hölderlin joins Aristotle and Augustine as the fundamental sources of Heidegger's analysis of ecstatic temporality.[35] Tragic transport to the eccentric sphere is the work of time itself; it is the arbitration, or necessitous arbitrariness, of Zeus, son of C(h)ronos, son of Ouranos. The midpoint of the most interior of inner lives is thus consumed in the fury of rhythm and counterrhythm, in the fire of time.

It is clear that the rhythm and counterrhythm of the caesura have everything to do with what Hölderlin calls the monstrous coupling of mortals and gods, their unbounded unification, limitless separation, and mutual betrayal, the infidelity of the gods being most memorable to oblivious mortals. The caesura has everything to do with the epoch in which we moderns live, the time of *désoeuvrement,* an epoch that assumes its place among the points of historical time only in order that the course of the cos-

35. See Krell, *Intimations of Mortality,* chap. 3, esp. pp. 49–50.

mos suffer no gaps. Rhythm and counterrhythm have everything to do with the infidelity of time itself, with the categorial reversal that human beings suffer when they try to make beginnings and ends meet. For even though time is rhythmic, it never rhymes (B, 735–36). Perhaps the tragedy that would best show this intense rhythm but lack of rhyme, the titanic struggle between daimonic mortality and arbitrary Zeus, the monstrous coupling of gods and mortals, and mortal women in particular, is a tragedy that Hölderlin does not translate and that Hegel never seems to have read—the tragedy of Io and Prometheus in the *Prometheus Bound* of Aeschylus. Another time, perhaps.

For the moment, let us be encouraged by Hölderlin's monstrous expansion of rhythm and counterrhythm. For what comes to appear in the dramatic action of tragedy is time, divinity, history, and mortality, including the mortality of failure—the failure, for example, of *thought*. Hölderlin to Isaak von Sinclair, on Christmas Eve, 1798:

> . . . the transient and transitory character of human thoughts and systems strikes me as being almost more tragic than the fates one usually·defines as the only truly tragic fates. And I believe this is natural. For if human beings are dependent on foreign influence even in the free activity that is most their own, in their independent thoughts; and if human beings are still modified by climate and circumstance in this regard, as we undeniably see that they are;—then where does anything like mastery prevail? . . . Even the purest thought of human beings . . . is as much an absurdity as a revelation. (B, 886)

During the Todtnauberg seminar on "Time and Being" in 1969, Heidegger refers at length to the following poem by Trakl. He does so perhaps in order to catch the rhythms of the rapturous but sober play of thought, rapturous because rhythm has seized it, sober because every revelation conceals its counterrhythmic fold, its dissolution, its surd. Caesura is seizure.

De profundis

Es ist ein Stoppelfeld, in das ein schwarzer Regen fällt.
Es ist ein brauner Baum, der einsam dasteht.
Es ist ein Zischelwind, der leere Hütten umkreist—
Wie traurig dieser Abend.

Am Weiler vorbei
Sammelt die sanfte Waise noch spärliche Ähren ein.
Ihre Augen weiden rund und goldig in der Dämmerung
Und ihr Schoß harrt des himmlischen Bräutigams.

Bei der Heimkehr
Fanden die Hirten den süßen Leib
Verwest im Dornenbusch.

Ein Schatten bin ich ferne finsteren Dörfern.
Gottes Schweigen
Trank ich aus dem Brunnen des Hains.

Auf meine Stirne tritt kaltes Metall.
Spinnen suchen mein Herz.
Es ist ein Licht, das in meinem Mund erlöscht.

Nachts fand ich mich auf einer Heide,
Starrend von Unrat und Staub der Sterne.
Im Haselgebüsch
Klangen wieder kristallne Engel.

Out of the Depths

It is a stubble field where black rain falls.
It is a brown tree standing all forlorn.
It is a hissing wind circling empty huts.
How sad this evening.

Beyond the hamlet
The gentle orphan gathers her meager harvest.
Her golden oval eyes feast in the twilight
And her womb awaits the heavenly bridegroom.

Turning homeward
The shepherds found the sweet body
Decomposed in the briar.

A shadow am I, remote from gloomy villages.
God's silence
I drank from the font in the grove.

Across my brow treads cold metal.
Spiders seek my heart.
It is a light that dies in my mouth.

At night I found myself upon a heath,
Bathed in filth and the dust of stars.
Among the hazels
Echoed again crystalline angels.

4 The Lunar Voice
of the Sister

In dieser Nacht lösen auf lauen Kissen
Vergilbt von Weihrauch sich der Liebenden schmächtige Glieder.

In this night, on pillows warm to the touch,
Yellowed by incense, the spent limbs of lovers unravel.

—Trakl, "Nähe des Todes," second version

Die Nacht ist schwarz. Gespenstisch bläht der Föhn
Des wandelnden Knaben weißes Schlafgewand
Und leise greift in seinen Mund die Hand
Der Toten. Sonja lächelt sanft und schön.

The night is black. A ghostly wind blows from the Alps,
The nightshirt billows about the boy who walks in his sleep,
And ever so gently a hand reaches into his mouth; it is
The hand of the dead. Sonja smiles sweet and fair.

—Trakl, "Die Verfluchten"

Daß endlich zerbräche das kühle Haupt!

If only that cool head would finally crack!

—Trakl, "Passion," third version

I swear I would love to follow the sister in the French language,
for which "I follow" *(je suis,* from *suivre)* also means "I am" *(je
suis,* from *être).* As matters stand, I will follow her at some distance, through a reading of Derrida's reading of Heidegger's
reading of Trakl. Heidegger's reading is to be found principally
in the essay discussed in the foregoing chapter, *"Die Sprache im
Gedicht";* Derrida's response to Heidegger's reading appears
throughout the *"Geschlecht"* series, but especially in the unpublished manuscript, *"Geschlecht III."* [1]

---

1. Martin Heidegger, "Die Sprache im Gedicht: Eine Erörterung von Georg
Trakls Gedicht," in US, 35–82. I cite the poems of Trakl in the edition by Walther
Killy and Hans Szklenar (Salzburg: Otto Müller Verlag, 1969–70), referring to

I swear I would love to follow her as her brother, but close upon her heels, into all the embroglios of love. The boundaries that separate us, or unite us, depending on how you look at it—I who merely *follow,* and she who undeniably *is* the sister, will remain invisible to me as I transgress them and trespass beyond them. That I know. For these boundaries are limits, borders, frontiers that I feel only in desire and pain; feel but never see, sense but never confront face-to-face. As I approach the limits, my pace and footfall will fail. If I should cross over and make the passage, it will be by stumbling blindly. I will have blundered into the foreign, thinking it is my home, dreaming of paradise, insistent and oblivious.

For here it is a matter of sisters. And of what Heidegger says about them or neglects to say about them. What does Heidegger say? And why the silences? I shall begin with some questions posed by Luce Irigaray in her remarkable book, *Oblivion of the Air in Martin Heidegger,* concerning Heidegger's reading of Trakl:

> That man is heading into his decline, into the decomposition of whatever up to now has gathered man—this he [Heidegger] has said. At least, by way of the poet Trakl. . . . That the dusk would offer the chance of a new dawn, that this November would offer the hope of a new spring to come, which would be granted by a gaze that is now lost in the night—this he has said. Again, that the destiny of this other sunrise has been confided to something foreign *[à l'étrange],* where all will be gathered, sheltered, and safeguarded otherwise. Where will our sojourn find another site? Where will habitation take place, no longer on the site of hate, but in the lodgings of the only tenderness there is?
>
> However, it is in a young boy, dead in order that he may safe-

---

this edition as T, with page number. I first discussed Heidegger's reading of Trakl, focusing on the situation of the First World War but also on the enigma of the sister in Trakl's poems, in the final chapter of *Intimations of Mortality,* "Strokes of Love and Death"; my reading of Heidegger's reading became more critical, and began to respond to the work of Jacques Derrida on Heidegger's Trakl essay, in *Daimon Life,* esp. chap. 8, "Something like Sexes, Something like Spirit." (See also pp. 76–77 of that book; for further comment on the unpublished "Geschlecht III," see *Daimon Life,* pp. 259–65.) I delivered an earlier version of the present chapter at the colloquium "*Le passage des frontières: Autour du travail de Jacques Derrida,*" at Cerisy-la-salle, in July 1992. See pp. 459–66 of the proceedings, cited in note 3 of chap. 3, above.

guard a profound childhood, that this setting and rising would find their possible future. A young boy, demented: sensitized otherwise than man, the old man, of the West. A dream dead at daybreak, a dream for the insurrection of spirit. Abandoned to the passageways of an underground memory.

The apparition and evanescence of a profound childhood, ungenerated by the difference between boy and girl, would find their place in the figure of an adolescent. It would be on the side of man's having yet to be engendered that a chance would be reserved for what is to come. Would it still be of man *[Encore de l'homme]*?[2]

A young boy, demented and defunct, a moribund lunatic, as the avatar of a childhood that is said to be more profound and serene than the first childhood, our lost childhood? Yes, there seems to be no doubt about it: Trakl's Elis is the figure of an oneiric, nostalgic, narcissistic intrauterine childhood.[3] Elis is so misty that he seems unborn, even ungenerated. He seems indifferently boy and girl—the dream of Empedocles.[4] He is the unengendered product of a sexual difference that is forever latent, the scion of a couple forever fraternal and familiar. (Why is the word *sororal* so uncommon as to be nonexistent? Why, as long as the sister remains in limpid latency, is she *fraternal?* But then why is Elis so uncannily *sororal?*) Elis, ungenerated, is the *ingénu,* the disingenuous creature, the *naïf.* He walks (if the dead do walk) in the simplicity of a different *Geschlecht* (a word that may be translated variously as sex, race, clan, family, branch or line, and so on, and which I shall leave untranslated throughout), promised since time immemorial and destined for an unlimited future, but, precisely for that reason, postponed forever. No doubt this is so for Heidegger.

2. Luce Irigaray, *L'oubli de l'air chez Martin Heidegger* (Paris: Minuit, 1983), pp. 108–9.

3. "Elis," an ancient city on the Peloponnesus, powerful during the Mycenaean period and associated with Arcadia, Olympia, and the worship of Zeus and Pelops, is an important figure in Trakl's *Sebastian im Traum,* completed in March 1914. See esp. T, 15, 47–49, 204–7. See also Jost Hermand, "Der Knabe Elis: Zum Problem der Existenzstufen bei Georg Trakl," *Monatshefte für deutschen Unterricht, deutsche Sprache und Literatur* 51 (1959), passim.

4. On Empedocles' dream—of having been boy, girl, bird, and bush in his prior lives—see Krell, *Postponements,* p. 111, n. 9.

However, in Heidegger's labyrinthine text on Trakl there are astonishing passages *on* the sister, or passages *to* the sister; or, at the very least, passages transfixed by the lunar voice *of* the sister. Hers is the voice of σελάννα, Selene or Semele, the moon. Her place, as we shall see, is (in) the place of God: it is her place to take the place of God, to relieve the solar deity of His burden and reassert the privileges of Astarte.[5]

It is Heidegger himself—who, as we know, had no sisters—who regularly and insistently calls upon the sister in his long text on Trakl. Nevertheless, this same Heidegger, ignorant of sisters, seems to block the advance of the sister's proper passage through Trakl's poems. Heidegger seems to want Trakl's figure of the sister to stop and freeze, as though he were afraid that she might blossom into a woman and a lover. He wants her to remain a little boy, or to become a little boy again, if that is what she ever was. Brother to brother.

Once again the shadow of Creon looms over Antigone. Once again the shadow of Hegel looms over Schlegel's *Lucinde* and abjures the wandering Venus, *Venus vaga*. To be sure, Hegel wants Antigone to preserve the unwritten law of the nocturnal gods—but to preserve them in her tomb. He wants Mary Magdalen, but at the feet of Jesus, a beautiful woman performing a beautiful deed—preparing the living corpse of Christ for the tomb of Hegel's piety.[6] Forever, it seems, the shadows of metaphysics and morals swallow the girl who is on the cusp, on the brink, on the very verge of becoming a woman. Always the growing girl sounds the death knell of systems of thought; always the systems order a preemptive strike. The sister? She is always al-

5. The topic under discussion is of course relevant to several debates occurring in feminist circles today: the desire of (some) women to have nothing to do with the nostalgic places of a (man's) god, the desire to be satisfied with a free and equal mortality, and the reply of (some) women that the proximity of women to what used to be called "nature," the region of the seas, the land, blood, and the moon, makes her confusion with divinity inevitable. I am not competent to engage in that debate, but hope that the present contribution helps to complicate it.

6. On these various figures of womankind in Hegel, see Krell, "Lucinde's Shame"; on the figure of Mary Magdalen, see Derrida's commentary on Hegel's *Spirit of Christianity* in *Glas* (Paris: Galilée, 1974), pp. 73–74, 82–83; English translation by John P. Leavey, Jr., and Richard Rand (Lincoln: University of Nebraska Press, 1986), pp. 62–63, 70.

ready marked—at least, as we shall see, for her brother—by the inevitable but unacceptable and inexplicable difference: the sister who is on the brink of adolescence is inadmissible, unassimilable, with regard to the fraternal system. Like Hegel, or a shade of Hegel, Heidegger recalls and then repels her.

An old story, you might say. But no, it is, or claims to be, an entirely new story, the entirely new history of a renovated Occident, the incipient history of an entirely new Geschlecht. Heidegger envisages nothing less than the transfiguration of man (and woman) as well as the transmutation of evil. Here, in his "Placement" of Georg Trakl's poetry, the end of all conflict and discord between men and women is taken to be in sight: what Schelling called the final, total scission or divorce of good from evil, *die endliche gänzliche Scheidung,* is at hand. It is a matter of an historic return, a homecoming, *Heimkehr* or *νόστος,* of a humanity once deformed but now in passage back to an altogether virgin site.

In this pristine historical region, which encompasses the locale of a Geschlecht until recently called "man," what is the situation of the sister? On the "site" of Trakl's poetry, in the "place" that Heidegger calls "apartness," *Abgeschiedenheit,* how is she discussed and where is she placed? I shall follow her, the sister apart, across seven stations of Heidegger's itinerary, through seven passages in and of "Language in the Poem."

The Selenic Situation of the Sister

At the end of Trakl's poem, "Spiriting Twilight," the following two lines appear:

> *Immer tönt der Schwester mondene Stimme*
> *Durch die geistliche Nacht.* (T, 65)

> Forever the sister's lunar voice resounds
> Through the spiriting night.

The sister's lunar voice carries across the ecstatic night sky. That opaque sky is in fact a pond or nocturnal weir, *den nächtigen Weiher.* "The waters," notes Heidegger, "sometimes blue, sometimes black, show humanity its proper visage, its returning gaze *[seinen Gegenblick]*" (US, 48). After the sudden descent of dusk and the onset of a night of stars, in which nevertheless the moon dominates all, the world is bathed in silvery chill. Of the night Heidegger says, "Its shimmer is cool *[Ihr Glanz ist kühl]*." He continues, approaching now the site of the sister:

> The chill light derives from the shining of her who is the moon *[dem Scheinen der Möndin]* (σελάννα). As ancient Greek verses tell us, in the precincts of her luminosity even the stars grow pale and frigid. All becomes "lunar." The stranger who treads through the night is called "the lunar one *[der Mondene]*." The brother hears the "lunar voice" of the sister when, on his bark, which itself is "black" and scarcely lit by the stranger's golden sheen, he tries to follow the stranger on the stranger's nocturnal voyage on the weir. (US, 48–49)

At the very moment when Heidegger hears the sister's voice, his gaze fixes on the brother's black boat, or on the golden stranger. With Heidegger, as we shall see, the scene that always eventuates is one in which a brother-friend follows the brother-stranger. On the Heideggerian scene it is always a matter of two brothers, not at war, but caught up in some mutual enchantment. What does the sister—she of the Selenic voice—have to do with fraternal enchantment? Her voice is scarcely heard, even as all the night "selenates," *wird monden*, becomes lunar. *The* sister? *Whose* sister? Is she the sister of the fraternal friend, the one who merely follows the stranger? Or is she the stranger's own sister—the sister, so to speak, of the strange—Irigaray's *l'étrange*—as such? That is hard to say. Passage to the sister, yes, but *whose* sister? Where is she, the one who radiates everywhere in this extravagant night? And why does Heidegger neglect to mention the poet of the stars and the moon—Sappho?

Upon the Being and Breast of a Girl

I swear I would love to follow the sister in the French language, crossing the Rhine into Germany only under the fitting phase of the waxing moon. Somewhere in the middle of that swift flowing stream, the Dionysian stream that for Hölderlin flowed through Plato's midnight *Symposium*, the German *Sein* (being) rises to meet the French word *sein* (pronounced *seing*), the breast. If I were to cross at Breisach, heading toward Heidegger's Freiburg and Todtnauberg, though not as far east as Salzburg, the breast in question would be that of a very young woman, a mere slip of a girl.

The stranger, the boy who died quite young and whose death rescued him from his *dementia,* is called Elis. Elis is the deceased. He is decease as such, if one may say such a thing. He is the one who guides his friend and brother-to-be into the country that is set apart, the land of *Abgeschiedenheit.* Such apartness or departedness proves to be the very locale, *der Ort,* of Trakl's poesy. For from the very beginning of Elis's brief and even negligible life, and throughout his haunting madness, the boy is called into downgoing, *in den Untergang.* Heidegger tries to situate or place that descent of Elis, the brother-stranger, in the following way: "Elis's downgoing enters into the primeval dawn that is older than the decomposing, decrepit Geschlecht; older because more meditative *[sinnender];* more meditative because stiller *[stiller];* stiller because itself more stilling *[stillender]*" (US, 55).

Once again we hear language that is akin to *rîme enchainée,* which we saw at work in the foregoing chapter, lending a peculiar rhythm to the lines of Heidegger's text, lines linked by repetitions of assonance and alliteration. *Sinnender, stiller, selbst stillender*—these words conduct a certain meditation that remains sentient (*sinnen* means to sniff out, to pursue a scent) into a state of surpassing serenity. The dawn is ancient in its sentient serenity; it is serene, and itself bestows serenity. One of the principal senses of the word *stillen* is to nurse an infant, to bring it to the breast and thereby to peace: the primitive scene, more primitive than the primal scene, more ancient even than the dream and the vision of the Wolfman, is the scene of the infant hallucinating and searching for the nipple of the breast, the scene that Freud first depicts in his 1895 "Project." [7]

The dawn of the downgoing is *stiller, weil selbst stillender.* Whence its serenity? What is its relation to nourishment and to the Milky Way of the night sky that precedes it, to the γάλα of the galaxy? What sort of nurse can the sister be?

One might object that when Heidegger writes *stillender* he is surely not thinking of suckling infants: the comparative form of

7. Sigmund Freud, *Aus den Anfängen der Psychoanalyse,* ed. Ernst Kris (New York: Imago, 1950), pp. 413–14; see also my *Of Memory, Reminiscence, and Writing,* pp. 131–35.

the present participle suggests something more nourishing and appeasing than any woman's breast can be. The objection is doubtless well taken. Yet what is it that is more nourishing and calming than the breast? What is Heidegger thinking of? What could that dawn or matinal moment be that bestows transcendent serenity and induces a calm that is more nurturing than the warm milk of a mother's or nursemaid's body? What does one find in the antiquity of the dawn, beyond all mothers, as it seems, upon the being and breast of a girl?

Heidegger continues: "In the figure of the boy, Elis's boyishness *[das Knabenhafte]* does not stand in opposition to girlishness *[das Mädchenhafte]*" (US, 55). What is bound up with the opposition here designated by way of avoidance—with boys-as-opposed-to-girls? What is implied in the apparently quite natural opposition of *das Knabenhafte* and *das Mädchenhafte*, the very naturalness of which Heidegger disputes? Elis does not incorporate the opposition of the two Geschlechter. Indeed, the boyishness of Elis seems to embrace both girl and boy: "*Das Knabenhafte* is the coming to appear of the more tranquil *(stiller)* childhood." Such a childhood of greater repose can be called "boyish" precisely because nothing mars its essential simplicity and oneness. "Girlishness" disappears from the text after this one appearance, and is replaced by the ever-recurrent "childhood," *Kindheit.* "The latter conceals and salvages within itself the gentle twofold of the *Geschlechter,* of the youth as well as of 'the golden figure of the young girl *[der Jünglingin]*.'"

The youth and the maiden, *Jüngling / Jünglingin,* are adolescents, perhaps. More likely, they are on the very verge of puberty, still embraced by the stiller, more serene childhood. A young boy and a young girl, in a childhood of chums who are always, it seems, boyish. When exactly does adolescence commence? Whatever the reply, whatever the limits of childhood, do not puberty and adolescence arrive always too soon? Do they not mark, in Heidegger's text, but certainly not in his alone, the end of all serenity? Do they not mark a duplicitous sexuality that in some sense will always be laid at the feet of the sister?

The question persists: When precisely—if not from the most primeval of pristine dawns, prior to all birth—is sexual difference marked? Heidegger himself insists on the "as well as" of the youth and the maiden, *des Jünglings sowohl wie der ". . . Jüng-lingin"* (T, 87). The "as well as" sews a narrow yet clearly visible seam of gender where there was to be only a gentle twofold, a folding of two into the fraternal one, without cease or crease. The neologism *Jünglingin,* denoting a female youth, traces the fine line of a scar in Trakl's poetry, the cicatrix of those ancient, duplex, duplicitous genders and genres of what used to be called "man."[8]

However, Heidegger nowhere cites those verses of Trakl that mix the genders and sexes without a palpable fold or visible seam. Trakl seems to make of the sister and her brother *one* strange being, embodied and desirous, *one* uncanny Ge-schlecht, as it were. Although Heidegger insists on the *oneness* of Trakl's "*one* Geschlecht," he never introduces lines such as the following:

> . . . *ein sterbender Jüngling, die Schwester* . . . (T, 83)
>
> . . . a dying youth, the sister . . .
>
> *Ein strahlender Jüngling*
> *Erscheint die Schwester in Herbst und schwarzer Verwesung.* (T, 62)
>
> A beaming youth
> The sister comes to appear in autumn and black corruption.

Or, finally, the following confusion of lids and eyes in brother and sister:

> *Da die Augen der Schwester sich rund und dunkel im Bruder aufgetan* . . .
> *Tief sinnt aus wissenden Augen ein dunkles Geschlecht.* (T, 177)
>
> When the sister's eyes opened round and dark in her brother . . .
> Deeply brooding are those knowing eyes of a darkling *Geschlecht.*

8. In German-speaking countries, back in the old days, a girl was a *Jungfrau* (a virgin) who might become a *Jungfer* (an old maid); nowadays she can become a *Junggesellin,* an unmarried apprentice or worker; she may *horribile dictu* once again have the opportunity to become a *Jungmädel,* one of the female auxiliaries of the Hitler Youth, which between 1933 and 1945 embraced young women during the crucial years of transition from ten to fourteen years of age; but only in the Trakl world can she be a *Jünglingin,* and only in Heidegger's version of that world will the mark of difference be both scarified and effaced in the specific manner this chapter is trying to describe.

Heidegger ignores or passes over in silence these notable confusions of gender and sex in the sometimes more gentle, sometimes more violent childhood of Trakl's poetry. Nor does he ever cite the "unholy childhood," *Unheilige Kindheit,* of Trakl's "Vestibule of Hell" (T, 73), or the "sad childhood" of "Evening Song" (T, 37), or the childhood "filled with sickness, terror, and gloom" of "Dream and Delusion" (T, 80). He passes over in silence the equally disconcerting lines that associate the sister with "Eve's shadow" (T, 24), "black corruption," and "putrefying azure" (T, 95). For blue is not always the blue of spiriting twilight in Trakl's poems, and certainly not always of the dawn: "At eventide Plague prepares her blue vestments" ("The Accursed," T, 58). The very multiplicity and indeterminateness of the hues and tonalities of the colors, which Heidegger himself underlines—for example, the red that is "carnal purple and gentle pink *[purpurn fleischig und rosig sanft]*" (US, 75), the carnal red that makes us (though never Heidegger, never *visibly* Heidegger) think of Sonja, "Wound, red, never shown / Lets us live in darkling chambers *[Wunde, rote, nie gezeigte . . .]*" (T, 59)—such multiplicity and indeterminateness remain far from the Heideggerian sister's silvery blue. Her pallid colors are remote, reduced to a kind of Hegelian gray-on-gray with cerulean undertones.

If I too now leave behind the multiple senses and confusions of the poet's palette, it will be in order to interrogate more closely that ostensibly more tranquil childhood in Trakl's poetry for which Heidegger yearns. Such childhood reserves in its latency, if only phantasmatically, a softer and more tender *doubling,* a duplicity that will *not* be of the sexes. A more gentle twofold, a softer, more delicate duplicity, something other than the discordant split of the sexes and genders—such is the promise that Heidegger sees reflected in the modestly lowered white eyelids of the bride, who is the very ornament of her race (*Die weißen Lider, die sein Schauen behüten, erglänzen im bräutlichen Schmuck* [US, 55]). The nuptial promise, the hymeneal hymn, pledges marriage, mating, and the nursery. Yet whose promise, and to whom? Elis, the one who remains apart in departedness, sees into the blue of the spiriting night; the white lids of protective modesty are both his own and the bride's ornament. It is as though Elis were Nathanael in E. T. A. Hoffmann's "The Sand-man," in which Coppelius's spyglass (that is, the *Perspektiv* of the *Doppelgänger*) returns to the viewer the gaze of his own eyes and precipitates his own death. Except that in Heidegger's reading of Trakl, presumably, the uncanny perspective promises a more gentle childhood than Nathanael ever knew. It is the childhood of a youth already departed, to be sure, so that the reference to "The Sandman" is more fitting and more disconcerting than it might at first seem.

At all events, the nuptial promise can hardly be a vow to pro-duce infants, a promise of further generation(s). It almost seems to be the tender duplicity of a child's game, as when boys and girls play "Mama's Wedding." How shall we find the promise of Elis, the dead boy? Where do we find (and why do we seek?) in the figure of Elis himself the girlishness that does not stand op-posed to boyishness? And if the moment should arrive when we find the promise and hold onto it, what nourishment will it grant to thought? What repose? What serenity do we seek upon the being and breast of Elis—*sein Sein und sein s e i n*—? What ineffable pleasure do we seek in the shade of young . . . boys . . . in flowers, *à l'ombre des jeunes . . . gars . . . en fleurs?*

The Generation of the Unborn

Heidegger cites the concluding lines of Trakl's "Lament" *(Klage)*: "Sister of stormy melancholy / See . . ." (US, 58). Yet he provides no commentary on the stormy sister. Much later in his "Placement," after having introduced and amply developed the themes of spirit, pain, and the flame, Heidegger also cites the concluding lines of "Grodek": "The ardent flame of spirit is nourished today by an overwhelming pain, / The unborn grandchildren" (US, 65). Heidegger's commentary takes up the question of these so-called "grandchildren":

> The "grandchildren" indicated here are in no sense the sons who remain ungenerated by the sons who have fallen *[die ungezeugt gebliebenen Söhne der gefallenen Söhne]*, those fallen sons who stemmed from the decomposing Geschlecht. If that were all that is involved, namely, a cessation of further generation of prior

Geschlechter, then our poet would have to celebrate such an end
[*müßte . . . jubeln*]. Yet he is in mourning. To be sure, it is a
"prouder mourning," one that gazes ardently on the repose of
the unborn. (US, 65)

I interrupt the quotation in order to concede that these
words of Heidegger's, no matter how hypothetical and tenuous
they may be, are in my view the most unnerving of his entire
corpus, even more disconcerting than all his silences.[9] The attribution of a *possible* exultation in the poet who confronts the dissolution of an entire Geschlecht—race, line, gender, generation, civilization, and so on—is more than disquieting. It attests
to the vast distance between Heidegger and Trakl with regard to
the accursed, decomposing Geschlecht. For Trakl never dreams
of jubilation, never sets himself apart from the Geschlecht that
suffers both generation and corruption; his apartness is not the
spurning, scornful distance that wishes a speedy demise for everything that has come to be under the old dispensation; his
voice is never that of either Mephistopheles or Silenos. Further,
the hypothetical attribution by Heidegger betrays the violence
of a "Placement" that insists on combing Trakl's poetry for
prophecies of a historic and fateful (not to say apocalyptic)
transformation of the Occident.[10]

At the risk of oversimplifying a reading (namely, Heidegger's of Trakl) that is nothing if not complex, I shall call this
(mis)reading of Trakl's "Grodek," and of the poem that in Heidegger's view is Trakl's poesy as a whole, its *verticalization*. By this
I mean that Heidegger always seems in a hurry to abandon the
horizon and horizontality of Trakl's Geschlecht, which is always
a race of *lovers,* in order to erect an entirely new race as the fateful historical apotheosis of the West. It is in my view a haste that
runs counter to much if not all that one reads in and of Trakl's
poetry.

However that may be, how would one erect to sheer verti-

9. See chap. 4 of my *Daimon Life* for a discussion of Heidegger's silences. See
also the discussion by Veronique Foti in chap. 2 of her *Heidegger and the Poets:
Poiesis, Sophia, Techne* (Atlantic Highlands, NJ: Humanities, 1992), p. 28.

10. On such "historial-destinal" transformation, see Dominique Janicaud,
L'ombre de cette pensée: Heidegger et la question politique (Grenoble: Jerome Millon,
1990), discussed in Krell, *Daimon Life,* pp. 165–70.

cality a Geschlecht, indeed, a *new* one? A novel race, generation, family, or sex? What is Heidegger thinking of, and by what transparent maneuver will he pursue that thought? I continue the quotation: "The unborn are called grandchildren *[Enkel]* because they cannot be sons; that is to say, they cannot be direct descendants of the fallen Geschlecht." It will therefore be necessary to skip. Three times. First, to skip an entire sex—for if the "grandchildren" cannot be sons, that certainly does not mean that they can be *daughters.* Second, to skip an entire generation. And third, to skip all generation (in the verbal sense) as such. Such skips or leaps are also shifts from *naming* to *being:* "The unborn are called *[heißen]* grandchildren because they cannot be *[nicht . . . sein können]* sons." The shift from naming to being involves skipping not merely one sex and one generation, a generation once removed, as it were, but all generation (of both sexes) as such, generation (by both sexes) removed once and for all. The newly erected (but forever unborn) race will sidestep all direct descendance, evade the downgoing inevitably implied in sexual generation, which in Heidegger's view is invariably struck by the curse of dissension. Yet what intercourse, if any, unites the two Geschlechter? "Between them [i.e., the fallen Geschlecht] and this Geschlecht [i.e., the unborn] lives another generation *[lebt eine andere Generation].*"

Lives? Whence the *life* of that unborn generation? How will it have come to be, this "other *Generation*"? Heidegger here writes the Latinate German word *Generation.* This is its sole appearance in "Language in the Poem." The word also appears in section 74 of *Being and Time,* at that perilous moment when Dasein, oblivious of its newfound finitude and rapt to the blandishments of a national heritage and a national destiny, prepares to choose its heroes and march off to war in the ranks of its "generation": "The fateful sending of Dasein in and with its 'generation' constitutes the full, proper occurrence of Dasein." [11]

Why the Latin? Why emphasize the *gen-* of generation, so redolent of the Mediterranean and Aegean, the root of γένος,

11.   In section 74 of *Being and Time,* Heidegger cites Wilhelm Dilthey's notion of "*Generation*"; see Martin Heidegger, *Sein und Zeit,* 12th ed. (Tübingen: M. Niemeyer, 1972), p. 385. I discuss this notion of "generation" in *Daimon Life,* pp. 178 and 339 n. 8.

γένεσις, and γίγνεσθαι, of *gens* and *genius*, of *gentilitas, generositas,* and *genitalis?* Heidegger writes the Latinate word *Generation* perhaps in order to stress a particular sense of *Geschlecht,* to wit, that of the temporal-historical sequence of human beings who follow generation upon generation, as we say. Or is it to gesture toward a far more potent sense of the word, skipping a generation and the entire process of generation in order to think something *like* generation in a novel, prodigious, phantasmatic way?

The new *Generation,* unmediated by fathers who have fallen in both war and peace, and also untouched by their fathers' unborn posterity, can only be called "other." Not "another" generation, but an "other" generation. "It is other *[anders]* because it is otherwise *[andersartig],* in accord with its other essential provenance from the dawn of the unborn" (US, 65–66). Such is the ambiguous maneuver attempted by Heidegger for the purpose of avoiding contamination by direct (as opposed to spontaneous) generation: between the "fallen" generation (Heidegger writes *verfallen,* and not simply *gefallen,* as though Dasein as such and in its very being were not forever "falling," or as though the novel Geschlecht were something other than Dasein, something other than the mortal) and the ungenerated generation, an "other" generation "lives," a generation that proceeds from the dawn of the very "unborn" whose origins we are seeking. In the phrase, *gemäß ihrer anderen Wesensherkunft aus der Frühe des Ungeborenen,* the very relation of "essential provenance" to the "dawn of the unborn" also is ambiguous: does the new Geschlecht have an *identical* or an *essentially other* provenance? In either case, whether the identity contaminates or the otherness causes the new Geschlecht to float freely in the air, the results are problematic. Heidegger's is less a maneuver than a vicious circle. "The child is the father of the man," said Wordsworth, and Heidegger's reply would be something like this: "The unborn-ungenerated is the only possible father of the generation that vacillates between its (unborn) father, its (ungenerated) sons, and its (parthenogenic) self." The structure of Heidegger's skipped generation, whether free-falling or generating in reverse, as it were, resembles the structure of the Logos father-and-son, that is to say, of fully present speech and bastard-orphan writing, as Derrida analyzes them in "Plato's Pharmacy." [12] For such a vacillating generation, for such an impossible posterity or ancestry of the unborn, for such recalcitrant *obsequence,* even the most agile maneuver will not suffice. There is no exit to the outer perimeter of the circle of the generation of generations of the living and dying.

The future of the race is in Heidegger's view to be "otherwise," *andersartig.* Of that there can be no doubt. The human Geschlecht to come, pyrified and distilled by the flame of spirit, will rise from the cinders of the corrupt Geschlecht, as though it were Hegel's spiritual Phoenix. *Andersartig,* except that the "otherwise" that would interrupt forever the generation of the corrupt generations, purging the infectious generations, is the selfsame "otherwise" that metaphysics and morals have always inflicted on the world. "Otherwise," except that the provenance of this *andersartig* seems to be of the selfsame spirit, namely, the spirit of rancor and revenge—Aureliano thirsting for endless Revolution, Amaranta weaving the shroud of Rebeca.

No doubt it would be necessary to complicate the reading at this point. For Heidegger does not dream of abolishing the race of mortals in order to fulfill the ancient desire for an incorruptible race. Indeed, the thrust of his reading, indicated by his resistance to any so-called "Platonic" or "Christian" interpretation of the line "It is a stranger on earth, the soul," is precisely to reject the pyrification that is craved by the metaphysico-moral tradition. And yet, no matter how essential this other side of the coin may be, a worry haunts readers of Heidegger's essay without cease, a worry to which these words of mine are trying to give utterance.

In the cinders so ardently desired by the pyrifying tradition, a tradition that Heidegger doubtless wishes to oppose but that he also seems to embrace or be embraced by, do we not uncover the final traces of the sister who was on the threshold of puberty? The final traces of the sister—as a pile of cinders sifting across bloodstained sheets, *blutbefleckte Linnen,* as Trakl says (T, 12, 38; cf. 9, 97)? Do we not find the final traces of the sister, her girlish-

---

12. See *Dissémination,* esp. I, 2, and II, 8, pp. 84–95 and 164–79; English translation, pp. 75–84 and 142–55.

ness purged and eternalized in a timeless boyishness, her incipient womanliness sterilized forever by fire?

Evil Most Furious:
Dissension between Brother and Sister

On the site of apartness, the flame of spirit gathers mortals, who are destined for a more tranquil childhood. Heidegger writes:

> That which gathers in apartness salvages the unborn from what has already withered away, saving it in a coming resurrection *[in ein kommendes Auferstehen]* of the coinage of humankind that advenes from the dawn. That which gathers, as the spirit of the gentle, at the same time soothes *[stillt]* the spirit of evil. The insurrection of evil waxes to utmost malignancy whenever it rages out beyond the discord of the Geschlechter and penetrates the relations of siblings *[in das Geschwisterliche einbricht]*. (US, 67)

The promise of a resurrection of matinal humanity—of the new Geschlecht that is to rise from the dawn of the unborn—is menaced by evil. Nevertheless, however threatened, the new humanity is destined to prevail. Paradoxically, the mark of the new humanity would have to be its irrevocable surrender of all dreams of resurrection: if the soul is a stranger on earth, that is because the earth has not yet become its sole abode. Yet even if we set this paradox aside, the problem of *evil* remains—that is to say, the problem of Heidegger's *discourse* on evil, which remains decidedly on this side of good and evil.

The flame of spirit is bound to soothe, appease, or still the spirit of evil. Yet the appeasement is as paradoxical as the resurrection. For, as we noted earlier in the chapter, one of the senses of *stillen,* indeed, the most current sense in modern German, suggests that the spirit of evil would be nursed, nourished, and nurtured, as one nurses a baby girl or boy. Or as one nurses a grudge, or a hopeless scheme of vengeance.

What is the evil, *das Böse,* that haunts Heidegger here? How is it to be tranquilized and brought to a standstill—or, on the contrary, nursed and nurtured? Heidegger explains nothing of this, just as in his lectures on Schelling and in his "Letter on Humanism" he has little to say about the dramatically conjured "rage of malignancy." [13] But in "Language in the Poem" he does indicate the worst of evils, the most maleficent of malfeasances, the gravest of ills, the outermost point of wickedness, *die äußerste Bösartigkeit.* The most malignant of evils is the irruption of discord between the sexes and/or generations, tribes, clans, etc. *(Zwietracht der Geschlechter);* more precisely, it is the spread of such dissension beyond the bounds of the erotic, where it has its seedbed, into that familial realm that should have been spared the ignominy—the realm of brother and sister.

In the German language, the sister gives her name to the relations between all the siblings. *Das Geschwisterliche,* homologous with *das Geschlechtliche,* is nevertheless separated from the latter, Heidegger would say, by an abyss of essence. Yet even if the sister lends her name to the privileged site of the siblings, we shall soon see that one can enter into relationship with her only by way of rapport with her brother.

Before we reach that moment in Heidegger's text, we might pose a question in the direction of this most maleficent of ills, the evil that contaminates the more tender childhood with troubles that should have remained outside the walls, forever *foris,* extramural and exogamous. What connection can there be between what Heidegger calls the most furious evil and what other discourses—let us say, certain discourses from Rousseau and Sade to Freud—call *incest?* Heidegger grazes this favorite topic of Trakl biographers, but does not cite or situate those poems of Trakl that give us to think incest, or more precisely, incest *prohibition,* where sex and generation meet in one Geschlecht. Such prohibition must have something to do with both the accursed, fallen Geschlecht and the most virulent spirit of evil; yet Heidegger remains silent before the testimony of Trakl's poems:

Im Park erblicken zitternd sich Geschwister. (T, 17)

In the park, brother and sister gaze on one another and shiver.

Die fremde Schwester erscheint wieder in jemands bösen Träumen.
(T, 31)

The strange sister appears once again in someone's evil dreams.

13. See my discussion of the sources in *Daimon Life,* pp. 138–42 and 296–300.

Wollust, da er im grünenden Sommergarten dem schweigenden Kind Gewalt tat, in dem strahlenden sein umnachtetes Antlitz erkannte. (T, 80–81)

Voluptuousness, when in the verdant summer garden he violated the silent child, recognized in its beaming visage the face of his own delusion.

Aus verwesender Bläue trat die bleiche Gestalt der Schwester und also sprach ihr blutender Mund: Stich schwarzer Dorn. (T, 95)

The pallid figure of the sister stepped out of blue corruption and spoke from her bleeding mouth: Prick black thorn.

Is there some connecting line between this fiery evil and the dissolution of the accursed Geschlecht? For here, as in the case of Hölderlin, it is a matter of ardor and dissolution—the fireball. Even if one were to eschew all biographical reductionism, how could one avoid the intertwining of evil and violation in Trakl's poetry, an intertwining as incontrovertible as it is disarming? By what force or debility of thought could one evade it?

Incest and the question of being? Incest prohibition and the sending of being? Heidegger would have recoiled. And yet, if the deeper harmony of a more gentle twofold can be deranged by some act of violence, by the violation that irrupts from discord between the sexes—and Heidegger himself attests to this menacing possibility—then how could Heidegger's thinking escape the legacy of the *Inzestverbot?* Heidegger anathematizes all psychoanalytic discourse, all the while himself approaching, *volens nolens,* the double-binds of encrypted desire, desire frustrated "from the dawn." Behind the silence of Heideggerian "sigetics," that is, the practice of hearkening to the rhythms of language and the raptures of thinking, the deathknell resounds, tolling the *glas* of every piety.

Of all the questions ensconced in the *Inzestverbot,* the following are perhaps among the most devastating ones: What if Heidegger's every effort to interrupt the march of generations, to truncate generation *(Fortzeugung)* as such; what if every attempt to safeguard a more profound and more serene childhood from the ravages of time, from latency's ineluctable passing; what if the dream of a more nourishing and more nurturing infancy, to be achieved by skipping a generation or reversing the flow of the generations; what if the phantasm that envisages for Occidental

humanity a kind of deferred, retroactive, or inverted blossoming—what if all this were precisely the phantasmagoria of a corrupted Geschlecht, the twisted dreams of the only race of mortals that ever lived? And what if Heidegger's role in this history
were to contaminate the budding Geschlecht with the malignant cells—the ressentiments—of the old? What if the ancient
Geschlecht, playing out the etiology of its illness from the historical dawn of day, were to infect the new with the disease of
rancor? What if the *crime* of incestuous violation were invented
only with the *prohibition* of the crime, so that the career of evil
would be coextensive with the phantasm of the good?

Heidegger does not permit himself such lugubrious
thoughts, even though his reading of Trakl prompts them and
makes them well-nigh inevitable. He does not go as far as Schelling would have gone, scalpel in hand, crying out for sutures.
Heidegger, in recoil, writes, "Yet at the same time," which is to
say, the time when sexual discord penetrates the more serene
childhood, "the fraternal twofold that is gathered in the human
Geschlecht conceals itself in the more serene onefold *[Einfalt]*
of childhood" (US, 67). The time in question is the metaphysical
time of the ἅμα, *zugleich,* the simultaneous; the main verb, *ver-
birgt sich,* is in the eternal present tense of a concealing latency,
a latency that enwraps, protects, and promises; and the gather-
edness of the twofold, *versammelte Zwiefalt,* precisely by means of
the past participle, functions to guarantee the always-already-
there of the onefold. Duality finds itself sheltered and gathered
in a prior fraternal unity, and the discord of a quarreling two-
some is but a grownup's nightmare. On the supposedly pristine
site of apartness, *Abgeschiedenheit,* apparently remote from every
possible contamination, immured in a futural past that is sealed
off forever from the depredations of a fallen present, "evil" is
transmuted once and for all:

> In apartness, the spirit of evil is neither annihilated and negated
> nor unfettered and affirmed. Evil is transmuted *[verwandelt].* In
> order to withstand the rigors of such "transmutation," the soul
> must turn to the grandeur of its essence. The magnitude of such
> grandeur is determined by the spirit of apartness. (US, 67)

The new locale for a new human race, new and yet always
already renovated since time immemorial, forever renewed as a

promise from the dawn, always rediscovered by humankind's re-
gressive march toward a more tranquil childhood—such are the
marks and re-marks of a fulgurating atavism of thought, a regression well beyond the "dreamy romanticism" that Heidegger
is happy to refute (US, 80). "Apartness is the gathering by which
the essence of humanity is rescued *[zurückgeborgen]* to its stiller
childhood; this childhood, in turn, is rescued to the dawn of
another beginning" (US, 67). Salvaged *(geborgen)* and brought
back *(zurück)* to a dawn that is both behind and ahead, humanity
inherits a past that is now absolutely accessible to it, in a future
forever to come but already absolutely present to it, if only as a
phantasm—the fragile shelter to which our being-apart is always
already abandoned, the place that since ancient times, since the
dawn, somewhere in the vicinity of mother, nurse, sister, and
lover, is called χώρα. "Apartness, as gathering, possesses the essence of place" (US, 67). Place is the mother and nurse who
grew old, except in a child's memory of her; the lover who grew
distant, except in the lover's obsessive brooding on her or him;
and, above all, the sister who in spite of the watchful eye of her
brother secretly, furtively, surreptitiously grew up: Caddy, the
fallen sister of Benjy and Quentin Compson—the sister who,
once upon a stiller time, in a gentler childhood, smelled like
trees in the rain.

How to Gain a Sister?

"A friend listens in on the stranger. Listening in this way, he pursues the one who is apart, and thereby himself becomes a wan-
derer, a stranger" (US, 68). The friend, all ears, becomes everything the stranger is. He is, or desires to be, the friend that
every Dasein carries with itself.[14] These strange friends share everything, absolutely everything they possess. Even their sister.
That is to say, the sister of the one (but which one?) becomes
the sister of the other (but which other?). As though hers were

14. In section 34 of *Being and Time,* Heidegger speaks of our "hearing the
voice of the friend that every Dasein carries with itself." See *Sein und Zeit,* p. 163.
This phrase is one of the guiding threads of Derrida's "Geschlecht IV," in John
Sallis, ed., *Reading Heidegger: Commemorations* (Bloomington: Indiana University
Press, 1993), pp. 163–218. See also Christopher Fynsk, *Heidegger,* chap. 1, esp.
pp. 42–44, where I first was drawn to this passage in Heidegger's text.

the voice and the narration that every neuter/neutral Dasein carries with itself.

The friend who listens invites the stranger to converse with him. He gazes on the stranger until the stranger returns his gaze. Through this exchange of regards, the friend becomes *a brother* to the stranger. The two are now confreres.

The friend, become brother, presumably obtains for himself all the mysterious serenity displayed by the stranger. Nevertheless, as though by way of supplementation, Heidegger now adds a final detail concerning the initiation into brotherhood, the rite of passage from friend to brother: "However, when the friend who listens in sings 'The Song of the Departed,' and in so doing becomes a brother to the stranger, the stranger's brother, through the stranger alone *[durch diesen erst]*, becomes a brother to his sister, the sister whose 'lunar voice resounds through the spiriting night'" (US, 69–70).

The lines of the "Gesang des Abgeschiedenen" that seem particularly relevant to Heidegger's reflections on brotherhood and the mysterious winning of a sister are these:

> *Und es leuchtet ein Lämpchen, das Gute, in seinem Herzen*
> *Und der Frieden des Mahls; denn geheiligt ist Brot und Wein*
> *Von Gottes Händen, und es schaut aus nächtigen Augen*
> *Stille dich der Bruder an, daß er ruhe von dorniger Wanderschaft.*
> *O das Wohnen in der beseelten Bläue der Nacht.* (T, 79)

> And a lantern glows, the good, in his heart
> And the peace of the repast; for bread and wine are sanctified
> By God's hands, and out of nocturnal eyes
> The brother serenely gazes at you, that he might rest from thorny
>   wandering.
> O to dwell in the ensouled azure of night.

Singing these lines, the friend becomes a brother to the stranger. And, although nothing in this poem directly names or invokes the sister, the friend, "through the stranger alone, becomes a sister to his sister." Two sets of remarks are called for, one on the "his" of "his sister," the second on the sister as inevitably the sister to a "brother."

In the phrase *wird der Bruder des Fremdlings durch diesen erst zum Bruder seiner Schwester,* what is the antecedent of the possessive pronoun *seiner*? Is the sister in question consanguineous with the stranger or with the stranger's friend and neophyte brother? The question is not without importance for an exogamous culture—Western civilization, for example—even if ours is a culture in decline, whether on account of the worst of evils or the best prohibitions concerning that evil. The French translation of Heidegger's "Language in the Poem" does not hesitate to answer the question concerning the sister. It translates the phrase as follows: " *ce frère devient, pour sa propre soeur, à son tour un frère,*" roughly, "this brother becomes in turn a brother to his own sister." [15] In other words, when the friend becomes a brother to the stranger, his fraternal relation to *his own* sister becomes somehow intensified, becomes now what it always should have been. The French words *pour sa propre* and *à son tour* correspond to nothing in the German text; they are expletives or *trouvailles* used to justify the translators' decision. Had Heidegger written " *seiner* eigenen *Schwester,*" one would know that the sister is initially related to the stranger's *friend*. However, the word *eigenen* is not there; neither is anything that might mean "in [his or her] turn." Had Heidegger written ". . . *des Fremdlings* . . . dessen *Schwester,*" one would know that the sister is first of all a sister to the *stranger,* and *only through him* a sister to her brother's new brother. In short, Heidegger's wording is ambiguous—or, as he would prefer to say, *mehrdeutig,* multiple in meaning.

And yet—passing now to the second set of remarks—in both cases the sister remains the sister to a brother, precisely as she does in Hegel's model of the ethical deed in the nascent ethical community.[16] She is a sister only by grace of the fraternal stranger. No matter whose sister she may be *ab ovo,* the brother remains the axis, the pivotal point, the active and controlling center of the sibling relation. The friend and brother enters into relation with her—no matter whose sister she is—exclusively by the action and efficacy of the stranger. *Durch diesen erst,* that is,

15. See Martin Heidegger, *Acheminement vers la parole,* translated by Jean Beaufret, Werner Brokmeier, and François Fédier (Paris: Gallimard, 1976), p. 72.

16. G. W. F. Hegel, *Phänomenologie des Geistes,* ed. Johannes Hoffmeister, "Philosophische Bibliothek" (Hamburg: Felix Meiner, 1952), pp. 318–42. See also Derrida, *Glas,* esp. pp. 163–71 and 184–211; English translation, pp. 144–51 and 163–88.

only through the stranger, does the friend become a brother to the sister: no multiplicity of meaning here.

Yet when the friend and brother-to-be listens in on the stranger, whose voice does he hear? Is not the stranger's a lunar voice? And is not the lunar voice the Selenic voice of the sister? Is not the stranger's sole voice the voice of the sister? If the stranger (himself) is lunar, *monden,* and if he is called "*der Mondene,*" does not the closest of ties bind sister and stranger? Is not the sister aligned with everything that is strange, including the extravagant, spiriting night, the night of decline and death—including, in a word, Elis, who haunts the forest rim of apartness in the company of blue game?

If the sister is *familial* in relation to all that is strange, there is nevertheless nothing *familiar* about her. She is the uncanny in all that is canny, the secret passage of the *(un)heimlich* as such. She is most uncannily lodged in the stranger's throat, as "his" larynx, "his" voicebox. She hears and understands herself while speaking, and gives herself out as her brother, her brother the philosopher. Everyone, including him, thinks it is he the master who speaks.

Heidegger would affirm much, if not all, of this. The order of stages in this rite of passage to the sister may be meant to protect the alterity of the sister from too hasty an appropriation, too indiscreet a "listening-in"—for *nachlauschen* is dangerously close to *belauschen,* "to eavesdrop." Perhaps the very difficulty of the passage is meant to protect the sister from an intuitive fraternal gaze that is insistent, insatiable, and totalizing. It would then be the brother's *modesty* that demands from him this fraternity with all that is strange *before* being granted fraternity with a sister he has always taken for granted.

Or, on the contrary (and this would be the inverse of a reading that must be at least double, if not duplex and duplicitous), do we discern in the phrase "through the stranger alone," *durch diesen erst,* a suppression of the very strangeness of the lunar voice of the sister and an obstinate obtuseness that is classic and absolutely typical, a resistance to all things touching woman, a self-assured and serenely arrogant fraternization with the sister? And precisely for that reason always on this side of her, always in spite of her, always absolutely deprived of her?

In (the) Place of God

The sister's uncanniest locale is her position in (the) place of God. Heidegger interprets her appearance in the last two poems of Trakl ("Lament" and "Grodek") as evidence of the lack of rapport between Trakl's poesy and what one might call, after Hegel, "the spirit of Christianity." Derrida, in *Of Spirit: Heidegger and the Question,* has posed his objections to Heidegger's strategy of dissociating Trakl from all that is "Christian." [17] Yet Derrida has not (yet) offered a detailed commentary on the sister in this regard—as he has, for example, throughout *Glas,* where the sister is a constant (and constantly anomalous) member of Hegel's Holy Family. Heidegger writes the following with regard to Trakl's Christianity:

> Why does the poet, here, in the uttermost need of his final saying, not call on God and Christ if he is such a decided Christian? Why instead *[statt dessen]* does he designate "the haunting shadow of the sister," the sister as "the one who greets"? Why does the song ["Grodek"] end, not with the confident prospect of Christian redemption, but with an allusion to the "unborn grandchildren"? Why does the sister also appear in the other final poem, "Lament"? Why is "eternity" here called "the icy wave"? Is that thought in a Christian way? It is not even Christian despair.
>
> Yet what does this "Lament" sing? Does there not resound in this phrase, "Sister . . . See . . . ," the intense onefold of those who, no matter how threatened they are by the uttermost withdrawal of the hale, continue to wander toward the "golden visage of humanity"? (US, 76)

Why *instead* does the poet call upon the sister? *Statt dessen.* Instead of invoking the Christian God, the poet invokes the sister. As though the two elements in the exchange—sister for God—were the most naturally interchangeable elements in the world. In (the) place of Christian redemption and salvation, the sister's salutation of the dead. Neither Trakl nor Heidegger alludes explicitly to Antigone or to the Valkyries; neither submits

17. See Jacques Derrida, *De l'esprit: Heidegger et la question* (Paris: Galilée, 1987), chaps. 9–10, esp. pp. 152–59 and 178–84; translated by Geoffrey Bennington and Rachel Bowlby as *Of Spirit: Heidegger and the Question* (Chicago: University of Chicago Press, 1989), pp. 94–98 and 108–13.

to a Hellenic or a Nordic paganism that would engulf Christianity. Yet how are we to think the *Stätte* of this *statt dessen;* how are we to think the region or place of this "in (the) place of"? Who is the sister who greets the dead? Is she the funereal maiden of Hegel's Holy Family, upholding the divine law of the night by embalming the bodies of all the sons of God? Is she somewhere between the plains of Attic Thebes, the house of a Pharisee where Jesus meets a woman who is saved by her tears and the chrism of her faith (Luke 7:36–50), and the gates of Valhalla? Heidegger does not reply in any detail. Having called and recalled the sister, he hesitates to say any more about her apartness. As he turns to the third and final phase of his "Language in the Poem," he hesitates in a way that is rare with him: "We scarcely dare *[Kaum wagen wir noch],* by way of conclusion, to ask about the locale of this place *[nach der Ortschaft dieses Ortes zu fragen]*" (US, 76).

Let me not dare too much where Heidegger fears to speak and Derrida himself "hesitates." If I seek greater proximity to the sister, it is with an awkward footfall, still not seeing the limits that are right up against my face.

One Geschlecht: (S)he-lovers, Sea-lovers

The apartness of the departed, of decease and demise, descendance, descent, and downgoing—these are some of the names of the region of Trakl's poetry. Heidegger identifies that region as the Western world from Plato to Nietzsche. According to Heidegger, the history of being, as the history of fateful sendings and propriations, remains a history of oblivion and abandonment. Of beings, by being. Of sisters by brothers, and of brothers by sisters. Of lovers by lovers, (s)he-lovers by sea-lovers, and vice versa. "*One* Geschlecht," as Trakl's "Western Song" says.

Heidegger scrutinizes this unique and unifying Geschlecht, marked by the sole use of emphasis, underlining, spaced type, or italic in Trakl's poetry. Heidegger nowhere reprints the whole of "Western Song," even though from the moment his placement of Trakl introduces the theme of Geschlecht (at US, 49) to the very end, where the *one* of "*One* Geschlecht" provides the focus (at US, 78–79), that song names the very locale of apartness, the Occidental region, the land of evening, which is the

site of (a vertical) history. Perhaps we can take a moment to read
the entire poem.

Abendländisches Lied

O der Seele nächtlicher Flügelschlag:
Hirten gingen wir einst an dämmernden Wäldern hin
Und es folgte das rote Wild, die grüne Blume und der lallende Quell
Demutsvoll. O, der uralte Ton des Heimchens,
Blut blühend am Opferstein
Und der Schrei des einsamen Vogels über der grünen Stille des Teichs.

O, ihr Kreuzzüge und glühenden Martern
Des Fleisches, Fallen purpurner Früchte
Im Abendgarten, wo vor Zeiten die frommen Jünger gegangen,
Kriegsleute nun, erwachend aus Wunden und Sternenträumen.
O, das sanfte Zyanenbündel der Nacht.

O, ihr Zeiten der Stille und goldener Herbste,
Da wir friedliche Mönche die purpurne Traube gekeltert;
Und rings erglänzten Hügel und Wald.
O, ihr Jagden und Schlösser; Ruh des Abends,
Da in seiner Kammer der Mensch Gerechtes sann,
In stummem Gebet um Gottes lebendiges Haupt rang.

O, die bittere Stunde des Untergangs,
Da wir ein steinernes Antlitz in schwarzen Wassern beschaun.
Aber strahlend heben die silbernen Lider die Liebenden:
E i n Geschlecht. Weihrauch strömt von rosigen Kissen
Und der süße Gesang der Auferstandenen. (T, 65–66)

Western Song

O the soul's nocturnal wing beat:
Once we shepherds wandered the rim of twilight forests,
With red game, green flowers, and the babbling source pursuing
Humbly. O, the ancient sound of my dear home,
Blood blossoming on the altarstone
And the lonely cry of a bird above the pond's green stillness.

O, you crusades and glowing martyrdoms
Of the flesh; purple fruits fall
In the evening garden, where ages ago pious disciples walked,
Warriors now, awakening from wounds and starry dreams.
O night, tender cornflower cluster.

O, you times of stillness and golden autumns,
When we peaceful monks pressed the purple grape;

And hill and forest shone round about us.
O, you hunts and castles; evening calm,
When in their chambers human beings contemplated justice,
Clamored in silent prayers encircling the living head of God.

O, the bitter hour of decline,
When we gaze on a stony image in black waters.
Yet, beaming, lovers raise their silvery eyelids:
One Geschlecht. Incense streams from pillows all roses,
And the sweet song of the resurrected.

Heidegger does not reproduce *this* hymn of resurrection in his "Placement." Yet he scrutinizes it in private, as it were, down to the two instances of the colon in it. (I swear I wish I could have written *colon* in French, or even German: *deux points,* two points, or *Doppelpunkt,* one double-point: the two single points that introduce *one* Geschlecht.) Heidegger scrutinizes the two instances of two points and the single known instance of italic or spaced type in Trakl's oeuvre: *one* italic, *one* Geschlecht. "It is, as far as I can see, the only word written in italics in Trakl's poetry" (US, 78). Heidegger's gesture "as far as I can see" is as modest as it is magisterial, his placement of Trakl's poem as preliminary and provisional as it is finalizing and apocalyptic. If he "scarcely dares" to name the locale of the place where Trakl's poesy as a whole dwells, he does not shy from the erection of yet another version of the propriative destiny of the West: the vertical rise of a new Geschlecht, the new dawn of a novel species of ek-sistent humanity, doubtless more mortal than ever mortal was mortal, yet no longer "fallen" and "accursed." The new humanity would occupy the very peak of the pyramid or "tip of the lance," *der Ort,* of history (US, 37). Strangely, the peak of the pyramid, the new spearhead of history, is something gentle, tender, and soft. Even more strangely, it is said to *flow,* as though it were an undulating *rhythm:*

This emphatic " *One* Geschlecht" conceals the tonic *[Grundton]* within which this poet's poem maintains its silence concerning the mystery. The unity of this *one* Geschlecht flows from *[entquillt]* the coinage that, rising from apartness, from the more soothing stillness that holds sway in it, from its "utterance of the forest," from its "measure and law," gathers by way of "the lunar paths of the one apart" the discord of the Geschlechter, gathering it in all simplicity to the more gentle twofold *[einfältig in die sanftere Zwie-falt versammelt].* (US, 78)

Heidegger scrutinizes this disingenuous gathering into a more gentle twofold. Concerning Trakl's " *One* Geschlecht" only *one* thing escapes him, I believe, the *one* thing that appears immediately before the second instance of the gathering by *deux points,* before the colon, and introduced by the particle "But," *Aber.*

First, let us note the matters Heidegger sees with perfect perspicacity, the things he never forgets:

> The " *one*" in the phrase " *One* Geschlecht" does not mean "one" instead of "two." Nor does the "one" mean the "they're all one and the same" of an insipid uniformity. The phrase " *One* Geschlecht" does not here indicate any biological findings at all, neither "monosexuality" nor "undifferentiation of sex." In the emphatic " *One* Geschlecht" lies concealed the unifying factor that unites from out of the gathering azure of the spiriting night. The word speaks in the context of the song in which the land of evening is sung. Accordingly, the word "Geschlecht" here retains the full multiplicity of its meanings, a multiplicity to which we have already alluded. (US, 78)

That is true: virtually the identical formulation concerning the multiple senses of the word *Geschlecht* appears twenty-eight pages earlier in Heidegger's "Placement" (at US, 50). As far as Geschlecht is concerned, nothing has changed during the long itinerary of "Language in the Poem." It is throughout a matter of the verticalization of Geschlecht into an event that marks the history and makes the destiny of the West; it is from start to finish a project that historicalizes Trakl's "poem," erects his *Geschlecht* into a *Geschichte.* Such verticalization departs from the apartness of Trakl's horizon, abandons the horizontality of Trakl's lovers; if Heidegger's reading is for an instant moonstruck, rapt to the voice of Sapphic σελάννα, it remains intent on brotherhood. However, let me continue the quotation:

> It [the word *Geschlecht*] designates, for one thing *[einmal],* the historical Geschlecht of man, humankind as opposed to other living things (plants and animals). Furthermore *[sodann],* the word *Geschlecht* designates the Geschlechter, the tribes, clans, and fami-

lies of his human Geschlecht. At the same time *[zugleich]*, the word *Geschlecht* everywhere *[überall]* designates the twofold of the Geschlechter. (US, 78)

The first time Heidegger refers to the plural *Geschlechter* in this passage, a plural that one is always prepared to translate as "the sexes," the apposition of "tribes, clans, and families" reinforces the decision to leave the German word untranslated. However, when the plural appears a second time, with no modifiers or appositions to qualify it, the translation of *Geschlechter* can only be "of the sexes." In this order or hierarchy of significations for *Geschlecht*, a hierarchy marked by the words *einmal, sodann, zugleich überall* ("for one thing," "furthermore," "at the same time everywhere"), the metaphysical *zugleich* or ἅμα asserts itself once again. Of all the Geschlechter, it is "the sexes" that remain the focal or nodal point: the convergence of "ontological difference, sexual difference," as the first of Derrida's *Geschlechter* indicates in its subtitle, is axiomatic.[18]

What Heidegger seems to forget in his grand history of forgottenness—although *seems* is the important word here, inasmuch as the attribution of forgetfulness is perhaps always a mark of one's own oblivion—is something that does come to appear in the texts of Trakl and even of Heidegger himself. It appears by disappearing, first of all in the *-schied-* of *Abgeschiedenheit*, the *-part-* of apartness. The imperfect verb *schied* ("parted") orders Heidegger's entire reading of "Autumnal Soul," the third stanza of which plays an important role in his "Placement":

> *Bald entgleitet Fisch und Wild.*
> *Blaue Seele, dunkles Wandern*
> *Schied uns bald von Lieben, Andern.*
> *Abend wechselt Sinn und Bild.* (T, 60; US, 49)

> Soon fish and game slip away.
> Azure soul, dark wandering
> Soon parted us from loved ones, others.
> Evening alters sense and image.

For Heidegger, the "others" constitute "the coinage of the decomposed configuration of man" (US, 49), the corrupted figure

---

18. Jacques Derrida, *Psyché: Inventions de l'autre* (Paris: Galilée, 1987), pp. 395–414; English translation in *Research in Phenomenology* 13 (1983): 65–83.

now ostensibly rejected and held at a distance for the sake of the
new Geschlecht. If these "others" are still "loved ones," if "love
and veneration nevertheless remain attached to them" (US, 50),
if, in other words, the apposition of alterity and love is undeniably affirmed in Trakl's line, then it is an embarrassment for Heidegger, and he is a little ashamed. What he desires is that the
stranger, Elis, (s)he of the lunar voice, be "the other with regard
to these others *[der Andere zu den Anderen]*" (US, 50), other than
those who are still loved but who are bound for a fall. Yet how is
one to be other to the others, especially if the ties still bind? How
is the "otherwise" of the new generation—even if like a crab it
could go backwards—to avoid all congenital contamination?
Unhappy dialectic! With Heidegger, the parting, split, separation, and scission have always already succeeded, apparently
without remainder or residue. Heidegger wants to exult. Unhappy jubilation! With Trakl, the others, the loved ones, remain
bound up with the others we are, inextricably *les-uns-les-autres,*
and also bound up with the poet himself. No passage to a brave
new race. "*One* Geschlecht."

What Heidegger seems to have forgotten appears in disappearing a second time, at the very end of "Western Song," immediately prior to the second instance of the colon, *deux points,*
or *Doppelpunkt.* This mark of punctuation, says Heidegger, encompasses "everything that follows," in this case the words "*One*
Geschlecht" (US, 78).[19] Here, immediately prior to the two

19. The colon, *Doppelpunkt,* or *deux points,* is clearly the cardinal mark of
punctuation for Heidegger. See his commentary on Stefan George's lines, *So
lernt ich traurig den verzicht: / Kein ding sei wo das wort gebricht,* in "Das Wort" (US,
222–23). There Heidegger distinguishes between the colon that merely introduces an assertion, opening up to some sort of statement, and the colon that
gathers up all that is to be said. In this second, essential instance, Heidegger says
of the colon that "the tone of the concluding verse gathers itself *[sammelt sich]* in
the word 'renunciation' *[verzicht],*" that is to say, in the word whose colon finally
gathers up the ultimate revelation of "Das Wort." Further, Heidegger expressly
concedes that the colon, as a mark of punctuation, is a characteristic of *writing*
rather than of speech (. . . *in der Schrift*): the colon marks the inevitable *writing*
of the saying of renunciation. Finally, the colon gathers nothing less than the
essence of language into the language of essence: in "Das Wort" Heidegger com-
ments at length on *Das Wesen der Sprache: [colon] Die Sprache des Wesens:* see US,
200–201 and 233. On this theme, see chap. 4, of Jeffrey L. Powell, "The Peculiar
Movement of Language in Aristotle, Hegel, and Heidegger," Ph.D. Dissertation,
DePaul University, 1993.

points that gather up and encompass *one* Geschlecht, are the words that a lunar reading will never fail to bring forward:

> *Aber strahlend heben die silbernen Lider die Liebenden:*
> *Ein Geschlecht.*

> Yet, beaming, lovers raise their silvery eyelids:
> *One* Geschlecht . . .

They are words that put a slightly different color on the matter of resurrection:

> *. . . Ein Geschlecht. Weihrauch strömt von rosigen Kissen*
> *Und der süße Gesang der Auferstandenen.*

> *One* Geschlecht. Incense streams from pillows all roses
> And the sweet song of the resurrected.

Lids of lovers, *two* silvery points, *one* Geschlecht. Beaming (s)he-lovers, sea-lovers, who breathe incense and speak with the voices of the moon: O my sister, the one I follow, the other I am: your hand in my mouth: your lips.

Part III

Blanchot

•

Kafka

•

García Márquez

5 "I, an Animal
of the Forest . . ."
Blanchot's Kafka

> She is like the sea, strong as the sea with its vast volume of
> water, and yet mistaken, tumbling down with all its strength
> when the dead and above all distant moon desires it.
>
> —Kafka to Milena Jesenská

> But Frank cannot live. Frank lacks the ability to live.
> Frank will never be healthy. He will soon die.
>
> —Milena Jesenská to Max Brod

It is odd that the Gallimard collection of Maurice Blanchot's essays on Franz Kafka, entitled *De Kafka à Kafka*, omits those pages
of *L'espace littéraire* that offer a reading of Kafka's *Der Bau*, "The
Burrow." For that tale, as read in *L'espace littéraire*, bristles with
one of Blanchot's most persistent and intense obsessions with
regard to Kafka. The present chapter will focus on the essays
contained in the Gallimard collection, especially the three most
recent essays, all of which deal with Kafka's life, especially his
love life—the engagements, the liaisons, the failures. I shall try
to relate what Blanchot calls "the feminine world" in Kafka with
Blanchot's own major themes as a critic, namely, the *narrative
voice* and the *neuter/neutral*. Even though the essays in *De Kafka
à Kafka* will serve as its principal source, my chapter will try to
keep in its peripheral vision "The Outside, the Night" of *L'espace littéraire*.[1]

---

1.   Maurice Blanchot, *De Kafka à Kafka* (Paris: Gallimard, 1981), cited in the
body of my text simply by page number within parentheses. See also Blanchot,
EL, esp. pp. 223–24, discussed at the end of the chapter. Since it will soon become apparent to the reader anyway, I had better note it at the outset: I am not
yet ready for a *thoughtful reading* of Blanchot: the backlog of Blanchotian texts,
texts which I have not read, does not cease to amaze me—the more I read the
more it grows. (I love hearing about those fabulous human beings who have
"read everything.") How then to *write* thoughtfully about Blanchot? *Captatio*   *117*

Most persistent and intense obsession? Which obsession is that? Among the many in Blanchot's relationship with Kafka—ambiguity, instability, solitude, the law, death, the narrative voice, the neuter/neutral, repetition, exteriority—the obsession depicted in one of Kafka's letters to Milena Jesenská, cited by Blanchot in "*L'échec de Milena,*" the obsession one might simply have to call by that mellifluous and precise name—*Milena* (165–66):

> It is something like this: I, an animal of the forest [*Waldtier*], was at that time barely in the forest; I lay somewhere in a muddy hollow (muddy only as a consequence of my being there, naturally); and then I saw you out there in the open, the most wonderful thing I'd ever seen; I forgot everything, forgot myself totally, I got up, came closer, anxious to be secure in this freedom that was new though familiar; I approached even closer, came to you, you were so good, I huddled near you, as though I had the right, I placed my face in your hand, I was so happy, so proud, so free, so powerful, so much at home; always and again it was this: so much at home—and yet, at bottom, I was only the animal, I'd always belonged to the forest alone, and if I was living here in the open it was only by your grace; without knowing it (because of course I had forgotten everything), I read my destiny in your eyes. It couldn't last. Even if you stroked me with your favoring hand, it was inevitable that you would observe my singularities, all of which bespoke the forest, this origin of mine, my real homeland; the necessary words ensued, about my "anxiety," necessarily they were repeated, about the anxiety that tormented me (as it did you, albeit innocently), until my nerves screeched; the realization grew in me, I saw more and more clearly what a sordid pest [*un-*

---

apart, this chapter is not what I had hoped it would be; it will not *situate* Blanchot's reading of Kafka in the larger contexts of their respective oeuvres. I am not prepared for either of these massive undertakings. Another time, perhaps.

The present chapter does try to do three things: (A) to give at least some sense of the scope of Blanchot's readings *of* and his persistent questions *to* Kafka; (B) to ask about Blanchot's Kafka with regard to what seems an obsessive preoccupation with the latter's "life," above all, his "loves"; (C) to reread Kafka's "*Der Bau,*" venturing to see in that tale—from Kafka's last year, the year also of "Josephine"—a figure of at least one of Blanchot's most peristent questions.

saubere Plage], what a clumsy obstacle I was for you in every re-
spect. . . . I recalled who I was; in your eyes I read the end of
illusion *[keine Täuschung mehr]*; I experienced the fright that is in
dreams (acting *[sich aufzuführen]* as though one were at home in
the place where one didn't belong), I had that fright in reality
itself; I had to return to the darkness I couldn't bear the sun any
longer, I was desperate, really, like a stray animal, I began to run
breathlessly; constantly the thought, "If only I could take her with
me!" and the counterthought, "Is it ever dark where she is?"
   You ask how I live: that is how I live.[2]

The Hades Complex? At all events, an obsessive return to
darkness. Yet without Persephone, in the absence of Milena. The
Orpheus Complex, perhaps? Orpheus pursuing the vanishing
Eurydice? In the myth of Orpheus, however, *Kafka* will always be
Eurydice; he will always be the first to return to the blackness of
darkness. Confusion of masks.
   Blanchot demands that we read Kafka's text as it was written—presumably, that is to say, in desperation. Or something
more than desperation. Rather, with an *intensity* (Hölderlin's
and Novalis's *Innigkeit*) that subsists beneath all the thresholds,
measures, and descriptions of desperation, in the throes of
which there can be no secure interval, no safe distance. The animal of the forest is not an *image* but a *life,* a life of exile from the
world and exclusion from the customary sources of hope. Must
one imagine the animal happy? Not necessarily. Blanchot cites
(167) a late note of Kafka's that contains the following phrases:
"silence, darkness, going underground, that is my way, I can
have no other." The upshot is that Kafka's very life is constituted
by "this subterranean menace": if the menace relents, "I too
cease." Most striking in the light of the two references to what
was "read" in Milena's eyes—a *destiny* that could not last and
hence the *end of illusion*—is Kafka's candid question at the end
of his cryptic remarks to Milena: "Wasn't it always there, from
the moment we met; would you have cast a fugitive glance in my
direction if it hadn't been there?"
   What sort of obsession possesses Blanchot? Blanchot is ob-

2. Franz Kafka, *Briefe an Milena*, expanded edition, ed. Jürgen Born and
Michael Müller (Frankfurt am Main: Fischer, 1986), pp. 262–63.

sessed with the relationship between Kafka's troubled confrontation with "the feminine world" and the seemingly sovereign
"narrative voice" of his fictions. That voice, while not triumphant, nevertheless transmutes all terror and trouble into la-
conic placidity: "You ask how I live: that is how I live."

Blanchot knows perfectly well how pointless it is to trace the
tortuous paths of Kafka's tortured betrothals and ephemeral liaisons with the world(s) of women; he knows how unreliable all
the accounts must be, especially those of the involved parties
(and all the parties are involved the moment passion seizes
them), Grete Bloch, Felice Bauer, the young Swiss woman in
Riga, the candystore girl, Milena, and—Franz. Nevertheless,
Blanchot devotes many of his later texts on Kafka precisely to
these tortuous paths or twisting tunnels: "*L'échec de Milena*"
(1954), "*Le dernier mot*" (1959), and "*Le tout dernier mot*" (1968).

Why should love affairs constitute the obsessive last word,
albeit an ironized, abashed, and constantly superseded last word
(244), for one whose sole obsession is writing? Perhaps because
they serve (in Kafka's case, but in his alone?) as the supreme
instances of the conflict or strife that prevails between *the law*
and *solitude,* or between *the shared word* and *silence.* Perhaps because such love relationships offer the writer at least some hope
that errancy in the desert, exile, and the surrender of every possible abode need not last forever. Perhaps because the most profound hopes, the most disarming illusions, the most alluring
temptations—that is to say, the best stories—reside there. Kafka
clutches at his engagements to his fiancées as at a last chance, a
final reprieve, a suspended death sentence; he also flings them
from him as the most dire contaminations, the most ignomini-
ous surrenders. Contamination with what? Surrender of what?
The contamination implied in all reconciliation with the world,
and the surrender of writing, which is the reason one must never
accept reconciliation.

Can Kafka really be convinced that marriage and his life as
a writer are in irremediable conflict? Or, more to the point, does
the writer's life necessitate conflict not only with marriage but
also with Milena? Does not the danger of massive self-deception
lurk here at every turn? Worse, does not the danger consist in
the fact that there are no turns at all, no discernible turns or
landmarks that would allow Kafka or anyone else to identify ei-

ther selves or deceptions? It is this, I believe, that fascinates and even obsesses Blanchot—the undeniable *factum* and *fatum* that a harmonious relationship between self and world, Hölderlin's dream, lies beyond all hope. It is this, I believe, that at a certain moment will cause Blanchot to be too abrupt, too impatient, even as he studies the ultimate patience of the narrative voice. Of course, *impatience* is in Blanchot's view both what Kafka fears most and what inevitably lies at the heart of all patience (EL, 234).

The institution of marriage—undergirded and circumscribed by the law—represents the more clearcut contamination and surrender, at least until Blanchot reminds us of Kafka's "debate with his father," his "dependence on his [paternal/maternal] family," and his failure to shine at those "virile tasks" that the world assigns him; and until Kafka himself confesses his compulsion to vomit at the sight of his parents' "conjugal bed," his nausea in the face of their bedclothes and nightshirts. To vomit, that is to say, "to drag my entire insides to the outside," a phrase that speaks the very dialect of the forest animal. The sight of these domestic evidences and embodiments of the law convinces Kafka that he too is tied to "these repugnant things" from which he would flee; yet, as in a nightmare, he cannot run away from the nausea, his feet are stuck in the "amorphous gruel of origins" (120). Thus the institution of marriage does not merely serve as an instance of the law; marriage, as connubiality, retains sordid traces of the natural order of love, ardor, and languor.[3]

Of his encounter with the nameless candystore girl, Kafka remembers only his sense of relief that it was not "*even more* abominable, *even* dirtier" (161). A "slight odor," a whiff of peppery sulphur, a "bad smell," "a trace of sulphur, a touch of hell" (162). And, somehow opposed to all that (for is it not possible that matters are quite different? that it is the love relationship that is tainted by marriage, and not the other way around?), the miracle of Milena: the electric storm of passion, where pepper delights and nausea is far. Yet Milena is already married, and Franz is already engaged, for the third time now; never mind

---

3. Hegel too was horrified and haunted by the thought of such a tainting; it is a scene of one his most violent dialectical (nondialectical?) repressions. See Krell, "Lucinde's Shame," *passim.*

that her marriage is troubled, and that his engagement will be a brief one. Never mind that Milena and Franz are outlaws, *vogelfrei,* free as birds, and as vulnerable. Never mind, because there are always obstacles enough to foil all the chances of a forest animal. Milena is young, she is Christian, she is willing to entertain and sustain a subterfuge in order to arrange the meetings, she is jealous, and she and Franz share friends who relish romantic intrigue. Misunderstandings abound. "Fewer of them would have sufficed," notes Blanchot, "for Kafka to become aware once again of the destiny that makes him an animal of the forest, foreign to the life of the world" (159). An animal as terrified of the electric storm as of the doldrums of domesticity.

The miracle of Milena does not avail. Not for him, not for her. Stories in our time, histories in this century, even love stories and histories of love, have denouements that no fiction would or could ever permit itself. Let the story (as history) come to a close now, at the outset: Milena grants to passion all its rights and privileges, she knows her desire and actively pursues it, she is inventive and focused and free enough to overcome all the obstacles; Franz meets her with passion, but also with "the intransigence of despair, the force of solitude, the ferocious desire to impose silence and to withdraw into silence" (Blanchot's words, 159); no, not even letters, letters torment; the lovers see one another again briefly in Prague; on June 3, 1924, Kafka dies; then, almost exactly two decades later, on May 11, 1944, Milena, at forty-seven years of age, dies of kidney failure in the concentration camp for political prisoners at Ravensbrück. Her husband was Jewish, her friends leftists, herself fiercely independent.[4]

---

4. Why do Kafka's biographers and the editors of Kafka's letters, who are very informative about Milena's relationship with Kafka, which was apparently unparalleled, say absolutely nothing about Milena Jesenská's life (and death) after 1924? Is hers the fate of all lovers? Or merely the fate of all unequal partners? Or the fate, precisely, of all *equal* partners? Or is it only a particular fate, a mere contingency, without relevance for the literary event we call "Kafka"? Would it not take a Kafka—not the event, the writer—to address these questions (on the oblique, to be sure), to write something about the silence that shrouds Milena's later life and death? For a corrective, and a stirring experience in biography, see Margarete Buber-Neumann, *Kafkas Freundin Milena* (München: Gotthold Müller Verlag, 1963), passim; translated under the (misleading) title, *Mistress to Kafka: The Life and Death of Milena* (London: Secker & Warburg, 1966).

The Feminine World and Literary Ambiguity

"Very ambiguous." Such are Kafka's relations with "the feminine world." "Very ambiguous"? What are the sites of *ambiguity* in Blanchot's essays on Kafka? Ambiguity of *language* in each of its parts but also in general; ambiguity of *literature,* which works and plays with the ambiguity of language ("In literature ambiguity is, as it were, delivered over to its excesses by the facilities it finds, and exhausted by the extent of the abuses it is able to commit" [57]); ambiguity of the *world* in general, in ways Maurice Merleau-Ponty was able to express incomparably well; ambiguity, in short, in all its seductive power. At the end (but only at the end, and only briefly) of "Literature and the Right to Death," Blanchot invokes Kafka's "struggle with women, which ends in bed." In bed? Ends? Perhaps. Yet perhaps also in a burrow or cave, and from the beginning, as the ambiguous case may be.

In the early essay, "Reading Kafka," Blanchot declares the word *ambiguity* insufficient to express the dilemma or malaise that every reading of Kafka confronts: "Ambiguity is a subterfuge that seizes upon truth in the manner of slippage *[glissement],* passage" (67).[5] In "The Wooden Bridge" (1964), Blanchot finds his way to a kind of hyperambiguity, as it were, an emptying-out of meaning so radical that there is neither an "interior" nor an "exterior" for the very emptying—Kafka's *Das Schloß* is "in possession of the principle of all ambiguity and of ambiguity as principle (ambiguity: the difference of the identical, the nonidentity of the same), the principle of every language and of the infinite passage from one language to another" (198). If, however, as Max Brod and Klaus Wagenbach insist, *Das Schloß* riddles on the failure that is called "Milena," one is perhaps justified in persisting with the question of ambiguity vis-à-vis "the feminine world."[6]

5. One is reminded of Derrida's doubts concerning "ambiguity" in *Of Grammatology,* these too highly reminiscent of Merleau-Ponty, if only by way of negation. See Jacques Derrida, *De la grammatologie* (Paris: Minuit, 1967), pp. 103–4; translated by Gayatri Chakravorty Spivak as *Of Grammatology* (Baltimore: Johns Hopkins University Press, 1974), p. 71.

6. Klaus Wagenbach, *Kafka* (Reinbek bei Hamburg: Rowohlt, 1964), pp. 123–35.

What has Kafka's rapport with the feminine world, his "very ambiguous" rapport, to do with the ambiguity and instability of language and literature? To trace in their own right the concepts or motifs of instability, of death as the possible impossibility and impossible possibility of human existence, of exteriority, the neuter/neutral, the other, the night, is no doubt a necessary task, but an arduous and demanding one. For the moment, let me persist with that ambiguous rapport of "the feminine world" and writing. Let me try to read "the forest animal" as it is written, not as an image or metaphor of Kafka's menaced, ambiguous life, but as a kind of reeking animal apparition: less Trakl's "blue game" than Ted Hughes's fox, albeit reduced in size, power, and slyness.

Not *altogether* reduced, however. Not wholly mousey and moley, not simply the victim, and not entirely without a taste for cruelty and torture (164). Kafka describes himself writing, that is, writes of himself writing, as "intrepid, nude, powerful, surprising" (81). "I am unhappy," writes the writer—who happily proceeds to unfold the entire world of unhappiness in his or her effervescent text. "You ask how I live: that is how I live."

Let us not call it literary mastery or know-how. Let us call it, with Kafka, a constantly surprising and powerfully intrepid nocturnal and therefore perhaps lunar nudity. At all events, not always the sibilant whistle of the performing mouse, Josephine, not always "research into the animal whimper."[7] At times a horrid and squalid metamorphosis; at other times an evolution from simian to urbane naturalist and philosopher; the first a terrifying secret, the second a success that one might report to an academy of science. In the present instance, in the letter to Milena from the forest animal, singularities that bespeak the forest: anxiety and torment, muddy hollow and pestilence, and the eventual return to darkness.

I shall try to read these moments of the letter to Milena in

---

7. Kafka's words, cited by Blanchot at 218. Paul Davies informs me of the importance of the animal's voice, the lizard's voice, the *other* voice that rises to disturb *Le dernier homme* (Paris: Gallimard, 1957), p. 113: "... *la voix est faible, grêle comme un crissement de lézard . . . a quelque chose d'animal, de trop physique. Imperceptible, elle nous ébranle. Bien qu'elle soit comme rituelle, l'entendre est une inquiétude, une sublime surprise.*" One should also heed the animal voices of *Thomas l'obscur* and *La folie du jour*, Paul Davies informs me. Another time, perhaps.

an admittedly desperate way—simply by retracing those places in the margins of my copy of *De Kafka à Kafka* where I took up my pencil and wrote the words *Der Bau,* as though that were commentary enough. I shall begin with the "preface" to the collection, "Literature and the Right to Death," [8] and then proceed through the articles, declining to order and catalogue these apparitions of the forest animal—sometimes reeking of sulphur, or of something more penetrating than sulphur, sometimes exuding but the faintest whiff—hoping that the cumulative effect of these marginalia will succeed where analytical animal husbandry fails. Succeed at what? At rendering more palpable the possible relations between the successes of Kafka's writing and the failure given the name *Milena*—but why given *this* name? *whose* failure is it? Is the genitive subjective or objective, or both? And what *sort* of failure are we talking about? [9]

The Animal Kingdom of the Writer

In the *Philosophy of Right,* Hegel is highly protective of the writer and the writer's spiritual production, that is, of literary (preferably philosophical) work. If he looks askance at fiction and the novel, especially Friedrich Schlegel's *Lucinde,* it is because the writer's work is so *geistreich,* so scintillating with ironic *esprit* that it threatens to outshine the more sober product of spirit's patient labor, which happens to coincide with Hegel's own. Blanchot makes no reference to the *Philosophy of Right* or the *Lectures on Aesthetics,* and this is regrettable inasmuch as "Literature and the Right to Death" has Hegel's *Phenomenology of Spirit* as its regnant genius, and like any tale of spirit, Hegel's *Phenomenology* stands in need of repetitions. Be that as it may, here it cannot be a question of evaluating Blanchot's reading of the *Phenomenology*—something he begs the reader in any case not to do

8. By what right can this text be called a "preface" to the "collection"? Even granting the problematic character, the outside/inside, of all prefaces? The text scarcely mentions Kafka. At least, the role that Kafka plays in "Inspiration," in EL, seems far more profound than the role he plays in the earlier essay here selected as a "preface."

9. Derrida shows just how dangerous the accusation of *échec* or failure is with regard to Georges Bataille's "*L'échec de Genet.*" See *Glas,* pp. 245–49; English translation, pp. 218–22.

(14n)—nor even of summarizing it adequately; here it can only be a matter of highlighting the relevance of certain themes in the *Phenomenology* for a forest animal.

According to Blanchot's Hegel, Hegel the phenomenologist, the writer condemns himself or herself to spirit's "animal kingdom," *au regne animal de l'esprit* (14). The writer is at best the slave or bondsman par excellence: although his or her labor depends on innate gifts (they are almost animal instincts, these writerly instincts) and on a consciousness of the goal to be attained in the work, it is only the actual labor *(travail, Arbeit)* that tells the tale. In a sense, the writer has talent only after he or she has written—and only *each time* the writing has actually occurred. The writer is subjected to the indignity of chasing after the prey of words as they unfold in time and irrupt into space. Thus it seems that the most spiritual of productions, the plenitude of spirit unfurling the proud banner of its life in letters, is like "a nothing" working (in) the nothing (15). The writer is not the beautiful soul, the effete soul, but the toiling creature whose precarious survival is in question: the law of the most ennobling spiritual production—bestowal of the Word, mimetic of divine creation—is the law of the jungle. Whoever dreams of abandoning the travail and tribulation of art and craft in order by some magic to become Rimbaud—or, for that matter, Schiller—"remains nonetheless, in the silence, someone who is incapable" (78). Failed as a writer, dead as a dog.

Nothing should be more surprising than this writerly animal kingdom and its law of the jungle, the Terror of freedom-for-all by means of death-to-each. Eve's Adam names the animals and thus completes the work of divine life and love. Yet (and here Blanchot stresses Kojève's implacable reading of Hegel's 1803–4 sketches toward a system of philosophy) to bestow the name is to slay the animal. Language bestows meaning precisely through assassination of the thing named (36–37). Blanchot might also have mentioned the 1808 *Propaedeutics*,[10] for which proper naming is the slaying *(ertöten)* of the images that have been captured in sensibility or intuitive feeling. Cognition depends on naming,

---

10. G. W. F. Hegel, *Texte zur Philosophischen Propädeutik,* from the "Nürnberger Schriften" (1808 and ff.), in *Werke in zwanzig Bänden,* "Theorie Werkausgabe" (Frankfurt am Main: Suhrkamp, 1970), vol. 4, pp. 9–302.

naming is iconoclastic, and the shattered paradigmatic icon is animal and vegetable *life*.

Here one is tempted to advance immediately and ever deeper into the Blanchotian labyrinth: the signature of my own name is the guarantor of my sense but also of my death;[11] the words and names of language are relics of the night, or of a day somewhere behind or beneath broad daylight, relics of the day as a fatality—what Blanchot will elsewhere call the *other* night (44); the word is scarcely detached from its "underground milieu" (42); it is as though bits of earth clung to its fur like an "inexorable affirmation," the residues that Merleau-Ponty struggled to identify as anonymous existence, generality, and the elemental; as though those grains of earth—*Mulm*, as the German language says, designating the powdery earth that the mole or *Maulwurf, talpa europaea,* tosses up in mounds at regular intervals—were material monuments of material words, words of a language that is "a thing that is eaten and that eats, devours, gluts itself and reconstitutes itself in the vain effort to turn itself into nothing" (51). Let me steer clear of the Blanchotian labyrinth, if I can. Let me merely mention the animal cited by Blanchot as an example of Adamic naming—naming as bestowal of meaning, appropriation, and assassination. Blanchot writes, "When I say, 'This woman' . . ." (36–37). Strange animal. Yet it is not so strange that she is named.

Language is the mystery of Hegelian spirit, inasmuch as spirit lives by confronting death: *la vie qui porte la mort et se maintient en elle.* Blanchot repeats Hegel's phrase (51 and 60; cf. PdG, 29)[12] without coming to terms with the *sich erhalten,* that is, the problematic *maintenance* that would arise from the *vain effort* of language. To be sure, it has to do with the possible impossibility and impossible possibility of death, that same labyrinth. Let me skirt it again by asking the obvious and too impatient question: What has all this to do with Kafka?

---

11. *De Kafka à Kafka,* p. 37. Is this the source, or one of the sources, of Derrida's seventh and final chapter of *La voix et le phénomène* (Paris: Presses Universitaires de France, 1967)? See esp. pp. 105–8. Translated by David B. Allison as *Speech and Phenomena* (Evanston, Illinois: Northwestern University Press, 1973), pp. 94–97. And the source of the many works in which Derrida meditates on *signature* and *seing?*

12. That is, Hegel, *Phänomenologie des Geistes,* p. 29.

Blanchot reminds us of Kafka's obsession with metamorphosis, itself a latter-day variation on the Cabalistic and Gnostic
theme of metempsychosis—the curse of being reborn in the
form of an(other) animal, say, an insect. Or a mole, which devours insects. Or that mole of the brine, a fish, as Plato's *Timaeus*
tells us, "at the bottom of the muddy sea." (There are some
blessed-accursed places where the Hellenic, Hebraic, and Christian traditions imbricate to indistinguishability, as though repeating one another, narrating the same mortifying tale, in
which integral greekjewchristian is integral christianjewgreek:
are these places always sites of supreme negativity vis-à-vis "the
feminine world"?) The errant ways of metempsychotics—
halfliving, halfdead—are depicted horrifyingly in Blanchot's
text (53), which in effect (and this effect is what Blanchot has in
common with Kafka) never skirts the labyrinth in which it
ever errs:

> Man enters into the night, yet night leads to the waking day; and
> there he is, vermin. Or perhaps man dies, whereas in reality he
> lives; he goes from city to city, borne on rivers, recognized by
> some, helped by none, the error of his past death sniggering at
> his bedside; it is a strange condition, he forgot to die. Yet another
> one believes he is alive, having forgotten his death; while another,
> knowing he is dead, struggles in vain to die; death? it is over there,
> the grand castle one cannot attain; and life? it was over there,
> one's native land, which one abandoned, following a deceptive
> call; now there is nothing left but struggle, the labor to die com-
> pletely, although to struggle is still to live; and everything that ap-
> proaches the goal renders the goal impossible.

The forest animal entertains this unstable, troubled relation
to its own life and its (im)possible death. Whether its death is
experienced as impending or as belonging to an irretrievable
past; whether the Heideggerian possible impossibility or the
Levinasian-Wahlian impossible possibility more aptly characterizes that animal's stance toward its own demise; whether the
ownmost, nonrelational, certain and yet indeterminate, impass-
able end of life or the unending pressure of the *il y a* depicts
Kafka's nightmare more accurately—these questions cannot de-
tain us here. Another time, perhaps. Instead, I want to insist ob-

stinately and blindly on the question of the relation between writerly death (or mortal writing) and the strange animal we saw Blanchot identify a moment ago as *cette femme*. Or the question of that strange animal's "world."

Solitude, Silence, and the Sister

In "Reading Kafka" (1943? 1945?), the oldest piece in the collection *De Kafka à Kafka*, Blanchot identifies the "two poles" of Kafka's meditation and oscillation: solitude and silence (the marks of the writer), on the one hand, and the law and the shared word (the "world" and the "man" Franz Kafka), on the other. No act of understanding or program of praxis will synthesize the two poles or flatten Kafka's experience to a single plane. As well try to understand the goal and purpose of the labor of the woodlouse: should one even pose the question of its meaning, the entire population of woodlice would be exterminated at one blow. Such is the anxiety that every reading of Kafka has to confront—every reading of these fragments and accomplished shards of texts. One might think of "The Burrow," the final pages of which (according to the chagrined editors) "went missing," when reading these lines of Blanchot's earliest text on Kafka (68–69):

> Kafka's major tales are fragments; his work as a whole is a fragment. This lack could explain the incertitude that renders the form and content of our reading of them unstable, without altering their tendency. Yet this lack is not accidental. It is incorporated in the very meaning it mutilates; it coincides with the representation of an absence that is neither tolerated nor rejected. The pages we read possess the most extreme plenitude; they announce a work with respect to which nothing is in default; furthermore, Kafka's literary production as a whole is given in its minute unfoldings, unfoldings that are interrupted brusquely as though there were nothing more to say. They lack nothing, not even the lack that is their object: it is not a lacuna, it is the sign of an impossibility present everywhere yet never admitted—the impossibility of a shared existence *[l'existence commune]*, the impossibility of solitude, the impossibility of holding to these very impossibilities.

"The torment of language is what it lacks by the necessity of being this very lack. It cannot even name it" (41). The impossibility of finishing with death and dying, of ending the day, of finalizing the meanings of things; the impossibility of being anything but survivors in a sanctuary that can never be refused but is never guaranteed, a refuge as secure as a penitentiary: these account for Kafka's hesitation in the face of birth rather than death. Blanchot cites it more than once: "My life, and my hesitation in the face of birth." The most terrible thing about "*Die Metamorphose,*" writes Blanchot, is the wave of voluptuousness that passes through its final page in the figure of Gregor Samsa's younger sister, Grete. What is most shocking is the young woman's (and, vicariously, her parents') will to live (". . . their ever more vivacious daughter . . . blossomed into a beautiful, buxom girl . . . to seek out a wonderful husband for her . . . she stretched her young body . . . [*"ihrer immer lebhafter werdenden Tochter . . . zu einem schönen und üppigen Mädchen aufgeblüht . . . einen braven Mann für sie zu suchen . . . ihren jungen Körper dehnte;"]*), a will perhaps reminiscent of the will of J. in Blanchot's own "*Arrêt de mort.*" The younger sister hesitating on the threshold of life, not yet surrendering to deformation, death, and decomposition, is perhaps Kafka's own sister, Ottla, whom Blanchot invokes on the final page of "The Altogether Last Word" (244); Ottla, whom the writer "prefers" to his lovers and fiancées; Ottla, who was, as it were, the writer's sister, mother, spouse, and lover—and well-nigh his Siamese twin.

In order to assist in thinking through Kafka's hesitation, and in order ourselves to hesitate on this side of the threshold of psychoanalytic categories and stratagems, one might also contemplate once again the sounds and soundings *(tönen)* of Georg Trakl's Grete, (and of) the poet's lunar sister. For it seems that Trakl shares Kafka's both enviable and execrable position in literature and life—*désastre absolu* (73), star-crossed, star-fallen, and star-cursed:

An die Schwester

Wo du gehst wird Herbst und Abend,
Blaues Wild, das unter Bäumen tönt,
Einsamer Weiher am Abend.

Leise der Flug der Vögel tönt,
Die Schwermut über deinen Augenbogen.
Dein schmales Lächeln tönt.

Gott hat deine Liber verbogen.
Sterne suchen nachts, Karfreitagskind,
Deinen Stirnenbogen.

To My Sister

Wherever you go it is autumn and evening,
Blue game sounding under the trees,
Lonely weir at eventide.

The flight of birds sounds softly,
The melancholy above your eyebrows.
Your narrow smile sounds.

God put the curve into your eyelids.
At night, Good Friday's child, stars seek
The curve of your brow.

The catastrophe and disaster in Kafka's case are so complete, writes Blanchot, that a minuscule margin encapsulates them: one cannot know whether that margin is a reservoir of hope or the final setting-off and sealing-off of hope forever. Kafka's work scintillates with the *vain effort* (again those words) to extinguish itself. That we have the work at all—the Kafkan corpus—depends partly on the betrayal of Kafka's wishes by a friend and partly on the lack of total efficiency on the part of the Gestapo. These external accidents seem to import something into the corpus itself, they seem to be represented in the work after the fact, as it were. Hence the anxiety of *reading* the work: ". . . and our reading turns anxiously about a misunderstanding" (74).

It is odd that it should be this earliest text on Kafka, "Reading Kafka," which puts us in closest touch with the very last word on him (1968), the word in closest touch with Milena. Should reading be as shattering as love? Reading should be as shattering as love.

The Narrative Voice

"Kafka and Literature" spotlights the animal once again; no, not *this* animal, the *other* one, the animal of the forest. "Intrepid, nude, powerful, surprising—which I normally am only when I am writing" (Kafka's words, cited at 81). Kafka rises on the afflatus of writing, from the misery of the "I" to the glorious *world* of misery in the third person singular, "he." From the depths of such writing, Blanchot does not hesitate to say, "surges the magnificence of life" (84). The incommensurable distance, the interval, the torsion toward infinity, the engagement in irresponsibility, the effort (not a vain effort, not in either sense) to write well—these themes could no doubt sustain the question of woman and writing and intensify the ambiguity it is pursuing.

Yet would it be possible, perhaps even necessary—or merely altogether dishonest and indiscreet—to demand, parallel to the shift from "I" to "he," a shift from "I" to "she"? Would it be possible to demand such a thing without an examination of the writer's generic, gender, and genital credentials? Not in the besotted hope that one can be and write everything, and with whatever hand one chooses, but in the sense that it may be important for both writing and living to try for more, and always to go for choreographies of many more than two, as Derrida says, both for writerly and survivorly reasons? "*Il est compromis,*" Blanchot says of the writer who lives; yet so is she, she who writes and who lives. "*C'est sa fatalité*" (78). Granted the fatality, one should perhaps seek the best positions, the eu-topia of the always-more-than-two, and let the mockers sneer "Utopia."

"Kafka and the Exigency of the Work," originally published in *L'espace littéraire,* elaborates the Cabalistic theme of metempsychosis as transmutation into the animal, and the less hallowed theme of the "gruel of origins," the nausea of the parental-conjugal bed mentioned earlier. The exigency of the work is in each case exile, the desert as the sole promised land, "the very bosom of dispersion" (112). The double-bind of patience and impatience in the preparation and elaboration of the work, the dilemma of figuration and idolatry, is no doubt crucial to the writer's anomalous position, and perhaps even to the failure that bears the name *Milena.* That such a figure—the figure of Milena—should present itself outside and beyond all labor, while Pygmalion is not at work but on a stroll; that such a figure, a figure herself intrepid nude nocturnal lunar powerful surprising, should loom prior to any moralizing iconoclasm, prior to any encryptment in tabernacle or codex or commentary, prior to all groveling before a capital-I Infinity; that she should walk and talk and approach and incline or recline or decline, that she should wistfully accept or passionately initiate love, in order there to co-constitute unspeakable joys terrors woes without patient elaboration, without rewrites, or sometimes with, sometimes without, unpredictably, as though she were the writer's *Einfall*, a windfall of great good luck, a chance so far outside the realm of plausibility that it cannot even be sought but only vaguely, albeit intensely, desired. As a writer, Kafka is capable of masterful strokes. Yet he imposes a discipline on himself, a minute labor in filigrain, "a slowness of approach, a precision of detail," very much visible in the exitings and enterings of "The Burrow." In that narrative, inside and outside prove to be equally treacherous and hence strangely identical or absolutely undecidable. That is tantamount to saying that for the artist there is no *chez-soi*, no command center of minute and confident control, no foyer of great good luck. "For him there exists only the outside, the stirrings *[ruissellement]* of the eternal outside" (131). The writer literally leaves *nothing* to chance—the nothing that is his or her sole element and only *modus vivendi*, a nothing working (on) the nothing.

"The Narrative Voice," however, is what we must now go to hear, inasmuch as the forces of life suffice only up to a certain point. "The forces of life suffice only up to a certain point." Blanchot begins with the sense of fatigue, reminiscent of Levinas's account of fatigue in *From Existence to the Existent*.[13] Life is limited by fatigue, yet is also expanded by language, which seems to draw every limit into its ken precisely by granting the limit a meaning. If the statement concerning life's forces comes at the end of a text, it seems to encircle life; yet the circle is undecidably within/without life, sustaining an altogether strange relationship with life. The tale or *récit* "would be like a circle that neutralizes life, which does not mean that it is devoid of relation to life, but that it relates itself to life by means of a neuter/neutral rapport" (172). Within the circle and circuitry of the tale, all given meaning is in *retrait*, both redrawn and withdrawn

13. Emmanuel Levinas, *De l'existence à l'existant* (Paris: Fontaine, 1947; 3d ed., Librairie Vrin, 1984), passim; English translation by Alphonso Lingis, *Existence and Existents* (The Hague: Martinus Nijhoff, 1978).

"by a distance in which all meaning and all lack of meaning are neutralized ahead of time." Not simply by authorial intrusion, whether didactic (Thomas Mann, *Doktor Faustus*) or ironic (Thomas Mann, *Der Zauberberg*); but by a shadow flitting behind every personage and event of a tale, by a feeling the reader has—Blanchot describes it deftly—that the hidden center of the tale lies *outside* the circle's circumference.[14] The problem for the philosopher would be that the distance instituted within the circle, the circuit of the tale or the narrative, is actually the distance opened up within language as such, and not only in poetry and fiction. The word *neutre* expresses the limit-situation of language itself, which would also be the situated limitation of language. Limit and limitation—a certain fatigue and a certain eccentricity—are the adumbrations of *le neutre* (173).

The third-person singular pronoun would in fact be the mark not of the masculine but of the neuter/neutral. Blanchot identifies it as the *il,* although his discussion tries to fend off any immediate reduction of it to either the third person (masculine) singular, *il aime,* or the impersonal, *il faut aimer;* to either "he weeps," *il pleure,* or "it is raining," *il pleut, es regnet, es gibt, es ist,* and so on. Blanchot does not here remark upon the (apparent? virtual?) gender specificity of the *il,* or upon the (apparent? virtual?) absence of the feminine and all plurals from it. Perhaps he does not need to. For neither person nor impersonality corresponds to the kind of distance that opens up in the neuter/neutral relation. "The narrative *il* [he/it] is the destitution of every subject, and the disappropriation of all transitive action or of all objective possibility" (180).

Blanchot identifies two forms of such destitution and disappropriation: first, the words of a narration somehow betray the fact that *no one is telling* the tale—the tale *parle au neutre;* second, those who speak or act in the tale, its "characters" or "personages," are not perfectly self-identical; it is as though, no matter how perfectly drawn they are, they were all amnesiacs. "It is the

14. Which is why Schelling too, and not only Hegel, would have to fear every work of fiction as a λογισμῷ τινι νόθῳ (*Timaeus,* 52b 2), "bastard reasoning" or "false imagination," as Schelling says, translating Ficino's *adulterina ratione*—for all of this implies the centrifugal motion of *evil.* See Krell, "The Crisis of Reason in the Nineteenth Century," pp. 13–32; and Krell, *Daimon Life,* chap. 9.

tale *[récit]*, independently of its content, that is a forgetting *[oubli]*: to recount a tale is to put oneself to the test of this pre-mier forgetting that precedes, founds, and ruins all memory" (181). Telling the tale—or, rather, *No one's* telling it, as the blinded Polyphemus cries out his tale of woe at the lip of his cave—is the very torment of language, its perpetual detour, its excess and shortfall, which in chapter 2 was called *hyperbollipsis*.

Even if it should endure as a kind of memento or monu-ment, writing is the architecture of contingency and residue. In the final lines of "Kafka and Literature," lines that speak of the monument, Blanchot gives the perfect model for what Derrida has recently called "the perverse reading of Heidegger." In the present instance, it is a perverse reading of the monumental function of the *temple* in Heidegger's "Origin of the Work of Art." [15] Kafka's art too raises a temple or a pyramid, elaborates a structure (*Bau*) of some kind, "but on each stone we find en-graved a sacrilegious inscription so deeply incised that the sac-rilege will last longer and become more sacred than the temple itself" (93). That is the deeper (that is to say, more perverse) reading of Keats's "Ozymandias," marking the endurance of inscribed transiency; it is the perhaps only slightly more per-verse reading of Yeats's "Under Ben Bulben"; it is the quite natural reading of Hölderlin's accounts of Empedoclean *nefas* or sacrilege.

Such is writing, and such is (its oblique, parenthetical rela-tion to) life. "To write—this relation to life, a relation diverted *[détourné]* in such a way that it affirms what does not concern it" (181). A statement that one would like to read alongside Freud's *Beyond the Pleasure Principle* and Heidegger's *Being and Time:* writ-ing as the very detour of life on its way (back) to an earlier state, a "how" of being that is called the death drive, writing as the undecidable limit-situation between *Sorge* and *Besorgen*, "care" and "concern," the undecidable mode of Dasein as *appropriately* inappropriate, already fallen into the "scribble" of *Geschreibe* yet always still falling, even as it is writing its fundamental ontolo-

15. For the perverse reading of Heidegger, see Jacques Derrida, *De l'esprit,* p. 153n; English translation, p. 134. For the temple in Heidegger, see the second part of *Der Ursprung des Kunstwerkes*, pp. 41–43; English translation in *Basic Writings*, 2d ed., pp. 167–69.

gies, a Dasein that can die only because, like all other forms of life, it is *alive* in its writing. Another time, perhaps.[16]

The neuter/neutral marks the invasion of the *other* into all discourse, the other neither as *autrui* nor as *l'Autre;* the other, not as personalized by an existential psychoanalysis or capitalized by an ethics of ethics, but as something even more recalcitrant to discourse. The *ne-uter* is precisely neither the one *nor the other* (201). It is, Blanchot writes, "aphonic." A statement one would like to read with Levinas *(Autrement qu'être)* and Derrida *(La voix et le phénomène)*, but also with Plato's *Philebus.* And, above all, with the large and small a's of LAcan. Another time, perhaps.

So far it has been a matter of the *il.* Yet something changes as Blanchot focuses on the voice, *la voix narrative* (though not *narratrice,* as he emphasizes; 181). The narrative voice is neuter/neutral, and yet she begins to resound strangely in Blanchot's own text from this point on.[17] Allow me to abandon Freud, Lacan, Heidegger, Levinas, and Plato for the frivolity of hearing her. (In English it is more than a frivolity—it is a perversion of the tongue. Precisely for this reason it proves impossible to abandon Derrida: it is a central perversion for *La carte postale,* in which one of the "she's" and "her's" so intensely desired and loved to distraction is assuredly *la voix.* And she is also at the very center of "The Law of Genre.") Yet one cannot even lipread such a perversion in the English language, where perversions, for even the most cunning of linguists, are harder to come by.[18]

16. Nor can I here elaborate the compelling remarks on the *neutre* and its alliance with night and with life in Blanchot, *Le pas au-delà* (Paris: Gallimard, 1973), pp. 101–107. (My thanks to Paul Davies for this and other references—reserved for that *other* time, perhaps.)

17. *De Kafka à Kafka,* pp. 182–84: ". . . *elle ne dit rien . . . elle n'ajoute rien . . . elle ne sait rien . . . elle sous-tend ce rien . . . ainsi ne s'entend-elle pas . . . elle ne s'y dissipe pas non plus . . . ,*" etc. etc.

18. See Derrida, *La carte postale: De Socrate à Freud et au-delà* (Paris: Aubier-Flammarion, 1980), pp. 15, 52, 84, 91, 121, 215 etc.; translated by Alan Bass as *The Post Card: From Socrates to Freud and Beyond* (Chicago: University of Chicago Press, 1987). But see esp. Derrida, "La loi du genre," in *Parages* (Paris: Galilée, 1986), pp. 249–87. Here Derrida juxtaposes the *il* and the *elle* as though juxtaposition were sufficient to engender a discourse of the neuter/neutral (284). Yet his own text shows that both the narrative voice and the law of genre are feminine in senses that transcend (or open a quasi-transcendental pocket for) the grammatical, the generic, and the genital; that the move from *je* to *nous* involves a touching of knees (*genoux*), genuflection, and an eccentricity. When the masculine genre

The narrative voice (182–84) is "radically exterior" to the
tale being recounted; it cannot be incarnated in the tale; it can
only be a voice that is "borrowed" from one or other of the characters (even if only tacitly, covertly, by ruse or strategem, so that
it *still* seems as though *no one* is telling the tale) or (if the narra-
tor is omniscient)[19] mediated by the ensemble of characters; it,
the voice, *la voix,* she "is always different from that which prof-
fers it, she is the indifferent difference that alters the personal
voice"; she is "spectral, phantom-like," self-effacing; she is in
withdrawal, not from beyond the tomb, but always, like Eurydice, reentering the tomb; by no means "central," the narrative voice is somehow always peripheral, always tasting and testing the limit, torquing and distending it, so that any possible
center is displaced; she deprives the text of any privileged foyer,
even if the hearth or place of reception and welcome (the χώρα,
in one of Timaeus' earliest descriptions of it: ὑποδοχή, δεχόμε-
νον) should be lack-of-focus, *afocalité;* she is therefore, we might
add, very like the *Venus vaga* that Hegel needs to localize (that
is, to cancel and preserve not in dialectic but in formaldehyde)
as Antigone, Antigone at home in the tomb; in short, the eccentric, nomadic narrative voice prevents the tale from "existing"
as something "achieved" and "accomplished."[20]

---

paints its self-portrait, the result is as follows: "I am [or follow: *Je suis*] woman,
the beautiful woman, my daughter the law is crazy about me *[folle de moi].* I speculate on my daughter. My daughter is crazy about me, that's the law" (286).
A curious neuter/neutral, to be sure: not a sterile outcome, but an engender-
ing configuration. See also Derrida's remarks in "*Survivre,*" also in *Parages,*
pp. 150–51. Derrida here effectively protects Blanchot from the more vulgar
forms of the question I have posed here concerning the (putatively) masculine
gender of the neuter/neutral *il.* For it would be easy at this point to engage
oneself to a polemic that has by now become familiar, indeed, has become a
regular member of the patriarchal family—Blanchot silences the *elle,* grants her
no voice, etc. Yet even if one should eschew all polemic, I nevertheless have a
worry that may or may not be worth voicing: I am uncertain about it, inasmuch
as both Blanchot and Derrida may already be far beyond such a worry. In which
case I only ask them to slow down, to come back, for my sake, and for hers.
   19.   Thanks to Geoff Bennington, belatedly, omnisciently.
   20.   This is true, we might add, even of a tale that seems fully accomplished,
rounded-off, and perfectly wrought—I think of Edith Wharton's "Roman Fever,"
or Flannery O'Connor's "A Good Man Is Hard to Find." These tales have their
jarring, disconcerting effect, the very disbelief or shock they induce, in the either
utterly calm or unspeakably violent withdrawal of the narrative voice in them. I

Blanchot offers three further characterizations of the narrative voice, which we might summarize as follows:

1. To speak in the neuter/neutral narrative voice "is to speak at a distance, preserving this distance, without *mediation* or *community*"; the distance is without symmetry or reciprocity of any kind; "(one cannot neutralize the neuter/neutral)."

2. Neuter/neutral speech neither reveals nor conceals; it stands outside the ontologies of the visible-invisible and of revealing-concealing.

3. Its speech is not attributive, not even enunciatory: to tell the tale, to write, is "to attract language into a possibility of saying that would be telling—without saying being and yet without denying it either *[une possibilité de dire qui dirait sans dire l'être et sans non plus le dénier]*" (184).[21]

Herself unheard, not understood even if and when heard, *inentendue,* the narrative voice gives us to understand, *donner à entendre.* Listening *out* for her, we believe we are listening *to* her; we tend to confuse her with "the oblique voice" of unhappiness or lunacy *(malheur, folie).* Of all animals, she is no doubt the strangest. Doubtless, she fascinates (in) Kafka.

An Incarnation Openly Bearing Its Emptiness

Let me now—not hearing, not understanding the narrative voice—skip blithely across Blanchot's "Wooden Bridge," which spans the emptiness at the heart of an inherently eccentric narration. Let me also avoid "The Last Word," which invokes the

---

believe this could be made palpable in a reading of these two short stories, so different from one another and from the tales of Kafka, where we are perhaps more "prepared for" absencing, withdrawal, and the tacit. Another time, perhaps.

21. One might well wish to challenge each of these characterizations from within the ontological framework of Maurice Merleau-Ponty's *Le visible et l'invisible,* ed. Claude Lefort (Paris: Gallimard, 1964), chap. 4, or the discourse of Heidegger's *Seinsfrage.* Whether brute being can be said without reference to beings; whether a discourse can invoke the elemental or the granting of time and being, whether it can venture the names *flesh* or *propriation*—none of these possibilities should be peremptorily excluded. There are no doubt resources in Heidegger's "The Way to Language" and Merleau-Ponty's "The Intertwining—the Chiasm" that Blanchot's abrupt denials concerning the neuter/neutral—influenced perhaps by Levinas—cannot ignore. Another time, perhaps.

solitude of the writer's mousehole, as well as the vanity and concupiscence of all the writer's constructions. Let me try to bring
these marginal cumulations of mine to a culmination by turning to "The Altogether Last Word," where she returns—she,
elle—both as the unheard narrative voice and as another kind of
absence, silence, withdrawal—call it what she wills. The altogether last word ironizes itself, simulating and dissimulating the
ultimate word on Kafka: especially in questions of "biography,"
and, in biography, questions of "love affairs," that is to say, affairs of passion and the pen, who would risk the altogether final
word? Only those who have never had the pleasure. Nor will
there be a final word on the writer's awesome, cavernous cellar
(226), which Kafka portrays in his letter to Felice Bauer, dated
January 15, 1913:

> One cannot be sufficiently alone when writing; . . . never enough
> silence around oneself when writing; the night itself is still too
> little night. . . . Often I've thought that the best way for me to live
> would be to set myself up—with my writing materials and a
> lamp—in the innermost space of a vast, sealed cellar. They would
> bring me something to eat, but always leave it far from the place
> to which I keep, outside the cellar's most exterior portal. My sole
> promenade would be to fetch my nourishment, dressed in my
> bathrobe, passing beneath all the vaults of the cellar. Then I
> would return to my table, eat slowly and punctiliously, whereupon
> I would immediately begin writing again.[22]

Nor will there be any altogether last word on the conflict between life and writing—now in Blanchot's own words:

> Writing, living: how could one abide the confrontation of pre-
> cisely these two words that are so poorly defined? Writing destroys
> life, preserves life, spurs life, ignores life—and vice versa. In the
> end writing has no relation to life unless it be by the necessary
> insecurity that writing receives from life, just as life receives it

22. Blanchot's ellipsis after the phrase "still too little night . . ." (226) omits
a phrase of some interest in the present context. Kafka compares the temptation
to flee the writing table (if I understand the passage well—it is not free of ambiguity) to the desire to return, *zurückzulaufen*, ". . . as though, quite by chance,
one were kissed by the mouth of one's best beloved! *[wie erst, wenn man unver-
sehens einen Kuß vom liebsten Mund bekäme!]*." See Franz Kafka, *Briefe an Felice*,
ed. Erich Heller and Jürgen Born (Frankfurt am Main: Fischer, 1976), p. 250.

from writing: an absence of rapport, such that what is written *[écri-ture]*, however much it gathers itself in dispersing itself, never re-lates itself to itself but to what is *other than* it, what ruins it or, worse, drives it off course. Kafka serves his apprenticeship with this *other than*—the other in the neuter/neutral *[l'autre au neu-tre]*—that pertains to writing. (228–29)

Yet in Blanchot's patient exposition of the (impossible) final word on the rapport between (love-)life and writing, there comes a moment when he writes perhaps too abruptly. Indeed, there seems to be a moment of thoughtlessness here. Impossible accusation! One looks for ways out: perhaps it is *Kafka's* thought-lessness, perhaps Blanchot has been ventriloquized by a Kafka who is in retreat, frantic, with no time left for thought. Yet this is not a promising escape either for Kafka or for ourselves. Thoughtlessness in either Kafka or Blanchot? Abruptness in two of the most painstaking writers and paragons of patience? The abruptness or thoughtlessness seems (to me) to occur in the very first point of Blanchot's seven-point analysis in "The Alto-gether Last Word," an analysis to which, admittedly, I cannot do justice here. Blanchot begins by characterizing the affirmative side of Kafka's "entry into relation with the feminine world" (220). Each time such entry occurs there is "a sort of grace, light-ness, a seducing and seductive temptation." "Even if difficulties arise very quickly" (221). Blanchot enters into those difficulties very cautiously. In this instance, they are difficulties with Felice Bauer, who, like the others, represents for Kafka a possible "chance to live," a chance to be "reconciled with the world" (222–23). By virtue of what? Not by any positive trait of hers, as far as one can discern, but by an "absence of trace," by a "non-culpability" which, while not "innocence," promises something in its very vacuity. Blanchot cites Kafka's first journal entry on Felice Bauer: "Miss F. B., . . . a bony and empty face openly bear-ing its emptiness" (223). Emptiness, "not as a trait of insignifi-cance, but as the discovery of an enigmatic possibility," adds Blanchot. The word *emptiness* enables Kafka to feel a presenti-ment—we are coming to the peremptory judgment or prejudg-ment, the moment of apparent abruptness or thoughtlessness—a presentiment of the attraction exerted "by a default that is like an absence of fault," like an " 'outside the fault' of which the feminine world incarnates the evidence."

What in the "feminine world" "incarnates the evidence" of either the "fault" or the " 'outside the fault' "? Why the parataxis of "feminine" and "fault," which perdures as a (neuter/neutral?) residue even after the "outside" is spoken? Blanchot quickly avows that we are not here confronting the familiar "naive Christian terror before the seductions of the flesh," yet he just as quickly footnotes Kafka's letter to Milena, which recounts with "implacable frankness" his first night of love—and peppery sulphur.

We must backtrack and read Blanchot's passage more patiently. It speaks of a fault *in default,* of an evidence utterly obscure, of an incarnation of phantom concealment. To repeat: the words *empty* and *emptiness* enable Kafka to sense an attraction incarnated in Felice Bauer, the attraction "of a default that is like the absence of a fault, this 'outside the fault' of which the feminine world incarnates the evidence [*cet attrait d'un défaut qui est comme l'absence de faute, cet 'en dehors de la faute' dont le monde féminin incarne l'évidence . . . :* '*dont*'? of *what* which? of the *fault?* of the *outside* the fault?], but also, by its presence [*mais, aussi, par sa présence . . . :* presence of what? of the evidence? of the feminine world? of the fault? of the 'outside the fault'?], already the equivocal separation *[déjà la séparation équivoque]."*

Equivocal indeed. Does the *dont* refer only to the word immediately preceding or to the entire phase within quotation marks? Are the quotation marks of "*en dehors de la faute*" sufficient to guarantee the "solidarity" of the *dont (don? dent? coup de?)?* What, in short, does the feminine world incarnate? Does it incarnate evidence of the fault or of the yon side of fault, the beyond or outside the fault—nonculpability, if not innocence? Whatever the case (and the case is ambiguous, very ambiguous, not only in Kafka, it seems, but in Blanchot as well), the remainder of the passage leaves the whole in inexpugnable ambiguity. "But, also": *mais, aussi:* already the equivocal separation, separation in its very presence as having always already occurred: *déjà.* Separation of what from what, in the presence of what to what? What is incarnation, such that it should incarnate either fault or absence of fault?

The next sentence confirms that it is the world, "the feminine world," that is under discussion. The world that the writer (normally? always? omnipotently?) institutes, the world that removes any asseveration—e.g., "I am unhappy"—from the *ich* to the *er,* or perhaps to the *es,* or beyond all these to the neuter/ neutral; at all events, from the wretched ego to the *world* of unhappiness. The oblique voice of unhappiness or lunacy, often confused with the silent narrative voice, here ostensibly narrates something about "the feminine world." Yet narrates it from what sort of distance or proximity, and in which sort of world? In what sort of neuter/neutrality? Off center, to be sure, inasmuch as the limit-experience of narration distends the circumference of language as such; yet how disconcertingly off-center? And in what region of the circle, world, or life? Is there only *one* sort of neuter/neutral? Is *she* the one and only? She—bearing her incarnate emptiness openly?

"From this world come in effect all temptations (which, however, need not be understood in the naive Christian sense, as seductions of the flesh, although there too, as we know, Kafka had his difficulties)." *En effet,* all temptations arise from or within "the feminine world." Temptations not to be taken in the "naive Christian sense," to be sure, as incarnations of the flesh. Should one be able here to distinguish between or among Jewish and/or pagan profundity and Christian naiveté? Has Nietzsche's genealogy of the ascetic ideal merely by some prejudice or oversight confused two or more readily distinguishable traditions? (There are some blessed-accursed places where the Hellenic, Hebraic, and Christian traditions imbricate to indistinguishability, as though repeating one another, narrating the same mortifying tale, in which integral greekjewchristian is integral christianjewgreek: are these places always sites of supreme negativity vis-à-vis "the feminine world"?) *En effet,* we are confronting a very specific temptation—or is it a very general one, a temptation that encompasses all temptations?

It is far rather the temptation of a life that attracts him because it seems at this strange point to remain foreign to culpability *[parce qu'elle semble à ce point étrange qu'elle reste étrangère à la culpabilité],* but in such a way that the attraction immediately makes the one who submits to it forever culpable by turning him away from himself *[mais telle que l'attrait fait aussitôt de celui qui le subit à jamais un coupable en le détournant de lui-même]*, subjected from now on to the deceptiveness of the detour and spoken for by the enchantment of oblivion *[voué désormais à la tromperie du détour et promis à l'enchantement de l'oublie]*. (223)

"Spoken for" by enchantment, "betrothed" to oblivion, "promised" in the sense that an adolescent girl is promised—is a young *man* ever promised or spoken for, in any of the traditions we might call "Western," whether Hellenic, Hebraic, Christian, or secular?—and thus bartered away, "alienated" in the sense of chattel released to foreign hands as the ultimate investment in, of, and for exogamy? The writer as bartered bride? As the source of *all* temptations, *in effect?* For example, the temptation of detour, which Freud's *Beyond* locates within the economy of life-death? But to continue the Blanchot passage: ". . . the enchantment of oblivion: this will be one of the meanings of *The Trial* and, also in part, of *The Castle*, both works written under the provocation of feminine foreignness *[sous la provocation de l'étrangeté féminine]*."

Perhaps we are being invited to think that the withdrawal to the innermost vault of a cavernous cellar and the emergence (in bathrobe) only in order to snatch nourishment back to the writing/eating table (elsewhere Kafka speaks of his desire to bite fast into his table so that he will never have to abandon it) have more to do with the enchantments of oblivion than with anything touching or touched by Milena. Perhaps we are being invited to think that *writing* is the detour—elsewhere, as we noted earlier, Blanchot explicitly calls it that. Which then is the diversion—the feminine world or writing, writing or living? Writing/living: they do not confront one another but engage in a ringdance of indeterminacy. Or is such indeterminacy the very incorrigible self-deception that would fascinate, even obsess, any writer? Detoured, diverted from the *writing self,* hence culpable; as though the writer possessed such a centered thing as a self, a self to be protected from the oblivion of other selves; a self diverted by and toward the strange figure that seems foreign to culpability. By virtue of what? Its vacuity. Its open bearing of and toward its own incarnate emptiness. Its candid bearing of its bony skull. Its being in default—as Heidegger says of *being* during the epoch of nihilism, *das Ausbleiben des Seins*.

Yet in the present instance *she* is in default. Of what? Of the fault incarnate? The fault incarnated in the feminine world? Or is she herself perhaps—ambiguity prevailing to the last—*default* incarnate? Is hers the lunar voice that can never be clearly heard, but also the voice that never allows the writer to ascend to a heaven of perfectly present ideas and ideals? Is hers the *engorged* voice? Is hers the turning-in of flesh, the turning-into flesh of an absence? Perhaps she herself is a cellar or cave, which Hegel calls the pristine interiority of sidereal Earth, the first involution of spirit in nature. A cave at whose innermost point, that strangest, least habitable point, someone writes. From Socrates to Kafka. From Kafka to Derrida and Irigaray. From Kafka to Kafka.[23]

Why "abrupt" or "peremptory"? Why "thoughtless"? Because Blanchot allows the memory of sulphur to evanesce in phrases that try to ward off Christian naiveté. Because the sight of pajamas and bedclothes that occasions Kafka's nausea is not held in queasy memory. Because "the feminine world" is invoked quite quickly and yet related still too reluctantly to the world of the neuter/neutral, the world beyond the *es* and the capital *Es* alike. Because the mystery of incarnation, fault, and default are invoked too automatically, too . . . naively Christianly, one might almost have said.

Or have I merely forgotten to remember "*la faute essentielle*" located in "Kafka and the Exigency of the Work" (124–31; EL, 91–98), the fault of figuration, impatience, and idolatry? For here Blanchot is careful to grant psychoanalysis its rights (not that analysis will wait upon any acknowledgement of its rights—the Church Militant never waits): "In this regard, the debate with the father remains essential, and all the new notes of the *Journal* confirm it, showing that Kafka dissimulates nothing of that which psychoanalysis could have revealed to him" (120). In short, it will not do to issue a few grammatical or ana-

23. See Luce Irigaray, "Le *hystéra* de Platon," in *Speculum de l'autre femme* (Paris: Minuit, 1974), pp. 299–457; English translation by Gillian C. Gill, *Speculum of the Other Woman* (Ithaca: Cornell University Press, 1985); and Jacques Derrida, "Envois," in *La carte postale*, pp. 5–273; English translation, pp. 1–256.

lytic pronouncements and close the file on Franz. Or on Milena. Or on Maurice.

Had I more space, time, and courage, I would pay more and better heed to pungent sulphur, gruel, vomit, mud, and moss. Elements of, on, or beneath the writer's earth, elements that cling to words as lint or talc or moonstain, incarnate elements that can never be neutralized. (Nor is it ever a matter of neutralizing *words* in Blanchot's meditation: for the very element of words, what clings to words and draws them out of work, "is" the *neutre.*) Perhaps the very distance, silence, absence, and withdrawal of the neuter/neutral narrative voice has to do with these elements that make us squeamish and/or lubricious. Irigaray would call them *mucous.*

Yet why, of all the elements, Dante's sulphur? Why the element that reeks of symbolism more than sulphur?

Why not the reek of fox?

Why not the taste of ozone in the electric storm of passion?

Why not, remote from the soursick stench of vomit, the sweet feast of a liquidity that gives as much as it takes?

Questions to Blanchot, perhaps. Yet, more likely, questions *de Kafka à Kafka.*

The Burrow

If "The Gaze of Orpheus" is the eccentric center that gathers—by desire—the fragmentary writing of *L'espace littéraire* as a whole, "The Outside, the Night" conducts us to the threshold of that eccentricity. It is here that Blanchot reads Kafka's "The Burrow." These are pages that ought to have been the self-displacing center or at least the "preface" of the compilation *From Kafka to Kafka.*

"The Outside, the Night" is the first section of chapter five of *L'espace littéraire,* entitled "Inspiration." (The second section of that chapter, as mentioned, is "The Gaze of Orpheus.") "The Outside, the Night" broaches the question of that *other* night which is more than the boundary of the day. In the bounded night, the "first" night, one confronts the possibility of oblivion and death; the *other* night "is the death that one does not find, the oblivion that forgets itself [. . . in] remembering without rest" (EL, 216). It is the unexpected gesture of death—Tolstoy's

Brekhounov "lying down on Nikita" in a gesture of death so intensely animal that it cannot be vulgar, a mortal gesture of tears and desire. In one of his most remarkable pronouncements concerning this night beyond all bounded nights and days, Blanchot says that we descry the *other* night "as a love that shatters all ties, a love that wants the end and that unites with the abyss" (EL, 222–23). What Blanchot does not go on to write (a sense of shame being no doubt vital to all writing) is the abyssal relation of such passionate love to polymorphous narratives: mysticisms of lips and members; murders by and of jealous husbands, wives, and lovers; mutual telepathies and terrors; the clichés of every vapid lovesong ever written experienced now as truths of a metaphysics gone physical at last; litanies of bodies that never knew what they were for or what they were about or what they could do; the stuff of fictions emitted by novel writing instruments in a world suddenly deprived of verticality and measure but granted a horizontality broader than any horizon and deeper than any abyss.

One possible path from the first night, the bounded night that belongs to the day, to the *other* night, appears in a seldom discussed note in one of Nietzsche's notebooks. It is the very notebook that contains his most important fragments on eternal return, the notebook we will examine more closely in the following, the concluding chapter. Whether Blanchot knows of this note concerning the night I do not know, but I interrupt this exposition of *De Kafka à Kafka* in order to present an excerpt from it. It appears as note 11 [260] (KSA 9, 539–40), dated Spring-Fall 1881:

> There is one part of the night about which I say, "Here time ceases!" After all these moments of nocturnal wakefulness, especially on journeys or walks, one has a marvelous feeling with regard to this stretch of time: it was always much too brief or far too long, our sense of time suffers some anomaly. It may be that in our waking hours we must pay recompense for the fact that we usually spend this time lost in the chaotic tides of dreamlife! Enough of that. At night between 1 and 3, we no longer have the clock in our heads. It seems to me that this is what the ancients expressed in the words *intempestiva nocte* and ἀωρονυκτί (Aeschylus), "in the night, where there is no time . . ."

Blanchot seeks the time of the *other* night. He comes close to finding it in Kafka's *Der Bau*, "The Burrow." To be sure, Blanchot cites "The Burrow" as an instance of the discovery of the "first" night, the binding and bounded night, rather than of the liberating, and perhaps *spiriting, other* night. Yet such a discovery is no mean achievement, and one night soon leads to another beyond or beneath all nights:

> To advance through this first night, however, is not a simple movement. It is the sort of movement evoked by Kafka's toiling beast in "The Burrow." One constructs solid defenses against the world above, but is exposed to insecurity from below. One edifies after the manner of the day, but is underground; what is erected caves in, and what rises bottoms out. The more the burrow appears to be solidly closed to the outside, the greater the danger that one will be locked in with the outside, will be delivered over to danger without end; and precisely when every foreign menace seems to have been excluded from this perfectly contained intimacy, the intimacy itself becomes the menacing foreignness, and the essential danger announces itself.[24]

By advancing through the bounded night, Kafka's burrower eventually breaches or at least broaches that *other* night which fascinates Blanchot. It is the night of the *other animal,* whose hissing or rustling sound is scarcely distinguishable from the subterranean silence. What the burrower hears is the sound of its imminent immanent absence, the perpetual ringing in the ears that is the unperceived horizon of all hearing, the hearing not of *Da-sein* but of *Fort-sein,* in the sense of Derrida's "Fors," the encrypted outside of an incorporated yet alienated desire.[25] Or what Heidegger in his *Contributions to Philosophy* calls *Weg-sein,* a being begone, a being bygone (*65,* 301–2). In the final pages of

24. EL, 223. For a commentary on Kafka's "The Burrow" that follows Blanchot's lead—but more explicitly the work of Gilles Deleuze and Félix Guattari, *Kafka: Pour une littérature mineure* (Paris: Seuil, 1975)—see Henry Sussman, "The All-Embracing Metaphor: Reflections on Kafka's 'The Burrow,'" *Glyph* I (1977): 100–131.

25. Jacques Derrida, "Fors," the Preface to Nicolas Abraham and Maria Torok, *Cryptonomie: Le verbier de l'Homme au loups* (Paris: Aubier-Flammarion, 1976; translated by Nicholas Rand as *The Wolf Man's Magic Word: A Cryptonomy;* Minneapolis: University of Minnesota Press, 1987), passim.

Kafka's tale, pages that are lost forever even if they never were written to be ever lost, the transition to the *other* night will always have occurred.

> The *other* night is always other, and the one who understands it becomes other; whoever goes to join it distances himself from himself, is no longer the one who goes to join it, but the one who diverts himself from it, the one who turns this way and that. Whoever searches intrepidly for the most profound limit of the first night, once having entered it, whoever tries to go toward the essential, at a certain moment understands the *other* night, understands himself, hears the eternally reverberant echo of his own advance, his advance toward silence; yet the echo returns him to himself as the murmur of the immense void, and the void is now a presence that rises to meet him. (EL, 224)

To construct the burrow of protective solitude is "to open the night to the *other* night" (EL, 225). Such is the night of Orpheus singing, desirous of Eurydice, gazing toward what will ultimately withdraw from him into the *other* night. What remains of the writer's inspiration and his travail is failure, *l'échec* (EL, 231). Perhaps the failure is given the name *Milena* only by way of indirection, diversion, and evasion. It is a failure that no patience can ever remedy, inasmuch as the heart of the most profound patience, to repeat, is and must be impatience (EL, 234). Yet the failing night is also the night of *Eurydice's* gaze, turning slowly toward the Orphic singer, refusing to turn back, feeling her body advancing, rising, falling, saying *yes* and doing *yes*. Eurydice now equally patient and impatient. With Orpheus now equally in withdrawal, uncertain, diverted, out of work, neutralized, spirited away. Confusion of marks. Confusion of masks. Confusion of moss.

The Moss

Two last words. Namely, *desire* and *exteriority*.

Desire. In "*L'échec de Milena*," that untranslatable title, with its unattributable genitive, two pages prior to the emergence there of the forest animal (163), Blanchot writes of Kafka's writing as a pact or alliance struck with "the danger of the night: 'abandonment to obscure forces,' 'unchaining of powers habitually held on edge *[en lisière]* at the forest's seam, on the rim of the domain of the forest animal,' 'impure embraces *[étreintes impures]*'—all this is in play when one writes." More concupiscence than vanity, unless vanity is the concupiscence of all asceticisms. (How are we to think, experience, and feel what our traditions still call *concupiscentia,* which is another name— perhaps the oldest—for the site of supreme negativity? How heed the *gift* without insisting on the poison, the silent and mysterious donation bestowed as if by magic, "but a magic that is essentially impure," the magic to which Kafka is committed, as "a privileged means of health.") Blanchot adds, altogether cryptically: "Perhaps it is the same in the case of desire." *Peut-être en est-il de même du désir.* Pollution as the grand health of which Nietzsche dreams, "health in small doses," as he says, the health that derives from "the closest things"? How would such thinking narrate itself—the thinking of desire and of impure magic as a privileged means of health? It would narrate itself while hovering in the moss outside the burrow—hovering in exteriority.

Exteriority. On the final page of "The Altogether Last Word" (244), Blanchot designates "this space *outside,*" this space *of* the outside (*du* dehors), this "radical exteriority," as Kafka's essential space, the space of the writer. His back to the wall of the deepest vault, farthest inside, the creature of the cellar can nevertheless only reside outside. Blanchot calls such radical exteriority *aorgic,* borrowing Hölderlin's word from the theoretical texts surrounding *Der Tod des Empedokles* (discussed above in Part I). "Aorgic" is that which resists the formative, organizing power of reason and even imagination, whether false or true. It is enough for the moment if we recall the troglodyte who must occupy the outside, the spelunker who advances to the outermost limit, the mossy lip of the cave or opening of the tunnel. The forest animal, barely in the forest, pacing its edge or lying there in a muddy hollow—muddy because of *his* presence, not because of the presence of "the feminine world," unless he too should *be* that world, be an essential *part* of that world—tasting and testing the freedom of the outside, very much at home, yet ultimately recoiling and returning to the forest that claims him as his true homeland (as the "masculine world"?), experiencing *himself* as a sordid pest, a plague, shuddering in the fright of dreams, acting as though he were at home in a place where he has no right to be, unable to bear the sun, fleeing alone into the dark, seeking in the writer's solitude and in the neuter/neutral narrative a life that would be intrepid nude powerful surprising. What is he writing there, this animal of the forest? From whom to whom?

•

— *There at that spot in the dark moss I am mortal. . . . As is unfortunately so often the case, caution itself demands the risk to life.*

—If it comes to that, I can match you, mortality for mortality. Look for me in the darkling moss, my love. Be cautious. But do risk it.

— *I live in peace in the innermost interiority of my house, and all the while the enemy tunnels its way slowly and silently from somewhere anywhere toward me. . . . I have never seen them as yet, but the sagas tell of them, and I firmly believe in them. They are creatures of the inner earth; not even the saga can describe them. . . . Here it cannot be said that one is in one's own house; rather, one is in their house.*

—I too firmly believe in them. I am afraid. Let me watch with you, deep in the forest where no one will see us. You have hollowed out your burrow, built your *Bau*. You have constructed and deconstructed your structure at once. I know something of these innermost interiorities of the inner earth: the sagas confuse and conflate me with those places.

— *Your house is protected, closed off in itself. You live in peace, warm, well nourished, lord, lord of a multiplicity of passageways and places; hopefully you will not sacrifice all this; yet if you merely surrender it to a certain extent, you may surely be confident that you can win it back again; but will you go for it? will you play a game in which the stakes are so high, so very high? You have reasonable grounds for doing so? No, for something like that there are no reasonable grounds. Still, I lift the trapdoor quite cautiously and am outside; I let the trapdoor drop and I dash from the treacherous spot as fast as I can.*

—Slow down! Slow down! How will you know when you are free? Are we in the clear yet? In the thicket? Or still in the dark? Which side of the door have you been listening from, the inside or the outside? Can you tell which side of the world you are on now? Tell me what you see, let me help you to decipher. I'll keep my ears open for you.

— *Then too I am not made for life in the open, I am not exposed to it. I know that my time is measured, that I need not be dashing endlessly here, that instead, when I wish it and am weary of my life here, someone will call to me, as it were, issuing an invitation I will not be able to withstand.*

—Come come!

— *It went to such lengths that I sometimes experienced the childish wish not to return to my burrow at all, but to settle down here near the entrance, to spend my life observing the entrance, retaining before my mind's eye—and finding in this my happiness—the thought of how secure my burrow could make me if I were in it.*

—No one can be more childish than you—unless it is I. Or less secure. A hollow near the entrance would be perfect, that is all I ask. Let us meet there. It needn't last forever, it needn't be for time without end.

— *I throw myself intentionally into the briar in order to punish myself, punish myself for the sake of a guilt that escapes me.*

—No not the bramblebush yes the mud yes and the moss.

— *It need not be a genuine enemy whose lust to pursue me I excite; it could as easily be some minor paragon of innocence, any little old repulsive creature that is on my heels out of curiosity; thereby, unwittingly, she becomes the leader of the world against me; that need not be the case either, but perhaps it is, and that is no less pernicious than the other, in many respects it is the most pernicious—*

—Why is *she* the leader? Why *Führerin?* Why a world of enemies in *her* train? Perhaps they are only after *her,* always and always only after *her?*

— *It is relatively easy to trust someone when one is keeping an eye on them, or at least can do so; it is perhaps even possible to trust someone from a distance; but from inside the burrow, that is to say, from out of another world, to trust someone fully who is on the outside, that, I believe is impossible. . . . I can only trust myself and the burrow.*

—Close your eyes. There. We can see nothing now. Trust me.

— *Always within my burrow I have endless time—*

—You trust your eviscerated structure and your bloodless

eternity more than me? Come out with me. For you never really let the hinged trapdoor fall, we are both still only on the verge of the outside. Why do you start so?

— *A hissing, scarcely audible in itself, wakes me. . . . It is sometimes like a hissing, but sometimes like a whistling.*

—It is the rustling of the leaves and layers of me. Don't be afraid.

— *Yet perhaps (this thought too creeps up on me) here it is a matter of an animal as yet unknown to me. . . . Implacably it hisses there, hisses from afar. . . . Someone is coming!*

—Are you afraid *for* me? Is that it? Are you afraid of what will become of me? Wait. Wait. Yes, I too can hear it now.

— *Perhaps I am in a strange burrow, I thought, and its occupant is now tunneling toward me.*

—Are they coming for me already, then? Yes? Then tell me when it is all over, tell me when all has changed. When will it all change? Has everything changed? Has anything changed? Has nothing changed?

— *The hissing sound remains the same, nothing has changed.*

— *Yet all remained unchanged.*——

—Aber alles blieb unverändert.——

6 Lunar Solitudes

The Eternal Return of Gabriel García Márquez

— *Tambien hoy es lunes.*
—Today too is Moonday.

It is still an unbearable contradiction, an unresolvable anomaly: the notebook that contains Nietzsche's first sketches toward the thought of "the eternal return of the same," his thought of thoughts, the thought for whose sake he wanted to be remembered, also contains a series of notes excoriating the fundamentally illusory notion of "the same."[1] Yet if the same notebook both celebrates and vilifies "the same," then the vaunted "return" of the same "same" is also cast in doubt. Further, if "eternity" is one of those thoughts against which we must always be "on guard," as Nietzsche says in both *The Gay Science* and notebook M III 1, then the "eternal return" of the "same" seems more a boondoggle than a boon, more a temptation than a thought, more a taciturn and sterile moon than a buzzing and fecund sun.

Add to this the further problem that for Nietzsche the ring of eternity is forged in and as the *instant* of our existence: if the ring of eternal return is forged at each point of its vast circumference, does everything always—or nothing ever—recur? Is

---

1. Nietzsche, KSA 9, 441–575. Among the most important passages on eternal return of the same, *die ewige Wiederkunft des Gleichen,* are these: 11 [141, 148, 152, 163, 197, 269, 318, 339]. Among the most strident criticisms of the eminently metaphysical notion of sameness or identity, *des Gleichen,* are these: 11 [138 ("Our *memory* depends on our seeing things as the *same* and taking them to be the same . . ."), 166, 202, 231–33, 237, 245, 254, 268, 293, 321. I wonder whether *any* interpretation of Nietzsche's "doctrine" of eternal return has paid heed to this textual anomaly? Perhaps the most demanding task for a sustained inquiry into Nietzsche's principal thought is the apparently straightforward preliminary task of *reading* M III 1 with meticulous care. See the eighth chapter, entitled "Eternal Recurrence—Of the Same?" in D. F. Krell, *Infectious Nietzsche,* forthcoming.

eternal return, as Derrida somewhere writes, nothing other than the unending return of nonreturn?

The Buendía family of Gabriel García Márquez's Macondo knows about these sorts of puzzles, even if Nietzsche never appears by name in those parchments of Melquíades that tell the Buendía story; the reader of *One Hundred Years of Solitude* knows about them too, as the eternal parade of Arcadios and Aurelianos passes by in motley review—generation gliding into generation and figure fading into figure—up to the final words of the parchments and the novel: " . . . and that everything written on them was unrepeatable forever and for always, because lineages condemned to one hundred years of solitude did not have a second opportunity on earth" (351/422).[2] Gabriel García Márquez elaborates the darker truth of eternal return—that its eternity is an undying mortality, and that mortality is the condition of receiving no second chance. The one hundred years of *One Hundred Years of Solitude* may be flexible, inasmuch as Úrsula and Pilar Ternera live well beyond the century mark. Yet the solitude of *One Hundred Years of Solitude* is adamantine, however many its facets and varieties. In the following reflections I would like to isolate two pairs of solitudes—those of love and rancor, on the one hand, and those of reading and writing, on the other—the solitudes (shades of Blanchot's Kafka) to which our several one hundred years of solitude condemn us severally. However, I shall introduce the solitudes by looking in some detail at the predicament of eternal return—the incessant return of no possible return, and the ending that never comes to an end—in the novel.

Eternal Recurrence? of the Same?

"Today too is *lunes*," mutters José Arcadio Buendía on the very verge of his pellucid madness. Soon the family will bind him to the chestnut tree in the courtyard. Soon the ghost of Prudencio Aguilar will touch his shoulder in an intermediate room of the infinite chain of the mirrored rooms of death, the intermediate

---

2. Gabriel García Márquez, *Cien años de soledad* (Buenos Aires: Editorial Sudamericana, 1967); translated by Gregory Rabassa as *One Hundred Years of Solitude* (New York: Harper & Row; and London: Jonathan Cape, 1970). I will cite the Spanish edition first, then the translation, in parentheses in the body of my text. On rare occasions, I depart slightly from Rabassa's rendering.

room where José Arcadio Buendía will stay forever, "thinking that it was the real room" (124/143). Yet the patriarch of Macondo, patron of the Gypsies and prophet of scientific lore, will tarry for years in the undecidable time of sameness and difference, the time of solitary madness. José Arcadio Buendía enters his son Aureliano's workshop and asks him what day it is.

> Aureliano told him that it was Tuesday. "I was thinking the same thing," José Arcadio Buendía said, "but suddenly I realized that it's still Monday, like yesterday. Look at the sky, look at the walls, look at the begonias. Today is Monday too." Used to his manias, Aureliano paid no attention to him. On the next day, Wednesday, José Arcadio Buendía went back to the workshop. "This is a disaster," he said. "Look at the air, listen to the buzzing of the sun, the same as yesterday and the day before. Today is Monday too." That night Pietro Crespi found him on the porch, weeping with the graceless sobs that old people weep,[3] weeping for Prudencio Aguilar, for Melquíades, for Rebeca's parents, for his mother and father, for all those he could remember and who were now alone in death. Crespi gave him a mechanical bear that walked on its hind legs on a tightrope, but he could not distract him from his obsession. He asked him what had happened to the project he had explained to him a few days before about the possibility of building a pendulum machine that would help men to fly and he answered that it was impossible because a pendulum could lift anything into the air but it could not lift itself. (73/80)

The pendulum of time—the pendulum of the pit of time, as it were—is not a lever in a perpetual motion machine. And if every day is lunatic, if every day is a Moonday too, then a buzzing eternity is no consolation for any lineage on this earth.

Twice in the novel Úrsula reflects on the massive hemorrhaging of time, which seems both rectilinear and circular in its motion, but in any case fleeting and dizzying, and also somehow wounded and bleeding. She visits her son Aureliano, the Revolutionary colonel, who has returned to Macondo to face imprisonment and the firing squad. Colonel Aureliano Buendía now speaks of his home town, so changed, so familiar:

---

3. This phrase is inadvertently missing from Rabassa's translation: ". . . *llorando con el llantito sin gracia de los viejos.* . . ."

"This morning, when they brought me in, I had the impression that I had already been through all that before." In fact, while the crowd was roaring alongside him he had been concentrating his thoughts, startled at how the town had aged. The leaves of the almond trees were broken. The houses, painted blue, then painted red, had ended up with an indefinable coloration.

"What did you expect?" Úrsula sighed. "Time passes."

"That's how it goes," Aureliano admitted, "but not so much." (111/127)

Decades later, during the drought, she visits her great-grandson in the deceased Aureliano's workshop, where the same dialogue (same, yet different) recurs:

José Arcadio Segundo was still reading over the parchments. The only thing visible in the intricate tangle of hair was the teeth striped with green slime and his motionless eyes. When he recognized his great-grandmother's voice he turned his head toward the door, tried to smile, and without knowing it repeated an old phrase of Úrsula's.

"What did you expect?" he murmured. "Time passes."

"That's how it goes," Úrsula said, "but not so much."

When she said it she realized that she was giving the same reply that Colonel Aureliano Buendía had given in his death cell, and once again she shuddered with the evidence that time was not passing, as she had just admitted, but that it was turning in a circle. (284–85/341)

The circularity of time's passage implies not so much a return of the same as a lapse in being and collapse in becoming. Many pages of *One Hundred Years of Solitude* puzzle over the decidedly vicious character of the circles or *vueltas* of time. José Arcadio Segundo sells his fighting cocks in order to buy tools and recruit men. He wants to transform the river, with its bed of prehistoric stones, into a channel deep enough for cargo ships. However novel his idea may be, Úrsula is reminded of the wacky schemes of her defunct husband: "'I know all of this by heart,' Úrsula would shout. 'It's as if time had turned around in circles and we were back at the beginning'" (169/199). Later, the proposed railway line, like the cargo boat line, confirms Úrsula's suspicions "that time was going in a circle" (192/226). To be sure, the endlessly proliferating bedazzlements of technical progress—the eternal return of novelty, but also of inevitable disillusionment—offer no solace. They confirm the matriarch's confused sense of "a progressive breakdown of time." "'The years nowadays don't pass the way the old ones used to,' she would say, feeling that everyday reality was slipping through her hands" (211/251).

The *vitium* of the circle and circuitry of time receives double corroboration in what one might call the Penelopean theme in the novel. Bitter Amaranta tries to fool death by unraveling the shroud that she weaves by day—the shroud she prepares first for Rebeca and then for herself. Similarly, the Colonel spends his last years producing tiny gold fishes with ruby eyes: when he finishes the twenty-fifth in a series he melts them down and starts all over again—Sisyphus in the goldsmith's shop, endlessly working the gold of flower petals, butterfly wings, and his own name, *Aureliano*.

The theme of political revolution is not spared this treatment, for it too is attached to the lurching carousel of breakdown and demise, the time of what the young Heidegger called *Ruinanz*. José Arcadio Segundo (who is actually misnamed Aureliano) takes up the life of political intrigue, secret meetings, and venal betrayals, of hapless and hopeless rebellion against the unholy alliance of the conservative, the military, and the gringo. "'Just like Aureliano,' Úrsula exclaimed. 'It's as if the world were repeating itself'" (253/303). This time the recurrence of the same takes the form of an intransigent *revisionism*, according to which no workers are ever slaughtered by the thousands when they strike against the banana company and no corpses are ever transported in cattle cars to be dumped into the sea. Nothing can resist the versions and perversions of the "hermeneutical delirium" (256/307) that envelops the workers when they make their demands on the company or that José Arcadio Segundo confronts when he recounts to others in Macondo the slaughter that he alone has survived.

When Mr. Brown announces that the banana company will suspend all activities "as long as the rain lasts," the rain cooperates by lasting "four years, eleven months, and two days," sufficient time to justify the company's abandonment of Macondo for more exploitable territories. This eternal recurrence of the rain makes nature herself complicit in revisionism: soon it will wash away every trace of the banana company's barbed-wire compound. It is as though the remorseless gringo who brings on the rains wears the mask of Quetzalcoatl, as though the banana company returns as the god in order to introduce a new Age of the Flood, the first of the four World Ages in Mesoamerican cosmogony, and then to withdraw in stately procession. Yet this new era of the rains is as undecidable as the era of drought that follows: the people of Macondo sit in their parlors "with an absorbed look and folded arms, feeling unbroken time pass, relentless time, because it was useless to divide it into months and years, and the days into hours, when one could do nothing but contemplate the rain" (273/327).

No doubt, return creates the *illusion* of renovation. When the rains finally cease and the drought ensues, all things in Macondo seem to return to their former state. Yet that seeming is the work of a merciless oblivion, first experienced during the "insomnia epidemic" of José Arcadio Buendía's day, but aggravated now, implacable and relentless, experienced the second time (as Marx prophesied all repetitions would be) as farce:

> That was how everything went after the deluge. The indolence of the people was in contrast to the voracity of oblivion, which little by little was undermining memories in a pitiless way, to such an extreme that at that time, on another anniversary of the Treaty of Neerlandia, some emissaries from the president of the republic arrived in Macondo to award at last the decoration rejected several times by Colonel Aureliano Buendía, and they spent a whole afternoon looking for someone who could tell them where they could find one of his descendants. . . . It was also around that time that the Gypsies returned, the last heirs to Melquíades' science, and they found the town so defeated and its inhabitants so removed from the rest of the world that once more they went through the houses dragging magnetized ingots as if that really were the Babylonian wise men's latest discovery. (292–93/351)

As the generations pass, and as each Aureliano, with the ghost of Melquíades at his ear, instructs the next Aureliano in the decipherment of the parchments that contain the history of the Buendía family, José Arcadio Buendía's lucid lunacy is vindicated. For those who dedicate their solitude to the Gypsy's Sanskrit scripts preserved in the goldsmith's studio discover that "it was always March there and always Monday *[lunes],* and then they understood that José Arcadio Buendía was not as crazy as the family said, but that he was the only one who had enough lucidity to sense the truth of the fact that time also stumbled and had accidents and could therefore splinter and leave an eternalized fragment in a room" (296/355).

If eternal recurrence of the same has any validity at all in *One Hundred Years of Solitude,* it is as contingency and oversight, lapse and implosion, fragmentation, rack and ruin. Time rolls on as the confusion it has always been since Aristotle—the confusion of rectilinear motion (itself a confusion of punctuated sequence or succession and seamless continuum) and circular motion (itself a multiple fracture of the tangent, resulting perhaps from the collision between Empedoclean and Aristotelian spheres, the collision of an erotic yet solitary divinity with unending Strife).

Which brings us to Gabriel García Márquez's most remarkable adaptation of the Nietzschean figure of the great wheel of recurrence. Whereas Nietzsche invokes the wheel's spinning *rim,* García Márquez focuses on the *axle* of the wheel and the inevitable wear-and-tear of time. The penultimate Aureliano tells Pilar Ternera of his love for Amaranta Úrsula:

> When Aureliano told her, Pilar Ternera let out a deep laugh, the old expansive laugh that ended up as a cooing of doves. There was no mystery in the heart of a Buendía that was impenetrable for her because a century of cards and experience had taught her that the history of the family was a machine with unavoidable repetitions, a turning wheel that would have gone on spilling into eternity *[dando vueltas hasta la eternidad]* were it not for the progressive and irremediable wearing of the axle *[por el desgaste progresivo e irremediable del eje].* (334/402)

The *axle* of eternal return gains in significance when we recall that the wheel, in Nietzsche's *Thus Spoke Zarathustra,* is the metaphor that the animals conjure up in their ditty or hurdy-gurdy song; it is the bauble they dangle before Zarathustra to tease him away from the dire consequences of his heaviest thought, to coax him into convalescence. Their invocation of the wheel is all "lovely talk" and "resounding lie":

—"Oh, Zarathustra," the animals then said, "for those who think as we do, all things themselves dance: they come and reach out their hands and laugh and flee—and come back.

"Everything goes, everything returns; the wheel of being rolls on eternally. Everything dies, everything blooms again; the year of being runs on eternally.

"Everything breaks, everything is joined anew; the same house of being is built eternally. Everything parts, everything greets again; the ring of being remains faithful to itself eternally." (ASZ III, "The Convalescent"; KSA *4,* 273)

What would transform the discourse of the wheel from a ditty into a hymn? Perhaps our focusing on that whirring axle—on the friction, the heat, the eventual breakdown? Nietzsche approaches this baneful side of his thought of thoughts constantly in his notebooks, where the "consolation" of eternal return is feared as much as any other metaphysico-moral gewgaw, and where the thought of recurrence would either transform its thinker radically or kill her or him who dares to think it. Nietzsche himself approaches the thought of the axle when he invokes the *double* rim of the wheel, the doubling that precludes all knowledge of motion, rest, space, and time:

Succession alone produces the representation of *time.* Supposing we sensed not causes and effects but a continuum: we would not believe in time. For the movement of becoming does *not* depend on points at *rest,* on identical stretches of stasis. ◎ The outer periphery of a wheel, like the inner one, is always in motion; in comparison with the inner periphery, the outer one moves more slowly, and yet it is *not at rest.* "Time" does not decide between slower or more rapid motion. In absolute becoming, force can never rest, can *never* be nonforce: "slow and rapid motion of said force" *cannot* be measured on the basis of a unit, for the unit is not given. A continuum of force is *without succession* and *without contiguity* [ohne Nacheinander *und* ohne Nebeneinander] (for this too would presuppose both human intellect and gaps between the things.) Without succession and contiguity there is *for us* no becoming, no multiplicity—we *could* only assert that such a continuum were one, at rest, immutable, devoid of becoming, without time and space. Yet that is precisely a merely human *opposition.* (M III 1, 11 [281]; KSA *9,* 549)

Eternal return is therefore not the eternity of which Hölderlin's Empedocles dreams and despairs, a time beyond succession, a feast of intimacy with one's beloved gods. Here too, in Nietzsche's notes on eternal return, all the points are consumed in fire. Gabriel García Márquez's insight arrives when he glances from the rim, from the outer surface of the double rim, to the wheel's hub:

Whereas the center of the axle might seem to hover suspended in motionlessness—in the eye of becoming's storm, as it were—its outer surface hums or grinds through the grease, producing friction, fervor, and inevitable if impredictable breakdown: spinning, spilling, somersaulting into eternity continues for what seems an eternity, a Great Year, a millennium, or at least a century, at which point "the progressive and irremediable wearing of the axle" ends it all. Or, rather, *begins* to end it all. For not even termination ensues once and for all, in order to serve as a unit of measure for all eternity. The eternity of return turns out to be the never ending of mortal ending.

When the Catalonian bookstore owner urges his circle of budding intellectuals to leave Macondo, one young man buys "an eternal ticket on a train that never stopped traveling . . . , a train with no return passing by" (339/408). The last of the circle to leave is "Gabriel" (Gabriel García Márquez?), who is reluctant to roam perhaps because of his "stealthy" girlfriend Mercedes, a clerk in last extant pharmacy of Macondo. "It was the last that remained of a past whose annihilation had not taken place because it was still in process of annihilation, consuming itself from within, ending at every moment but never ending its ending *[acabándose a cada minuto pero sin acabar de acabarse jamás]*" (339–40/409).

In the final pages of the book, the ultimate Aureliano, the monstrous *nouveau né*, is carted off by the ants, who presumably now wear the mask of Quetzlcoatl. The last Aureliano's father, the penultimate Aureliano, the neophyte widower, deciphers aloud the parchments to which the reader has long since been secretly introduced. Something like eternal return prevails in the closing pages of the book—a recurrence forged in the instant of apocalyptic time, when every reader's decipherment of the pages of this magnificent literature coalesces with Aureliano's, and the sighs of disenchantment become as heavy as the sighs of love:

It was the history of the family, written by Melquíades, down to the most trivial details, one hundred years ahead of time. He had written it in Sanskrit, which was his mother tongue, and he had encoded the even lines in the private cipher of the Emperor Augustus and the odd ones in a Lacedemonian military code. The final protection, which Aureliano had begun to glimpse when he let himself be confused by the love of Amaranta Úrsula, was based on the fact that Melquíades had not put events in the order of man's conventional time, but had concentrated a century of daily episodes in such a way that they coexisted in one instant. Fascinated by the discovery, Aureliano read aloud without skipping the chanted encyclicals that Melquíades himself had made Arcadio listen to and that were in reality the prediction of his execution, and he found the announcement of the birth of the most beautiful woman in the world who was rising up to heaven in body and soul, and he found the origin of the posthumous twins who gave up deciphering the parchments, not simply through incapacity and lack of drive, but also because their attempts were premature. At that point, impatient to know his own origin, Aureliano skipped ahead. Then the wind began, warm, incipient, full of voices from the past, the murmurs of ancient geraniums, sighs of disenchantment that preceded the most tenacious nostalgia. He did not notice it because at that moment he was discovering the first indications of his own being in a lascivious grandfather who let himself be frivolously dragged along across a hallucinated plateau in search of a beautiful woman who would not make him happy. Aureliano recognized him, he pursued the hidden paths of his descent, and he found the instant of his own conception among the scorpions and the yellow butterflies in a sunset bathroom where a mechanic satisfied his lust on a woman who was giving herself out of rebellion. He was so absorbed that he did not feel the second surge of wind either as its cyclonic strength tore the doors and windows off their hinges, pulled off the roof of the east wing, and uprooted the foundations. Only then did he discover that Amaranta Úrsula was not his sister but his aunt, and that Sir Francis Drake had attacked Riohacha only so that they could seek each other through the most intricate labyrinths of blood until they would engender the mythological animal that was to bring the line *[estirpe]* to an end. Macondo was already a fearful whirlwind of dust and rubble being spun about by the wrath of the biblical hurricane when Aureliano skipped eleven pages so as not to lose time with facts he knew only too well, and he began to decipher the instant that he was living, deciphering it as he lived it, prophesying himself in the act of deciphering the last page of the parchments, as if he were looking into a speaking mirror [*espejo hablado:* literally, a *spoken* mirror]. Then he skipped again to anticipate the predictions and ascertain the date and circumstances of his death. Before reaching the final line, however, he had already understood that he would never leave that room, for it was foreseen that the city of mirrors (or mirages) would be wiped out by the wind and exiled from the memory of men at the precise moment when Aureliano Babilonia will finish deciphering the parchments, and that everything written on them was unrepeatable forever and for always, because lineages *[estirpes]* condemned to one hundred years of solitude did not have a second opportunity on earth. (349–51/421–22)

Solitudes of Love and Rancor

What recurs? What is forged in the neuter/neutral instant of eternity? Solitude. Or *varieties* of solitude. Among them, the desperate loneliness of love and the bitter isolation of rancor and ressentiment. A technowizard or a computer could calculate quite precisely the appearances of the words *solitary* and *solitude* in *One Hundred Years of Solitude.* There are at least sixty-one such references for a mortal reader counting by finger and eye, and many of them are solitudes of love and rancor. Herewith a sampler rather than a survey, a brief catalogue rather than an inventory.

When José Arcadio Buendía, son of José Arcadio Buendía, first tiptoes through Pilar Ternera's house in the black night, he experiences the terror of a "fearful solitude," the solitude of a first love. After their lovemaking bears fruit, José Arcadio Buendía flees Macondo with the Gypsies into the solitude of rancor. First, the solitude of love:

> Then he gave himself over to that hand, and in a terrible state of exhaustion he let himself be led to a shapeless place where his clothes were taken off and he was heaved about like a sack of potatoes and thrown from one side to the other in a bottomless darkness in which his arms were useless, where it no longer smelled of woman but of ammonia, and where he tried to remember her face and found before him the face of Úrsula, confusedly aware that he was doing something that for a very long time he had wanted to do but that he had imagined could really never be done, not knowing what he was doing because he did not know where his feet were or where his head was, or whose feet or whose head, and feeling that he could no longer resist the glacial rumbling of his kidneys and the air of his intestines, and fear, and the bewildered anxiety to flee and at the same time stay forever in that exasperated silence and that fearful solitude *[aquella soledad espantosa]*. (30–31/27–28)

And then, seemingly inevitably, the new solitude of rancor and ressentiment: "Anxious for solitude, bitten by a virulent rancor against the world *[Ansioso de soledad, mordido por un virulente rencor contra el mundo]*," the unexpectant father storms into the Gypsy camp and lights out for the world beyond Macondo.

His brother's solitude is less mercurial and more continuous with his nature since birth. Aureliano, destined to be Colonel Aureliano Buendía, is perhaps the most irremediably solitary of Gabriel García Márquez's characters: not even Remedios, his child bride, can shatter Aureliano's "private and terrible solitude" (63/67), which is somewhere between the poetry of his love and the warfare of his bitterness. Whether the Colonel is "lost in the solitude of his immense power" (146/171) or captured and imprisoned, he is in each instant of his life "more solitary than ever" (111/127; 146/171). He remains fundamentally unchanged, whether in tumult or in silence, and when each of his seventeen bastard sons is born they bear Aureliano's look of incorrigible solitude. As he grows old, the Colonel's solitude becomes a hard shell that not even he can crack: "Taciturn, silent, insensible to the new breath of vitality that was shaking the house, Colonel Aureliano Buendía could understand only that the secret of a good old age is simply an honorable pact with solitude" (174/204).

Both his sister Amaranta and his foster sister Rebeca share— without sharing, without the remotest possibility of sharing— the Colonel's solitude. Although Amaranta finds in the innocent embraces of her nephew Aureliano José "a palliative for her solitude" (127/146–47), neither her nephew—who is dispatched to an "abrupt solitude" (127/147) when she finally bolts her door against him—nor her brother's comrade, Colonel Gerineldo Márquez—who likewise is "lost in solitude" (144/168) after Amaranta's final rejection of him—can interrupt "her solitude unto death" (143/167). Both Amaranta and Rebeca are locked into solitude, whether in their love for Pietro Crespi or their hatred for one another. Amaranta weaves shrouds for her arch rival and herself, "not with any hope of defeating solitude" (222/264), while Rebeca squats adamant in her empty house after the murder of José Arcadio Buendía the younger, "her face wrinkled by the aridity of solitude" (189/224). And while the unflagging matriarch, Úrsula, occupies "the impenetrable solitude of decrepitude" (213/253), shut off from the rest of the world by her cataracts and her bewilderment, her young granddaughter, Remedios the Beauty, "wanders through the desert of solitude" (204/242) to which her savage beauty condemns her up to the moment she ascends body and soul into the ultimate solitary haven of heaven with the family laundry:

> Amaranta felt a mysterious trembling in the lace on her petticoats and she tried to grasp the sheet so that she would not fall down at the instant in which Remedios the Beauty began to rise. Úrsula, almost blind at the time, was the only person who was sufficiently calm to identify the naturalness of that irreparable wind and she left the sheets to the mercy of the light as she watched Remedios the Beauty waving good-bye in the midst of the flapping sheets that rose up with her, abandoning with her the environment of beetles and dahlias and passing through the air with her as four o'clock in the afternoon came to an end, and they were lost for-

ever with her in the upper atmosphere where nothing could reach her, not even the highest-flying birds of memory. (205/ 242–43)

Most of the novel's characters endure on the earth, however, living the life of Santa Sofia de la Piedad, that is to say, a life of solitude, whether in or out of love. Aureliano Segundo suffers "the bitter solitude of his revels" (232/277), "dying of solitude in the turmoil of his debauches" (346/417), while his neurasthenic wife Fernanda remains utterly solitary in her paranoid puritanical fervor. Only with Petra Cotes, and only then in their postdeluvial dotage, does Aureliano Segundo come to know "the paradise of shared solitude" (288/345), a sharing that is as unlikely and as rare as anything can be in a town's one hundred years. Aureliano Segundo's elder daughter's passion for Mauricio Babilonia causes her too to be "anchored in her solitude" (247/296), a solitude that is interrupted by brief encounters at sunset in the bathhouse—until the evening when Meme's lover is shot in the spine, crippled, and dies "of old age in solitude" (248/297). Only Aureliano Segundo's younger daughter Amaranta Úrsula and his grandson Aureliano seem to break the shackles of solitude by grace of passionate love. Yet it would be more correct to say that the fetters are bent rather than broken, and that they soon enough are mended. Solitude, whether of love or rancor, is less a contingency or accident than the inevitable concomitant of what Sartre and Merleau-Ponty would call an *existential solipsism*. Not even one hundred years of solipsism would be enough for lineages on this earth. "Lineages," *estirpes*, being yet another word that might translate the untranslatable *Geschlecht*, the "*one* Geschlecht" we encountered in Trakl's "Western Song."

Even though Aureliano is marked by "the pox of solitude" (333/400), he and his young aunt enter what Robert Musil calls "the millennial realm" of passionate, incestuous love.[4] In the

4. Musil, *Der Mann ohne Eigenschaften*. The third part of the novel is entitled, "Into the Millennium (The Criminals)." It would be something—something stupendous—to write a chapter or a book on Ulrich and Agathe, Grete and Georg, Grete and Gregor Samsa, Franz and Ottla—those Austrian brothers and sisters who confuse the sibling relation with something Hegel said it could not be confused with. Not to mention Freud, who did have sisters but who does not count, since he too was Austrian. Another time, perhaps.

final pages of the book, their love seems to leave behind all rancor and bitter defeat: "In that Macondo forgotten even by the
birds, where the dust and the heat had become so strong that it
was difficult to breathe, secluded by solitude and love and by the
solitude of love *[recluidos por la soledad y el amor y por la soledad del
amor]* in a house where it was almost impossible to sleep because
of the noise of the red ants, Aureliano and Amaranta Úrsula
were the only happy beings, and the most happy on the face of
the earth" (340/409–10). The rancor reemerges in Amaranta
Úrsula when her husband Gastón abandons her with no apparent sign of distress or even discomfort; it dissolves again during
her pregnancy, as she and Aureliano become "more and more
integrated in the solitude of a house that needed only one last
breath to be knocked down" (345/415). Amaranta Úrsula and
Aureliano, son of Meme Buendía and Mauricio Babilonia, are
"the solitary lovers" who tenaciously sail against the sublunary
tides of disenchantment, oblivion, red ants, and whistling weeds:

> Aware of that menace, Aureliano and Amaranta Úrsula spent the
> last months holding hands, ending with the love of loyalty for the
> child who had his beginning in the madness of fornication. At
> night, holding each other in bed, they were not frightened by the
> sublunary explosions of the ants or the noise of the moths or
> the constant and clean whistle of the growth of the weeds in the
> neighboring rooms. Many times they were awakened by the traffic
> of the dead. They could hear Úrsula fighting against the laws of
> creation to maintain the line, and José Arcadio Buendía search-
> ing for the mythical truth of the great inventions, and Fernanda
> praying, and Colonel Aureliano Buendía stupefying himself with
> the deception of war and the little gold fishes, and Aureliano Se-
> gundo dying of solitude in the turmoil of his debauches, and then
> they learned that dominant obsessions can prevail against death
> and they were happy again with the certainty that they would go
> on loving each other in their shape as apparitions long after other
> species of future animals would steal from the insects the paradise
> of misery that the insects were finally stealing from man. (346/
> 416–17)

Amaranta Úrsula gives birth to the last Aureliano, an infant
"with the open and clairvoyant eyes of the Aurelianos, and pre-
disposed to begin the race again from the beginning and

cleanse it of its pernicious vices and solitary calling, for he was the only one in a century who had been engendered with love" (346/417). Yet the eternal recurrence of the Buendía line is marked and marred by the bestial coil and recoil that Úrsula most fears: the final Aureliano is born with the tail of a pig jutting from his coccyx. When his mother bleeds to death in childbirth, and his father wanders distraught through the town, "searching for an entrance that went back to the past" (347/ 418), and when, finally, baby Aureliano himself is carried off by the conqueror ants, only one solitude remains amidst the rubble of love and rancor: the solitude of reading and writing—

The Solitude of Parchment

Melquíades the Gypsy scribbles "his enigmatic literature" in the solitude of Aureliano's workshop (67–68/73). Melquíades has returned there "because he could not bear the solitude" of death (49/50). The gypsy's return accords with the sleepy resurrection of Prudencio Aguilar, the man José Arcadio Buendía kills at the outset of the novel when Prudencio imprudently ridicules Úrsula's precautions against the conception of pig-tailed progeny. Prudencio returns not to haunt his murderer but to seek his companionship "on the tedious Sundays of death" (124/143), not to mention the eternal Moondays of literature. No mortal reader can know the meaning of Melquíades' parchments until he or she reaches one hundred years of age. This means that the parchments are reserved for Úrsula and Pilar Ternera, who never read them, and closed to the long line of Aurelianos, who always try. The only thing that "prospers" in the parchments themselves is a lifeless, livid flower. Colonel Aureliano Buendía opens Melquíades' room,

> looking for the traces of a past from before the war, and he found only rubble, trash, piles of waste accumulated over all the years of abandonment. Between the covers of the books that no one had ever read again, in the old parchments damaged by dampness, a livid flower had prospered, and in the air that had been the purest and brightest in the house an unbearable smell of rotten memories floated. (209/247)

José Arcadio Segundo begins to labor over the unintelligible parchments only after the revisionist forces have condemned him to the radical solitude of the victim whose disastrous experience of history all the world denies. He classifies the ciphers of the parchments, which prove to be Sanskrit, and teaches them to young Aureliano, the penultimate Aureliano, the bastard son of Meme and Mauricio Babilonia.

The eighteenth episode of the novel (301–17/361–81) finds young Aureliano occupying Melquíades' room, learning by heart "the fantastic legends of the crumbling book," legends that turn out to be stories about the Buendía family, stories that are also contained, as fate would have it, in the book *One Hundred Years of Solitude*. The parchments themselves attain one hundred years of age, thus offering themselves to an Aureliano who otherwise would be no match for them. Fernanda ignores her bastard grandson all the while he reads—for the two "did not share their solitude"—and corresponds with her invisible celestial doctors, while he, over three toilsome years, translates the first page of the parchments. When four mischievous children break into the room and try to destroy the parchments, an "angelic force" causes the text to levitate and hang suspended in the air. Aureliano likewise suspends his life outside that room, devoting himself entirely to the parchments that are both "encyclicals" and "encyclopedias," both sacred and profane literature, containing all the lore by means of which, as he says, "Everything is known *[Todo se sabe]*." Only his passion for his sisterly aunt, Amaranta Úrsula, interrupts Aureliano's decipherment of the parchments; only "the same spongy release in his bones" disturbs his reading, writing, decoding.

True, his friendship with "the wise Catalonian" and the three young friends who form the Catalonian's circle also serve as a kind of interruption. It is the wise (and cynical) Catalonian who teaches him "that literature was the best plaything that had ever been invented to make fun of people" (327/394). And yet, whether in love or rancor, adoration or mockery, the solitude of literature is precisely that which never leaves one alone, never abandons either reader or writer to *absolute* solitude. For reader and writer alike are haunted by family and friends—Gabriel, the great-great-grandchild of Colonel Gerineldo Márquez, the friend whose first name (Gabriel) and patronymic (Márquez) point us unmistakably to the matronymic of our author, Gabriel García Márquez, so that (the novel's) Gabriel's (unknown) *sister* would be the mother of (our) Gabriel, if only the genealogies and *Geschlechter* of *One Hundred Years of Solitude* respected the *Inzestverbot.*

Incest apart, or incest included, it is Empedoclean friendship, love, passion, and the mating strife that tie the fortunes of literature to the fatality of family, tying with the ties that bind. Mortals are invariably haunted by families, the others, the loved ones, hounded by the destiny that an absolute solitude would most desire to spare itself—whence the desire to be a single parent, or even better, to be an invisible parent, to produce or be produced from neuter/neutral genetic material in a chaste Petri dish, to produce or to *be* Faust's witty *homunculus,* the sprite of humanity in a bottle—but not in a family.

As the reader of Gregory Rabassa's English translation of *One Hundred Years of Solitude* is driven back in desperation again and again to the family tree or genealogical table that Editorial Sudamericana never provided for the Spanish edition, and as that reader struggles to learn the precise nature of the incestuous relations between Aureliano (the *fourth* Aureliano, not counting the seventeen Aurelianos of the first Aureliano, Colonel Aureliano Buendía) and Amaranta Úrsula (who combines not only the bitter rancor of Amaranta and the indefatigable efficiency of Úrsula but also the icy beauty of Fernanda and the savage glory of Remedios the Beauty), the solitudes of passionate love and of the family hit home. They are the solitudes of the night behind the night, solitudes of lunar voices, of forest animals, and of literature, where every day is Moonday.

Aureliano abandons the parchments at the moment they begin "to reveal themselves as predictions in coded lines of poetry" (330/397). Gastón scans the skies for the airplane that should be coming from Europe but is lost in Africa, and his wife enters the library of her nephew Aureliano, more her brother than a nephew, the ancient workshop where something like an intrepid literature is being pursued: " 'Hello, cannibal,' she said to him. 'Back in your cave again?' "

> Trying to overcome his disturbance, he grasped at the voice that he was losing, the life that was leaving him, the memory that was

turning into a petrified polyp, and he spoke to her about the priestly destiny of Sanskrit, the scientific possibility of seeing the future showing through in time as one sees what is written on the back of a sheet of paper through the light, the necessity of deciphering the predictions so that they would not defeat themselves, and the *Centuries* of Nostradamus and the destruction of Cantabria predicted by Saint Milanus. Suddenly, without interrupting the chat, moved by an impulse that had been sleeping in him since his origins, Aureliano put his hand on hers, thinking that that final decision would put an end to his doubts. She grabbed his index finger with the affectionate innocence with which she had done so in childhood, however, and she held it while he kept on answering questions. They remained like that, linked by icy index fingers that did not transmit anything in any way until she awoke from her momentary dream and slapped her forehead with her hand. "The ants!" she exclaimed. And then she forgot about the manuscripts, went to the door with a dance step, and from there she threw Aureliano a kiss with the tips of her fingers as she had said good-bye to her father on the afternoon when they sent her to Brussels.

"You can tell me later," she said. "I forgot that today's the day to put quicklime on the anthills." (330–31/397–98)

When Aureliano confesses his love and Amaranta Úrsula spurns him in horror, he seeks solace at the house of the ancient Pilar Ternera. Recognizing "the oldest sobs in the history of man" (334/402), the wise old woman—Pilar Ternera is by now 145 years of age—sends him back to the Buendía house. The struggle between nephew and aunt, raised as brother and sister, commences:

Amaranta Úrsula defended herself sincerely with the astuteness of a wise woman, weaseling her slippery, flexible, and fragrant weasel's body as she tried to knee him in the kidneys and scorpion his face with her nails, but without either of them giving a gasp that might not have been taken for the breathing of a person watching the meager April sunset through the open window. . . . Then she began to laugh with her lips tight together, without giving up the fight, but defending herself with false bites and de-weaseling her body little by little until they both were conscious of being adversaries and accomplices at the same time and the affray degenerated into a conventional gambol and the attacks became caresses. Suddenly, almost playfully, like one more bit of mischief, Amaranta Úrsula dropped her defense, and when she tried to recover, frightened by what she herself had made possible, it was too late. A great commotion immobilized her in her center of gravity, planted her in her place, and her defensive will was demolished by the irresistible anxiety to discover what the orange whistles and the invisible globes on the other side of death were like. She barely had time to reach out her hand and grope for the towel to put a gag between her teeth so that she would not let out the cat howls that were already tearing at her insides. (334–35/402–3)

"It was the end." The end of literature. Where it always ends? In bed? At the writing table? When a member of his circle loses the wise Catalonian's own manuscripts in the local whorehouse their author proclaims the loss "the natural destiny of literature" (337/406). Perhaps he is only making fun. Yet when the Catalonian quits Macondo, urging his circle to do likewise, the end of eternal return commences: the eternal ticket on a train that never ceases, a train with no return passing by, with its wheels that would have gone on spilling into eternity were it not for the progressive and irremediable wearing of the axle. It is an ending that consumes itself from within, ending at every moment but never ending its ending. Secluded by solitude and love and by the solitude of love, Aureliano and Amaranta Úrsula work at the final twists and turns of Gabriel García Márquez's amorous tale of pig and ant and parchment:

But when they saw themselves alone in the house they succumbed to the delirium of lovers who were making up for lost time. It was a mad passion, unhinging, which made Fernanda's bones tremble with horror in her grave and which kept them in a state of perpetual excitement. Amaranta Úrsula's shrieks, her songs of agony would break out the same at two in the afternoon on the dining-room table as at two in the morning in the pantry. "What hurts me most," she would say, laughing, "is all the time that we wasted." In the bewilderment of passion she watched the ants devastating the garden, sating their prehistoric hunger with the beams of the house, and she watched the torrents of living lava

take over the porch again, but she bothered to fight them only
when she found them in her bedroom. Aureliano abandoned the
parchments. (340–41/410)

As her pregnancy with the ultimate Aureliano proceeds,
their love mellows and deepens. They recall the lost days of their
childhood together in that same house, the house of Buendía,
the paper house that is now losing the final battle "in the age-
old war between man and ant" (345/415). They share a love, a
passion, a sexuality, and a solitude that of all the couples in the
book only Aureliano Segundo and Petra Cotes have known. After the deaths of Amaranta Úrsula and their pig-tailed son, the
last of the Buendía line, Aureliano becomes aware "that he was
unable to bear in his soul the crushing weight of so much past"
(347/420). When he sees "the dry and bloated bag of skin that
all the ants in the world were dragging toward their holes," the
epigraph that opens Melquíades' parchments returns to him in
a flash of lunar lucidity. Aureliano has read this story before, as
we are reading it now but will always have read it before: "*The
first of the line* [estirpe] *is tied to a tree and the last is being eaten by
the ants*" (349/420).

With that epigraph commences one of the most remarkable
endings (or refusals ever to end) in all literature. The final three
pages of *One Hundred Years of Solitude* compress one hundred
years of time into an intense instant and all the space of Me-
soamerica into several dozen lines of text. A century of daily episodes, themselves recurrent and rhythmical, both amorous and
rancorous, are drawn by the centripetal force of writing into
ever-tighter circles of the same until the friction and the ardor
of that writing cause the center or hub to smoke and crack. The
Sanskrit of Melquíades and the Spanish of Gabriel García Márquez coalesce, the reader rushes headlong to the prediction of
his own immanent and imminent end, the tenses of the verbs
catch up with themselves and overtake one another in a moment
of ultimate fusion and confusion. In the affirmation of the return of nonreturn, affirmation of the irreparable fragility of
mortal lineages, affirmation of the unalterable mortality of the
inhabitants of earth, an affirmation repeated now a second or a
third time in these pages of mine as splinters or eternalized frag-

ments in a room, as though a second opportunity could be negotiated:

> Aureliano had never been more lucid in any act of his life as when he forgot about his dead ones and the pain of his dead ones and nailed up the doors and windows again with Fernanda's crossed boards so as not to be disturbed by any temptations of the world, for he knew then that his fate was written in Melquíades' parchments. He found them intact among the prehistoric plants and steaming puddles and luminous insects that had removed all trace of man's passage on earth from the room, and he did not have the calmness to bring them out into the light, but right there, standing, without the slightest difficulty, as if they had been written in Spanish and were being read under the dazzling splendor of high noon, he began to decipher them aloud. It was the history of the family. . . . [A]nd he began to decipher the instant that he was living, deciphering it as he lived it, prophesying himself in the act of deciphering the last page of the parchments, as if he were looking into a spoken mirror. Then he skipped again to anticipate the predictions and ascertain the date and circumstances of his death. Before reaching the final line, however, he had already understood that he would never leave that room, for it was foreseen that the city of mirrors (or mirages) would be wiped out by the wind and exiled from the memory of men at the precise moment when Aureliano Babilonia will finish deciphering the parchments, and that everything written on them was unrepeatable forever and for always, because lineages *[estirpes, Geschlechter]* condemned to one hundred years of solitude did not have a second opportunity on earth. (349–51/420–22)

Index